ANDRÉ GIDE

And the Crisis of Modern Thought

---

*Chaque homme porte
la forme entière de
l'humaine condition.*

MONTAIGNE

à Klaus Mann   avec l'affection d

André Gide.

ANDRÉ GIDE

And the Crisis of Modern Thought

By KLAUS MANN

Creative Age Press, Inc.

DESIGNED BY STEFAN SALTER

Manufactured in the United States of America
American Book–Stratford Press, Inc., New York

55

TO

JULIAN GREEN,

the French Novelist and
American Soldier

PREFACE

I do not believe in prefaces. The significance of a book should be self-evident. Introductory notes reveal, if anything, an embarrassing lack of confidence on the part of the author. By pointing out the timeliness of his work, he indicates that he distrusts his book or his reader or both. The author's voice sounds shaky and unconvincing when he apologizes for the choice of his theme or his hero. "It may seem surprising that I have picked just this or that topic," he begins, pathetically. "And yet . . ."

It may seem surprising that I picked André Gide. Of course, he is one of the most illustrious living writers and well known everywhere: nobody will contest his literary rank. But why devote, just now, a whole book to the work and character of a French writer, however meritorious? Are there not more vital things to write about, at this juncture of history? Why not tackle, bravely and directly, the great, urgent issues confronting us?

But that is precisely what I try to do, by writing about André Gide. His work is a microcosm that involves the complete scope of modern man's experiences and obsessions. He does not dodge the crucial conflicts of our time but integrates them with his personal drama. All human values on which our civilization is based are at stake in his inner dialogue. He echoes our uncertainties; he articulates our dilemmas. His biography mirrors, and in part anticipates, the tremendous crisis we are passing through. His vision and message will prove relevant to future intellectual developments.

One has called Gide undecided and volatile as he accepts and candidly confesses his inherent contradictions and polarities. To me, his spiritual courage and integrity are more valid and more constructive than any orthodox program. The politicians and partisans simplify and thus distort the vast complexity of our situation. Gide is truthful and bold. His self-scrutiny delves into the innermost recesses, not only of his own soul, but also of ours.

His grace and his gravity, his conscientiousness and his pride, his subtleties, his moral fervor, and his adventurous spirit—everything he stands for is now mortally challenged. The barbarians mean to exterminate the human type represented by men like Gide. It behooves us, therefore, to reaffirm our faith in his imperiled grandeur. In doing so, we participate in the crucial struggle between the forces of darkness and the forces of light.

CONTENTS

I. LEGEND AND REALITY

*Fame is the sum of all misconceptions circulating
about one individual.*
RAINER MARIA RILKE

Ne me comprenez pas si vite, je vous en prie!
ANDRÉ GIDE

W H E N the First World War was over, the muddled and martyred peoples knew nothing about each other, or rather, they knew the wrong things. Only too well informed of their respective enemies' disgraceful or fatuous features, they completely ignored each other's spiritual efforts and accomplishments. International fame was reserved to generals, female spies, the inventors of new formidable weapons, and the victims of such inventions—that is, to the unknown soldier. Four years of hateful, relentless struggle had sufficed to sap, or to destroy, the concept of cosmopolitan culture.

The very nation that was most responsible for these ominous developments was also most painfully affected by them. If the average German groaned under the economic blockade, the German intelligentsia—not yet quite corrupted or exterminated, at the time—suffered even more cruelly from their intellectual isolation. For the Germans are less equipped than any other people for cultural self-sufficiency. The Latin races, together with the Anglo-Saxon world,

3

constitute a vast and independent unity, which may remain creative and intact even when disconnected from the Germanic or Slavic spheres. Nor does Russia actually need the West; she can always withdraw to her Asiatic sources and memories. But the German genius becomes sterile or inimical as soon as it loses touch with the currents of international life. The land of Europe's middle can be productive only when it receives and gives. Its spiritual equilibrium, indeed, its very existence as a cultural potency, depends on a world-wide system of interconnections and affinities. Control and stimulus from abroad are indispensable to that highly gifted but dangerously unbalanced people.

In 1919, a bankrupt and exhausted Germany—or at least her intellectual élite—was eager to resume the international contacts disrupted by the war. The cultural vanguard of the defeated Reich wanted to know what had happened out there, in the world, while they, the nation of poets and thinkers, had had to content themselves with the dashing *bons mots* of their Kaiser. What was *en vogue* in London and New York? How had Italian music, the Russian novel, developed, since 1914? What were the newest discoveries of international science? Where stood the American film? What direction prevailed in the realm of French letters?

In the beginning this thirst for knowledge was unbiased and comprehensive, not confined to any particular country or tendency. Gradually, however, the general curiosity took on more definite shapes and oriented itself according to certain prejudices or interests. There were young Germans who seemed exclusively concerned with the Russian experiment, while others looked for inspiration to Italian Fascism, Oriental wisdom, or the business-conscious idealism of a Henry Ford. Others again looked to France.

To many of us the goings-on in Paris seemed more attractive and significant than what occurred in Moscow or in Rome. France—most bitterly loathed by German nationalists —remained, or became again, the love and hope of German liberal intellectuals. It was there, in the sphere of French civilization, that we sought the patterns and formulas to complete and counterbalance our own intense but fragmentary vision.

We, who had been children when the war began, could hardly be familiar with the amplitude of French culture. In fact, we did not even want the advice of older generations, but spurned their vapid clichés. It was our ambition to discover our own France independently, just as Nietzsche and Heinrich Heine had once discovered theirs.

For too long a time already, we thought, the concept of French culture had been reduced to the classical Latin tradition, plus a touch of frivolous Gallic *esprit*. At once flippant and boisterous, lascivious and pedantic, the French genius was represented (in the opinion of the international cultured bourgeois) by Voltaire's acrid wit and by the admirable legs of *la* Mistinguette. According to this cliché, the pompous rhetorics of Victor Hugo are typically French, as are the fierce probity of Georges Clemenceau, the rakish elegance of Maurice Chevalier, and the hackneyed grandeur of *les* Dumas, *père et fils*.

Anatole France was accepted as the essence and acme of the French contribution.

But in 1920 the time of Anatole France was over. Not that he ceased to be a superb stylist and sagacious mind— naturally not. But his voice no longer was the voice of his nation and of our epoch. His sparkling wit had become somewhat stale. His prose and his ideas were too transparent and too smooth—too reasonable, bare of mystery. The great skeptic utterly ignored—at any rate, he failed to dramatize—our innermost desires and anxieties. He did not find adequate gestures and formulas to express our protests and longings.

Anatole France did not suffice, any more.

Evidently, the Paris of 1920 was not the Paris of 1890 or 1902. The Dreyfus Affair seemed immeasurably remote —a mythic event, something like the Trojan War or Sarah Bernhardt's first appearance. A new time requires a new myth.

Emile Zola's myth had become dusty and cumbersome. The ponderous devices of his naturalism appeared devoid of all relevance and persuasion, as did Symbolism and all esoteric subtleties of the *fin de siècle*. Baudelaire and Degas were memories like the histrionic patterns of the *Comédie Française* or the stunning picture hats of the Empress Eugénie.

We sensed that new, thrilling things were in the making on the banks of the Seine. No doubt, French genius had undergone, or was just passing through, one of its amazing transformations. It quivered, capered, phosphoresced—all in raptures with new insights, new uncertainties. Bewitched, rejuvenated, it revealed new, disquieting aspects —a stringent gravity and youthful impetus, both of which it seemed to have lost long ago.

We were not disappointed when we came to France, in those rousing, riotous days following World War One. We found, indeed, what we were looking for—new ideas, new

8 février 40   40 rue Verdi
                      Nice
                      Alpes Maritimes

Mon cher Klaus

    Je suis profondément touché par votre
longue et excellente étude de Tass und
Wert, sensible à l'extraordinaire attention
et à toute la sympathie dont elle fait
preuve. Les pages sont d'une perspicacité
singulière et témoignent d'autant
d'intelligence que de cœur. Je les ai lues
avec l'intérêt le plus vif ; mais aussi (et
de cela surtout je vous suis reconnaissant)
elles m'ont beaucoup instruit. Grâce à vous
j'ai pris conscience des pénibles déficiences
de mon Journal. Non plus que je n'y
donne la première place aux amitiés qui
ont eu le plus d'importance dans ma vie,
je n'y rends l'hommage dû à ceux que j'ai

les plus admirés, & qui ont été mes maîtres et
m'ont formé. Vous me donnez désir d'écrire
des _Retouches_ à mon _Journal_, comme j'ai
fait pour mon _Retour de l'U.R.S.S._, et, si
j'arrive à bien ce projet, j'aurai plaisir
à vous le dédier, car c'est vous qui m'en
avez donné l'idée. J'y remettrais en place
voulue les dieux de mon Parnasse intime.
Eh quoi ! dans ces 1300 pages, je n'ai même
pas une fois nommé Heine, ou Kafka !... C'est
honteux. Voici bien le grave inconvénient
d'un _Journal_, où qui, tenu par à-coups,
sans ordre, sans composition, ne met rien
à sa place et ne tient compte d'aucune
de proportions ni d'hierarchies.

Je relève à peine d'une assez longue
grippe et suis encore trop fatigué pour
vous en écrire plus long ; mais pense à vous
très affectueusement et me sens plus que
jamais votre ami

André Gide

rhythms, a new vision of life. There were new passions and problems, a new expansion of human consciousness.

There were new names, too. Or rather, most of these names were new to *us*, at that point, while the French vanguard was long familiar with them. But it was only now, in those post-war days, that French letters reflected—visible to us all—the influence of such pioneers as Rimbaud and Lautréamont. Bergson's philosophy challenged and refuted the evaluations of the nineteenth century. A new generation deserted the onerous doctrines of materialism. The new spirit played off intuition against knowledge and experience: the concept of creative evolution, against the idea of progress. Bergson glorified change and motion, not as means for any empirical purpose but as mystic principles— autonomous, irresistible.

If Rimbaud's image of *Le Bateau ivre* transported French and European youth towards unprecedented adventures, it was Bergson's notion of the *élan vital* which swelled the sails of the magic vessel.

The seditious vagabond, Rimbaud, unmasked, mercilessly, the cracks and the corruptions of our way of life; his uproarious drama anticipated disasters and illuminations to come. Had the French genius ever indulged in idle subtleties or complacent optimism? If so, Rimbaud's appeal ended the epoch of elegant weariness. Tragic and hazardous, he sings anguish and inspiration—a new experience, a new violence. His approach to God, life, and art defies all compromises and contrivances.

"Le combat spirituel est aussi brutal que la bataille des hommes," says Rimbaud. *"Dure nuit! le sang séché fume sur ma face!"*

From such brutal and ecstatic auguries a new vision could spring, and also a new faith.

Charles Péguy, killed in the Battle of the Marne, was obsessed with this new faith and vision. His were the sober discipline of a Roman legionary and the compelling fervor of an authentic prophet. This militant lover of France revived the myth of Jeanne d'Arc; his passion and purity were the mirror in which French youth recognized their task and their tradition.

Charles Péguy had the passion of integrity and also of heroism.

Paul Claudel has the passion of faith. His song is burdened with faith as trees are burdened with too heavy fruits. His powerful mind seems at once illuminated and darkened by his constant preoccupation with God. An eerie twilight prevails in the dome of his work; everything is bathed in a solemn and somber purple. The austere splendor of Gothic sculptures emanates from his invocations and tragedies. All sacerdotal zeal and stern gravity, his work offers bountiful comfort to those who believe with him, but challenges and condemns the lukewarm and faithless ones.

Paul Valéry has the passion of purity, the quasi-religious fervor of artistic, more-than-artistic, conscientiousness. In the prime of his life he renounced poetry for two decades and concentrated on mathematics. When he began to produce verse again, shortly after the war, his style had assumed the crystal lucidity of mathematic formulas. "The life of the gods is mathematics," says the German poet Novalis. And the French poet, Paul Valéry: *"La philosophie est une affaire de formes."*

André Suarès, whose analytical prose soars at times to the height of real inspiration, has the incurable obsession of a Christian who does not want to be saved, of a God-seeker who refuses to find what he is looking for. *"Vous êtes né pour la vie sainte, et moi pour la vie tragique,"* he concludes his imaginary dialogue with Pascal.

Romain Rolland, like Suarès, has a sense of tragedy, but combined with an ardor of compassion typical of great reformers and humanitarians. The monuments he erected for Beethoven, Tolstoi, Michelangelo seem designed primarily to immortalize the mortal tribulations besetting those tragic heroes. "My beloved Beethoven!" exclaims this cosmopolitan Frenchman, herald of German music and social consciousness, "You are the greatest, most reliable friend of those who struggle and suffer." The same may be said of that understanding biographer of genius and helpful comrade of the underdog, Romain Rolland.

He reaffirmed and deepened the ethical awareness of the French and European spirit. But while he was concerned with issues of such spectacular magnitude and of such revolutionary impact, another French novelist, Marcel Proust, even more audacious, ventured on the most devious and most delicate recesses of the individual drama. An explorer, he too delved into the abysmal secrets of time and memory, and, *à la recherche du temps perdu,* discovered new zones and potentialities of our undiscovered soul.

Thanks to Proust, our psychological insights were widened and clarified. It was as if he had presented us with miraculous glasses through which we could recognize the most minute details and implications of our own experience

—shades and overtones we could not discern before Proust's prodigious sensibility disclosed their meaning to us.

Thus the genius of France uncovered long-forgotten treasures or traced out new aspects of our lives—the younger generation no less ingeniously than that of Rolland and Proust.

Jules Romains attempted to integrate his own individual adventure with the collective drama of one indivisible social organism. Abandoning himself, he strove for a mystic unification with the universe. *"Je cesse d'exister tellement je suis tout,"* he asserted, while multiplying, simultaneously, his literary existence through the foundation of a poetic school called *Unanisme*.

The Surrealists, some time later, unveiled the rampant mysteries of the unconscious, and publicized the splendor of paranoia as if it were a new toothpaste or fashionable resort.

Others established themselves as experts in international sex habits. Paul Morand, a dashing Baedeker of cosmopolitan vices, compiled and analyzed the erotic particularities of all capitals from Shanghai to Stockholm. He too, for all his snobbism and triviality, contributed his bit to the intensification of the *élan vital:* if only by introducing prize fighters and jazz into the sphere of French letters. His streamlined exoticism has at times the juicy wit of a high-class *cocotte* and the sauciness of a successful *gigolo*—engaging qualities which neither Chateaubriand nor Pierre Loti commanded.

If Paul Morand has the temperament and talent of an unusually gifted pimp, Jean Giraudoux remains always the diplomat he happens to be by profession. With remarkable tact and skill he juggles incoherent patterns and images, bringing about ever new and ever delightful cocktails. He has a lot of charm and fantasy but no backbone. His poetic devices and cerebral caprioles—though infinitely more refined and more original than Morand's obvious gags—are curiously lacking in persuasion and validity. Yet, his sensitive craftsmanship has added a new dimension to the traditional elegance of French prose. For the Parisian drawing rooms have an inevitable tendency to become a little provincial. Time and again, they need the tonic touch of fresh air from abroad. That is what Jean Giraudoux brought along when he returned from Bombay or Budapest. An agile messenger of the Quai d'Orsay and of French literature, he rushed from continent to continent, picking up whatever he could digest and fusing it with his innate heritage—the heritage of Marcel Proust and of La Rochefoucauld, Madame de Sévigné and Charles Baudelaire.

The danger of provincialism in French literature, if it ever existed, was definitely done away with in 1920.

Henri de Montherlant, the spirited bard of bull fights and of other forms of sublime sadism, introduced a Spanish glow and rhythm into the receptive climate of the Paris Parnassus. The cocky verve of his prose reminds us of those *toreros*, whose truculent grace he extols.

In the wondrous tales of the Franco-American writer, Julian Green, the stifling air of French provincial towns is imbued with the nostalgia of homelessness and with the saturnine echoes of British and German masters. The bleak and idyllic setting of Madame Bovary's tragedy assumes, in Julian Green's novels, the sinister grandeur of *Wuthering Heights* and the fathomless melancholy of romantic adagios.

The lascivious secrets of the boudoir assume a flavor of serene innocence in Colette's subtle idiom. An experienced and tactful guide, she takes us to quite hazardous festivities and makes us witness the most peculiar *divertissements*. But the air in her charming stories is never fulsome and sultry. A tonic fragrance prevails—a refreshing aroma, as from flowers and kittens. The young people she portrays have the appetites and the attractiveness of young animals; their pranks and vagaries are as disarmingly graceful and natural as are the plays of guileless foals of fawns. Colette has added a new color and a new aroma to the great French tradition of erotic literature. Her attitude toward life in general, and in particular toward sex, is as sovereignly elegant and understanding as that of a grande dame in the eighteenth century may have been, and as that of a twentieth-century woman may eventually become.

Jean Cocteau contributes a new magic ritual—the staggering *tours de force* of an inspired illusionist. His art seems to be derived from bewitched zones where the realities of our life, the laws of gravity and of ethics are no longer relevant. A clairvoyant clown and clownish visionary, he gushes puns and prophecies, performing indefatigably the uncanny stunts of his repertoire.

Colorful and yet monotonous, the program of Jean Cocteau includes acrobatic acts and macabre antics, great poetry and morbid dislocations. The august characters of antique myths and medieval legends, pacing the scene of a Parisian music hall, display the feverish agitation of twentieth-century neurotics, while the *enfants terribles* of a decaying *bohème* stylize their games and agonies according to mythic patterns. The magician-poet—frail but dynamic, like one of Picasso's ravishing *arlequins*—supervises the show, which is accompanied by the glorious discords of Stravinsky's music for the Russian Ballet. An opium pipe serves him as a baton to direct his opalescent parade.

What a delightful spectacle! And how frightfully chimerical . . .

Cocteau realizes, at bottom, that his astounding performance has as little to do with human and living things as opium has with religion. *"L'opium ressemble à la religion dans la mesure où un illusioniste ressemble à Jesus"*—the confession of an opium smoker.

He has long made his choice, in favor of the illusion.

Something is lacking in all these brilliant efforts—even in the work of the one genius among so many admirable talents, Marcel Proust. With the diligence of a monk or an ant, he is all absorbed in his specific mania: to perceive the unperceivable; to articulate the unspeakable. The rôle of a moral leader has never appealed to him. How could he be interested in changing or in explaining a phenomenon as sweet and as intriguing as is life on this earth? He contents himself with registering its fluctuations and vicissitudes, anxious not to miss the tiniest detail and to integrate everything into the meticulous structure of his useless, immortal work.

Men like Péguy and Rolland, on the other hand, are completely possessed by their respective political and ethical missions. The former violates the idea of Occidental culture by insisting on the primacy of the Latin, Cæsarian tradition over all its other components. The latter deprives the

idiom of Voltaire and Rabelais of its tonic aroma, dena-
tionalizing it for the sake of an anæmic idealism, *au-dessus
de la mêlée*.

If their approach is biased and one-sided, the architectonic perfection of Paul Valéry's accomplishment is hardly
relevant to our troubles and tasks. It may be that his aristocratic detachment and august universalism anticipate a
higher and finer state of human civilization to be attained
in the future.

Messages like those of Suarès and Claudel have a more
direct bearing on the problems we have now to cope with.
But, again, these two disclose only some special aspects of
our plight. Besides, both are slightly irritating, for all their
authentic greatness: Suarès, because of his mulish persistence in asking questions which he obviously does not wish
to have answered; Claudel, as he accepts an axiomatic system as a priori truth. His apodictic faith banishes uncertainty, thus negating the cardinal and innermost experience
of our uncertain lives.

Where is the synthesis of so many fragmentary vistas
and revelations? Where could we find a mind ample and
open enough to integrate all potentialities of this epoch?
Whose intuition and intelligence do live up to the spiritual
crisis we pass through?

We kept asking and seeking. There were plenty of
prophets and pedagogues who offered us their advice—in
Paris, and elsewhere too. Some of them were attractive;
most of them turned out to be fakes.

One name, however, sounded like a promise to us. It was
frequently mentioned, that name, and in contradictory

ways—with hatred, admiration, fear, or tenderness, but never with indifference or disdain.

What sort of a character might he be, that much-praised, much-slandered man, André Gide?

When I first came to Paris, in 1925, André Gide was still comparatively unknown in Germany. Only one of his works, *The Return of the Prodigal Son,* enjoyed a certain popularity, thanks to Rainer Maria Rilke's admirable translation. As for his other books, some of them were available in German adaptations but were almost completely ignored by the public. Not even the intellectual vanguard—excepting a few experts—was aware of Gide's significance.

One of these experts, however, happened to be a great friend of mine. Ernst Robert Curtius, Professor of Romance Languages at the University of Heidelberg, was undoubtedly one of the most thorough connoisseurs of French literature outside France. His books and lectures were instrumental in revealing to German youth the treasures and surprises of contemporary French thought.

Urbane and open-minded, Curtius combined the conscientiousness and profundity of a real scholar with the easygoing charm and sparkling wit in which German professors usually are lacking. He could not only lecture but could also laugh. Small wonder, then, that a lonely and fastidious man like Gide was attracted by this mellow and engaging personality. Curtius could pride himself on André Gide's cordial friendship.

While the professor elucidated, to his students and readers, the structure and the impact of Gide's literary message, he amused me with many an inside story about Gide's private hobbies and habits. The picture of the great writer as it emerged from the ancedotes of his friend and admirer was lovable, if somewhat involved and capricious.

"One has to know him long and intimately to understand and like him," Curtius said, beaming as usual when he dwelt on his favorite subject, Gide. "And one has to be familiar with his writings, too. Otherwise you'll see just his vagaries and the bewildering paradoxes of which his character consists entirely—so it seems. But in reality and at bottom, there is nothing paradoxical about the man. On the contrary, he is more harmonious, in a sense, than anyone I've known. Harmonious in a complicated way, if you know what I mean. The way our grand old Goethe might have been—all self-assured and serene, notwithstanding those notorious two souls dwelling together in his breast, alas. But why shouldn't a strong and intelligent fellow master half-a-dozen souls, if need be?" he concluded. "It's all a question of wit and equilibrium, I suppose."

When I left for Paris, Curtius gave me a letter to introduce me to André Gide. Before we separated, at the station in Heidelberg, he furnished me with some last-minute advice.

"You'd better not ask him questions about his literary work," Curtius admonished me. "He doesn't like to discuss why he wrote this or that, or what he is planning to write. That's one of his peculiarities: he loves to write about himself and to talk about other people. But it bores him to talk about himself or about what he's writing."

After a while he added, "The best thing is not to *talk* too much with him, anyhow. It's much more fun to *do* things with him—things he enjoys doing. We had a won-

derful time together, he and I, when we went to an aquar-
ium and looked at the fishes and the carnivorous plants. In
fact, he got quite a kick out of watching those ravenous
blooms. They look so innocent; but when it comes to catch-
ing a worm or something, they are as swift and relentless
as a shark—or a man." He laughed in memory of the
greedy flowers and of Gide's excitement when he studied
them.

Before the train left, I received this last piece of advice:
"And, above all, don't you allow any gossip-monger to fool
you with dire stories about Gide's conduct and character!
People talk a lot of nonsense, as you know. So you'd better
just laugh at them when they try to tell you that Gide is a
fiendish creature, full of vices and wiles. He is not so diabolic as all that—really not. Take it from me, he is an unusually nice old chap. And now, good luck to you! And
give him my best regards!"

During the first weeks of my stay in Paris, Gide was out
of town. "*Parti en voyage*," was the succinct information I
got when calling up his apartment. "Naturally, he would
be," people told me, with an odd mixture of respect and
malignancy. "That's exactly what you'll always hear when
you try to reach the great man. He becomes more and more
inaccessible."

It did not take me long to realize how right Ernst Robert
Curtius had been when warning me against the venomous
rumors circulated by Gide's enemies and fostered, unwittingly, by certain naïve admirers. At that time—in the
spring of 1925—the gossip around Gide flourished rampantly, in consequence of his recently published book,

Corydon (1924). In this series of Platonic dialogues Gide had dared to tackle an untouchable topic—namely, the phenomenon of homosexual love. The treatise is a frank and semi-scientific examination rather than a eulogy of the matter it deals with. Yet even the more liberal critics were shocked by this detached, candid study. The only response *Corydon* received from the press was a glacial silence or inordinate abuse.

However, the campaign against Gide had already begun some time before the appearance of this hazardous publication. The growth of Gide's international reputation got on the nerves of certain chauvinistic gentlemen. Of course, the antagonism between Gide, the cosmopolitan, and the Nationalistic camp dated back to pre-war days, when the young author of *L'Immoraliste* and *La Porte étroite* challenged such powerful conservatives as Maurice Barrès and Charles Maurras. The old quarrel gained new momentum now, thanks to the rabid malice of a popular mediocrity named Henri Béraud.

In a sheet called *L'Eclair* this jolly citizen started a crusade against what he termed "the long faces" of certain dreary scribblers—that is, the literary circle around André Gide and the magazine *Nouvelle Revue Française*, of which Gide was a founder. M. Béraud disliked the whole lot of them —Marcel Proust, Paul Valéry, Jean Giraudoux, and the like. In Béraud's opinion, they were treacherous as well as tiresome, pretentious bores who believed neither in sound fun nor in the Holy Church nor in *la grande nation*. Gide was the worst one of the unpleasant lot, according to *L'Eclair*— at once stuff-shirted and immoral, poisoned by German philosophy, utterly devoid of *esprit* and patriotism.

"And what was Monsieur Gide doing during the Great War?" asked Monsieur Béraud. "Who has ever seen a patriotic statement from that uprooted internationalist?"

In reality Gide, instead of making statements, had worked throughout the War for a vital organization, the Franco-Belgian Center. But he did not condescend to rectify Béraud's distortions. On the contrary, the rampant invectives rather seemed to amuse him. He even considered dedicating his new book to M. Béraud, as an expression of his gratitude for all the good laughs due to him.

But meanwhile the scandal started by *L'Eclair* assumed alarming proportions. The meanest, most reactionary journalists of Paris wrote luridly about Gide's devastating influence on French literature and French youth.

The slanderers asserted by turns that Gide was powerful and wicked enough to corrupt the entire nation, and that he was deplorably unsuccessful and isolated, without any following, a pathetic figure. "M. Gide does not even represent a literary clique," jeered the Nationalist *Revue Française*, "not even the magazine for which he himself writes" (i.e., the *Nouvelle Revue Française*). After this almost sympathetic beginning the concluding statement sounds unduly excited: "His work is the most revolting moral and intellectual scandal of this century."

Don't we recognize these shrill, hysterical accents? Accusations of a similar type were darted against D. H. Lawrence in England, against Frank Wedekind by the German press. Those who challenge the hypocrites and disregard their taboos, must expect to be stoned, or, even worse, to be smeared with dirt.

In some cases the denouncements became almost humorous. To publish a pamphlet under the title, *Un Malfaiteur: André Gide*, sounds like a practical joke. Yet the anonymous moralist who thus made an ass of himself did not realize how very funny he was. He meant it seriously—if only in a symbolic way—when he blamed that "evildoer," Gide, for the suicide of his—the anonymous author's —son. The imaginary young man had ostensibly taken his own life, out of sheer depression and bewilderment, after having read one of André Gide's books, *Les Nourritures terrestres*. The saddened father suggested that many a fine French youth might follow his son's baleful example unless public opinion and the Government prevented the *malfaiteur* from continuing his literary practices.

It was all very well to sneer at such a primitive slander. But the matter became much graver when men of talent and reputation joined in the infamous chorus. A shrewd Catholic philosopher like Henri Massis, the most gifted representative of the Neo-Thomist movement, was more dangerous an enemy than that insidious old busybody of a Henri Béraud. Massis was cruel and sagacious, a real fanatic, not a garrulous fool. With acrid wit and fierce determination he kept hurling maledictions against that paragon of vices and blasphemies, André Gide. Evidently, the sacerdotal polemicist deemed it his duty as a Christian and a patriot to exorcize the tempter and impostor like an evil ghost. Many distinguished minds of literary French 'Catholicism assisted Massis in his dogged, passionate efforts. It is noteworthy, however, that some of the purest and most eminent Catholic writers—men like François Mauriac and

Georges Bernanos—abstained from joining the furious "anti-Gideans." As, incidentally, did many of the Nationalist camp. While the rank and file jingoists vied with each other in abusing Gide, some of the more enlightened patriots came out in favor of him. Léon Daudet, for one, the editor of the royalist paper, *L'Action Française*, disapproved expressly of the "absurd malignancy" of certain attacks directed against Gide.

Yet the virulent campaigns sufficed, not to sap Gide's intellectual influence, but to distort his legend. Thanks to Béraud, Massis, and some dozens of less prominent enemies, he attained the problematical distinction of a veritable demon. No mortal being could combine so many contradictory features in one character. The prodigious villain whom those imaginative gentlemen described appeared as a desultory will-o'-the-wisp and at the same time as a pedantic bore—half Cagliostro, half schoolmaster; at once dry and stagy. He was defamed as un-French, un-Christian, and un-European. Some of his foes thought him too irreverent; others, too eclectic. They blamed him for his mysticism and his flippancy, for his wit and for his seriousness. To them, he was both a hypocrite and a cynic. "There is one thing worse than hypocrisy: cynicism," proclaimed Paul Claudel, referring to André Gide.

His destructive teachings, they said, undermined the ancient French ideals but offered nothing in their place. Without faith and without direction, an irresponsible adventurer, he lured youth away from the Pantheon of their race, into a maze of lies and paradoxes.

His whole life was a challenge and a mystery. Descended

from a wealthy, bourgeois family, he did whatever he could to hold in derision the dignity of bourgeois institutions. An aristocrat by nature and upbringing, he seemed attracted by all sorts of perilous eccentricities. "To live dangerously" was one of his main aspirations. So he did, by falling from one extreme into the other: one day, given to a paroxysm of religious feeling; the next, to veritable ecstasies of carnal lust. He posed as the immoralist but was constantly preoccupied with moral issues. His married life was full of happiness, according to his report; but he prided himself on his objectionable penchant for dark-skinned Arabian boys.

Even his friends and followers were puzzled by his iridescent character, which fascinated even his opponents. In fact, his adversaries seemed as much under his spell as were his admirers. Whether they called him fiendish or tiresome, they kept talking and wondering about him.

I recall the bewitched, apprehensive smile on the face of a young French writer—a recent convert and Catholic priest in the making—with whom I looked at a portrait of André Gide. As usual, I was taken with the noble shape of this physiognomy, and expressed my delight.

"*Mais oui,*" admitted the devout young man, "*il est beau.*" And he added, with a transient shudder, "*Que voulez-vous? C'est la beauté du diable.*"

Early in the summer I had word from Gide. He was back in town—only for a short while, though, as he indicated. Yet he wanted to see me. Could I make it for luncheon, next Tuesday, about one o'clock?

I called on him at his apartment, in the *rue Vaneau*—a

drowsy and dignified little street, *"la tranquille rue Vaneau,"* as Gide calls it in one of his narratives, *Les Caves du Vatican.*

The young man who received me introduced himself as Marc Allegret. He was svelte and swarthy, pleasant to look at, with jaunty, self-assured motions and a hard, handsome face. I found him occupied with rummaging through books and papers, which were piled up on shelves, chairs, and tables, inundating even the floor.

Allegret apologized for the mess and told me that Gide and he were on the point of leaving for a long journey to the interior of Africa. Gide needed badly a drastic change of air—the young man explained to me—whereas he, Allegret, was looking forward to the expedition mainly as an opportunity to test and to improve his ability as a cameraman.

As for the books, they were destined to be sold at auction. I opened one of them at random, and was surprised to find it adorned with a cordial dedication autographed by the author, a well-known, respected man. Wouldn't the writer in question be rather hurt, I dared ask, by such an obvious lack of esteem and courtesy? Marc's smile was wry and not without bitterness. Precisely this, he told me, was what his friend was driving at. He meant to shock some of his dear colleagues and to teach them a lesson. For most of them had let him down, in the most weak-spirited way, when it would have behooved them, as friends and as intellectuals, to defend the author of *Corydon* against the insults of half-wits and hypocrites.

"Not that the whole hullabaloo is anything to worry about!" young Allegret assured me with a defiant laugh.

"Why should we get excited because of some greasy fools? It really isn't worth-while. Ridiculous, that's what it is. I can't help giggling when I see a lot of so-called French patriots rioting against the man who has been elected, unanimously, by the Royal Academy of London to take over the membership of the late Anatole France. It's too silly for words! The nation of Voltaire and Rabelais apparently has become more prudish than even those demure gentlemen on the other side of the Channel."

Curiously, I cannot recall the moment of Gide's entrance, nor do I recollect what he said or looked like when I was presented to him. It is as though he had insinuated himself into the room, noiselessly—emerging from a trapdoor, as it were—and spirited me away in the pleats of his loose, weather-worn cloak. The first picture of him that looms up in my memory is that of a quaint, haggard wanderer striding by my side.

Lean and vigorous, he makes the impression of a man who is in the habit of spending a good deal of time outdoors in physical exercise. (In reality, Gide is fond of extensive walks but refuses to engage in any sport.) His gait has a swinging, energetic quality, although he stoops a little. In his wide, discolored pelerine and his broad slouch hat, he might be a slightly eccentric professor or a somewhat diabolic priest. His face is expressive and delicate, with a high, admirably shaped forehead, straight, narrow lips, and strangely Mongolian eyes peering from under dark, bushy eyebrows.

His whole attitude is that of a man who tries very hard to appear placid and sedate while quivering with inner nervousness. All his gestures, even his voice and the scholarly elegance of his speech, seem to vibrate with disciplined agitation. Only some minor habits, such as a frequent snuffing and his constant smoking of cigarettes, betray the tension behind this conscious and consistent self-control. There can be a sudden, disconcerting twinkle in his eye, an uncanny flash like a warning sign from the volcanic depth of his being.

During this first luncheon I had with him, in a modest *brasserie* near the Luxembourg Gardens, it happened twice that such a flitting sparkle altered the placidness of his brow. The first little "explosion" took place when I offered him a cigarette. He had smoked incessantly before and during the luncheon. Surprisingly, he forgot to light himself another *Gauloise Bleue* when our meal was over. As I offered him a Lucky Strike, he shook his head and raised his right arm, with a gesture expressing protest rather than ordinary refusal. "It's a terrible vice," he said with an ambiguous grin—and there was the twinkle! He added, suddenly pensive and grave, "Usually I am too weak to resist. It is really disgraceful . . ."

Later he took up the cigarette theme once more in a different context. We discussed a mutual acquaintance who was addicted to morphine, and I asked Gide whether he had ever tried narcotics. He said curtly, "No," and then stared into space for a moment. "Cigarettes are devilish enough," he said, musing and absent-minded, as if talking to himself. "If I ever touched an opium pipe, morphine, or such as that, I would be certainly doomed. I don't have the fortitude to resist evil. Yes, in wanting things I am strong, and I usually get what I want. But when it comes to rejecting a temptation . . . *alors ça, c'est une autre histoire* . . ."

The second incident to provoke the flash in his eyes was equally harmless and undramatic. A young boy passed by and tried to sell us a bunch of roses—withered, colorless stuff. He couldn't have been more than ten or eleven years old, a rickety little creature with large, shiny eyes in a sallow and clever face. Gide gave him a handful of change but did not take any flowers—a caprice which obviously perturbed and puzzled the lad.

"Did you notice the wry glance he gave me?" Gide whispered, exceedingly animated, as soon as the boy had left. "He is *profoundly* shocked. How extraordinary! Of course, he stole the flowers, and he would steal my money if he had the opportunity. But no charity! A helpful, disinterested gesture upsets his philosophy and even offends his honor. *C'est bien curieux ça! C'est tout à fait remarquable . . .*"

We talked about other things—about Goethe or Proust or the beauties of Tunisia. After a short while, however, Gide interrupted himself with a nervous start, electrified, as it were, by something I could not see. "I have a hunch," he said, half-gravely, half-roguishly, "in fact, I am positive that the little one is still around somewhere. He is making faces behind my back. I am afraid he is cursing me just now! I feel it in my spine . . ."

Then he shrugged his shoulders, as if resigning himself to an unescapable danger, and resumed the literary conversation. He has an odd way of talking without opening his mouth, producing, between his teeth, sibilant sounds punctuated by brief, nervous sniffs.

There was no mention of his own work or projects, nor, remembering Ernst Robert's admonition, did I ask any questions.

I am not positive as to the exact date on which this first meeting took place; it must have been some day between the seventh and the fourteenth of June. Years afterwards I read, under the date of June 8, 1925, this laconic entry in Gide's diary: "Finished *The Counterfeiters.*" And the next note, of June 14: "Leaving for the Congo."

He is always on the point of leaving. It seems incompatible with his temperament to settle down, to stay anywhere. To a superficial observer, and according to the gossipy legend, Gide's life is rampantly nomadic, an aimless, neurotic roving from place to place. In reality, however, his vagrant habits are not as inordinate as all that. He is a vagabond, all right; but a vagabond with a system. The direction and the scope of his wanderings are determined and limited by certain preferences and definite aversions. I remember how surprised, almost shocked, he was when I told him about a journey to the polar zones that I was planning at the time. "To go up there, to the foggy North, for the fun of it?" he exclaimed. "What a weird thing to do!"

His own route is confined to the Mediterranean sphere and to Central Europe—Germany, Austria, Switzerland, Czechoslovakia. Also, he went to London repeatedly, but not nearly as often as to Berlin or to Marseille. For half a century North Africa—Morocco, Tunisia, Algeria—remained for him the essence and the symbol of adventure and relaxation. He has never crossed the Atlantic, nor did he carry out his long-cherished project of a Far-Eastern voyage. His two most extensive journeys were those to the Congo, in 1925, and to the Soviet Union, in 1936.

He kept moving, throughout the years; but it was not an erratic zigzag, rather an endless revolving around certain traditional centers—Berlin and Biskra, Nice and Naples, Munich and Marrakech, Geneva and Genoa. And if it is true that his flat in the rue Vaneau meant hardly more to him than an occasional *pied à terre*, it is also true that there was a place to which he could always return and feel truly at home—Cuverville, the estate in Normandy, where his wife, almost invisible to the world, would be always waiting for him. "*Ma pauvre femme . . .*" Gide would say, with a curious expression of embarrassment and infinite affection. He has never acknowledged, not even in his *Journal*, what all his intimates knew, that Emmanuèle and Cuverville were really indispensable to him—the heart and harbor of his restless life.

Is he a particularly puzzling man, that evasive nomad and devoted husband, André Gide of Cuverville and the world? But, then, all men are puzzling. One has to be fond of a human being to understand his actions. One has to consider the whole complexity of an individual character before evaluating the gestures through which this character manifests itself.

In the special case of Gide it is comparatively easy to grasp the interrelations between the accessories of his life and its essence. Even his most casual, prosaic actions are somehow relevant to his general philosophy. Already my first meeting with him yielded some information as to this remarkable congruity.

The seemingly trivial action of the sale of his books, for instance, assumes a new, significant aspect when visualized in this context. Gide parted with his library, certainly not for the sake of a few thousand francs nor exclusively or mainly in order to annoy his colleagues. He had to do so, rather, compelled by one of his basic obsessions—namely, his aversion to, indeed, his fear of, any earthly possession. Even innocuous souvenirs can become a burden; they stick to their owner as sin sticks to the sinner. Belongings *are* sin, perhaps? Or what else is the meaning of Christ's ominous parable about the rich man, the camel, and the eye of a needle?

It may be that Gide remembered this dreadful warning when he wrote in his journal, "There are extremely few things that really mean something to me. But I do not know how to get rid of them in a decent fashion. At times I undertake journeys, just in order to escape from my belongings."

Satan has many faces, he employs many traps and baits. Are cigarettes a contrivance of the Evil one? Gide seems to think so. At any rate, that is the impression he gave when he discussed the cigarette issue with such extraordinary gravity.

I was all the more startled when I noticed, some time afterwards, that the whole tobacco incident was a sort of paradoxical self-quotation—*paradoxical*, because Gide amused, or tortured, himself by assuming the character and actually using the words of a rather unpleasant personality he had just portrayed—namely, Pastor Vedel, an unctuous hypocrite who belongs to the personnel of *Les Faux-Monnayeurs*. His inability to resist cigarettes is one of Vedel's petty obsessions—an unending source of struggle and remorse.

What a strange discovery! Why did he choose, among

all disguises, all identities at his disposal, just the one that must be most hideous to him? Why did he quote, or even impersonate for a while, that canting pedagogue, when his fantasy was pregnant with so many more attractive characters? Evidently, he ridiculed and humiliated himself by repeating Vedel's petty scruples as though they were his own.

The pastor's ethical views are primitive and distorted; Gide's, complicated and truthful. Vedel adheres to clear-cut principles (which he transgresses by stealth), whereas Gide strives for a new moral code, in the complex structure of which "good" and "evil" overlap and can hardly be separated. He realizes that it is by no means always good, and not even always Christian, to avoid risks and resist temptations. To comply with evil can be advisable, indeed, necessary, in the interest of both God and man.

Gide, constantly preoccupied with such problems, goes as far, at times, as to feign hypocrisy and accept the rôle of a liar, as a sort of self-chastisement and paradoxical self-denial.

He was more like himself—in fact, he was typically, strikingly "Gidean"—when he wondered about the little peddler's feelings and grimaces. As a psychologist and an ethical thinker, Gide has always been fascinated by precisely those reactions and impulses people try to conceal. From his early youth he was haunted by the ideas of exciting things occurring behind his back. "At times it seemed to me," he tells us in his memoirs, "that I might catch a glimpse of I-do-not-know-what, if only I turned around swiftly enough."

Moreover, he takes it for granted that others are

possessed by equal curiosity. When one of his friends, Julian Green, complained to him about the indiscretion of a chambermaid, Gide smiled mysteriously and said that he expected, in fact, rather liked, his servants to be inquisitive. Time and again, Gide disclosed, he would leave some slightly objectionable letters or diary notes on his desk, unlocked and visible, with the definite purpose of inciting the curiosity of his butler or chambermaid. "Of course, I would be deeply disappointed, even a little hurt, if I had to find out that they did not care to penetrate my secrets. Such a reserve would simply prove an offensive lack of interest in my private affairs."

Are Gide's enemies right, then, when they call him "morbidly indiscreet"?

Maybe they are not quite wrong; but, at any rate, they are grossly indiscreet themselves. For what they do is to exploit malignantly Gide's own voluntary confessions. Slander becomes all the more unfair and indelicate when the slanderers use material provided by their candid and generous victim.

How cheap and mean, to "discover" and denounce Gide's curiosity, since he has said himself, not once but hundreds of times, that this inquisitive impulse is one of his basic and essential features. True, this fervent thirst for knowledge, the main source of Gide's inspiration, can manifest itself as wanton intrusiveness. But this danger is balanced, in Gide's particular case, by another fundamental element inherent in his being—his inexorable, absolute sincerity.

It is bad taste to blame a man for certain qualities which he himself constantly exposes and analyzes. It strikes me as superfluous and vulgar to arraign the "vanity" of a writer who divulges in his diary that his "perpetual question" and "morbid obsession" is: *Am I lovable?*

No doubt, Gide is coquettish; he wants to please, to seduce; in fact, he is a bit of an actor. Whoever has listened to him when he reads aloud from his writings is inevitably charmed, even spellbound, by the subtle effectiveness of his histrionic technique. He can be irresistible when he wants to conquer a person whose affection seems worth-while to him. But this coquetry is controlled, or mostly suppressed altogether, by virtue of his tact, reserve, and self-irony.

According to his legend Gide is arrogant. He may actually seem so when he keeps a morose, discouraging silence in the face of an elegant crowd, or of an obtrusive journalist. There are things that get on his nerves. The society woman who succeeds, by some miracle, in getting hold of him for her literary *soirée* may have a terrible time. The "lion," whom she expected to thrill her party with his daring talk, is likely to hide in a corner, petrified by boredom, or to pace the room, near the door through which he intends to sneak out as soon as possible.

He may appear conceited when one of the ladies addresses herself to him with an idle but innocuous remark, say, about the current best-selling novel. I, for my part, do not forget his disgusted grimace when I asked him whether he liked *David Golder*—a sensational success, at the time. "Golder?" he said, as absentminded and scornful as a Proustian snob when asked about a social parvenu who is not admitted to the exclusive *monde*, "David Golder? *Je regrette. Connais pas.*"

I ventured to say that I had a prejudice against best-

sellers myself, but that the thriller in question happened to
be indeed fairly interesting. Whereupon Gide shrugged
his shoulders. "Maybe it is," he said. "I don't care."

It was impossible to demur from this scathing verdict.
Without having read the book, Gide knew what sort of
stuff it was, and to what type of readers it owed its sweeping popularity. He considered the whole affair not worth
talking about.

Despite his modesty and his qualms concerning his own
achievement, he is aware of his rank. Used to compare his
efforts with the sublime patterns of classic literature, he refuses to condescend to the sphere of sensational, trashy
writing.

But while exclusive in the realm of letters, he is genial
and responsive in all other domains of life. The same man
who can be chilly, even frightening, when dealing with
lion-hunters or tawdry celebrities, will always be of ex-
quisite politeness in his attitude towards those socially inferior to him. An old gardener's tale about flowers and
animals, the gossip of an experienced concierge, are much
more attractive to him than the eloquence of an Academi-
cian.

He enjoys the company of primitive, unspoiled people
more than being with highbrows, and he seems more fascinated by children than by any grown-ups. His penchant
for Arabian adolescents constitutes an integral part of his
"wicked" legend. But I have seen him enchanted with the
most innocent intention, also by ordinary, white children.

When he was our guest in Munich, my youngest brother
and sister were presented to him. The little girl was about
eleven, the boy about ten years old, at the time. Gide's face

was flushed with delight and with curiosity as he looked at them and asked them various questions in his quaintly well-turned German.

"How do you like my youngsters?" the proud mother inquired as soon as the two had withdrawn. "Michael already is quite a fellow, isn't he?"

"*Mais, Madame!*" Gide exclaimed, beaming with admiration. "*Mais vous savez bien qu'il est superbe. Il est robuste comme tout: c'est un plaisir de le voir.*"

It was more than just a compliment. His *Journal* confirms the sincerity of his enthusiasm. We read, under the date of July 1, 1931, "Excursion by car to the Lake of Starnberg, with Thomas Mann and his family. The two youngest children accompany us, both gloriously handsome . . ."

He seemed in high spirits, throughout that fine summer day. Yet in his diary he complains about a headache that harassed him at that time. It was this disturbing migraine he held responsible for what he thought his "*mauvaise grace*" —his poor manners. What actually happened was a bantering argument between my mother and him concerning a zoological question—the propagation of butterflies, to be quite precise. The whole incident was as harmless and inconsequential as could be. And still Gide worried subsequently about his imaginary incivility.

His rueful report continues, "Curious, this disposition to impolite obstinacy which often results from headache. At the dinner, which succeeded Thomas Mann's lecture at the University, I was placed between Thomas Mann and Bruno Frank, whose conversation is unusually enjoyable. I maintained against both that there is, besides Goethe's *Prometheus* monologue, a short play in three acts of which the monologue is a part, and that this play is *not* the *Pandora*; moreover, that the Hafiz translation by Hammer is the one Goethe studied and which stimulated him to write his *Divan*. To be verified. . . . Was it also the migraine which induced me to leave a very inadequate tip for the waiter?"

To the published version of his *Journal*, Gide added a special footnote to the effect that "Bruno Frank actually mistook the Hafiz translator Hammer for another man of the same name, born considerably later, after Goethe's time."

So Gide is indeed a pedant?

His minute conscientiousness even in trifling matters is but one aspect and manifestation of his extreme intellectual probity. A misquotation is to him as shocking as a crime may be to us. His extraordinary memory not only protects him from making mistakes himself but also renders him particularly sensitive to the mistakes of others. I am sure that he often renounces, out of modesty and politeness, an argument in which he could easily prove his point. An incorrect citation of his own text can annoy him more than the meanest invective. His Puritan righteousness revolts against every lie. But no other deceit vexes him so much as does a wanton distortion of the written, verifiable word.

A second detail occurring in the Munich diary note seems to confirm another unpleasant feature of Gide's legend. His remark about the inadequate tip suggests a certain pettiness in financial matters. It sounds as if he tried—but unsuccessfully!—to overcome his inborn avarice.

One of the most-repeated anti-Gide anecdotes is the one

about the penniless young writer whom he took for luncheon to a fairly expensive restaurant. When the meal was over, Gide continued to chat, oblivious, as it were, of so trifling a necessity as paying the bill. A quarter of an hour passed—half an hour, and more. The last diners left the restaurant. The waiter, lingering near the table, repeatedly cleared his throat to remind "*ces messieurs*" of their duty. The broke young man became more and more fidgety. He glanced at the ominous piece of paper, then at Gide, at the waiter, then at the bill again. Gide still did not move. Was he gloating over the embarrassment of his guest? Finally he said, with one of those notorious twinkles in his eyes, "*Que voulez-vous, mon ami? Je suis avare—c'est tout.*"

Of course, the story is pure invention. But even presuming that Gide had actually pulled such a cruel trick on a poor little fellow, it would by no means prove his stinginess. He might have done so out of sheer curiosity, in order to watch the perplexed face of his victim. Or he wanted the incident to be repeated, perhaps, as an additional touch to his demoniac nimbus. An inverted impostor, he attempted at times to appear more diabolic than he actually is. While others display their virtues and conceal their vices, it is the other way round with him.

In a character sketch entitled "Conversation with a German"—a queer piece, in various respects—Gide describes a rather unpleasant man, who came from Cologne to Paris for the sole purpose of paying a visit to him. For one reason or another, Gide expected the stranger to ask him for a loan, and prepared in advance his refusal. But the visitor spared him the speech; surprisingly, he did not ask for money. Why, then, does Gide emphasize his determination to deny what was not entreated of him?

And why is he so unduly discreet, on the other hand, as regards his generosity? I happen to know that he frequently gives very substantial sums, not only to friends in need, but also to strangers who come to him with their sorrows. Such noble deeds he performs secretly, as if ashamed of his kindness. But he sounds almost boastful when he dwells on his less impressive actions or impulses.

No doubt, Gide is in part responsible himself for some of the falsifications concerning his character. Especially in his youth it amused him too much to shock the Philistines and to bewilder even his friends. It was in reference to Baudelaire that he spoke, most revealingly, of certain "bizarre contradictions and almost absurd antagonisms which might be easily taken for feints—all the more as he also indulged in feints."

Gide may be right when he asserts that Baudelaire's *"feintes de parade"*—designed to scandalize the mob—irritated some of his most exacting readers, particularly as certain other readers admired him just on account of these tricks.

Evidently, Gide, in describing Baudelaire, disclosed certain trends and potentialities of his own character. He certainly did not dislike to be scandalous. Nobody will be defamed (or praised) as a demon and demoralizer, unless he aspires to this curious glory, if only unwittingly or temporarily. It is not by accident that Gide quotes, with the accent of amused approval, the answer Flaubert gave when asked what sort of reputation would please him most. *"Celle du démoralisateur,"* said the author of *Madame Bovary.*

Gide is even more outspoken when he cites a German diatribe against Nietzsche, climaxed in this remarkable sentence: "And thus Nietzsche will be always remembered as a corrupter of youth." "Which is maybe the most attractive career," adds André Gide.

But even if he thought this sort of fame desirable—as he did, perhaps, in certain capricious moments—it remains surprising that the public and even a number of critics should have been deceived by his occasional "gala feints." His signal integrity, the candid seriousness of his being, ought to have refuted and foiled his own playful efforts to appear diabolic.

Or has he been misunderstood, not because of his feints, but because of his truthfulness? Has he been called a cynic because he refused to lie? Has he been labeled as an anarchist because he defied outdated conventions? His authentic purity is more shocking, perhaps, than his faked wickedness? And what critics have denounced as "mannered" or "obscure" in his writings might turn out to be the accurate expression of his innermost complexity.

"*Ma valeur est dans ma complication*," says Gide.

Those who could not grasp the complications of his character blamed him for the contradictions inherent in his work.

> Do I contradict myself?
> Very well, then, I contradict myself;
> (I am large—I contain multitudes.)

It may be permissible to apply Walt Whitman's self-assured words to his more fragile, but equally complex brother, André Gide of France.

Of course, it is impossible to define the "multitudes" contained in his character without first describing this character and its background. The various energies focused in Gide's work and nature have to be visualized as an entity, a living, indivisible organism whose growth is insolubly linked with developments of a larger scale and of more general relevancy.

To understand André Gide, we have to conceive his work and character as a product and an expression of both his specific background and our epoch at large. It is a difficult, dangerous epoch, rich in paradoxes and polarities, which has molded the substance of André Gide and manifests itself in his writings. How, then, could we expect—how could we want his work and faith to be simple?

II. THE HEIR

Quite apart from the fact that I am a décadent, *I am also the contrary.*
FRIEDRICH NIETZSCHE

Oh! naître de nouveau. Oublier ce que les autres hommes ont écrit, ont peint, ont pensé, ce que l'on a pensé soi-même. Naître à neuf.
ANDRÉ GIDE

ANDRÉ GIDE was born in Paris, on November 22, 1869.

"On November 22," his diary informs us, "our planet shifts from the influence of Scorpio to that of Sagittarius."

And he adds, addressing himself to those who blame him for his "uprootedness," "Is it my fault that your God elected to make me come to this earth between two stars, as a product of two races, two provinces, and two confessions?"

The "two races" are the peasant stock from which he is descended on his father's side, and the well-to-do, patrician family of his mother, Madame Juliette Gide, née Rondeaux, from Rouen. His maternal clan is rooted in fertile Normandy, whereas the Gides came from a barren mountain zone in the south of France. Those are the "two provinces" he refers to.

As for the "two confessions," Gide alludes to the Catholic-Protestant polarity which is such an integral part

of his heritage. True, his childhood and youth were dominated, almost exclusively, by a Puritanism of almost Calvinist austerity. Yet the Catholic streak, derived from certain
sectors of his mother's parentage, never ceased altogether
to influence the atmosphere of his home.

As a half-grown youth, André toyed with the idea of
becoming a convert to the Catholic creed. It was at the
time when a Protestant pastor prepared him for the solemn
ritual of the First Communion. The dryness of these perfunctory lessons could not satisfy the metaphysical appetites of a passionate, striving heart. André began to wonder
whether the form of religion in which he was being in-
structed did actually respond to the innermost requirements of his soul. The more colorful apparatus of the
Catholic faith intrigued and attracted him. Naïvely, he
went to the minister with his qualms and desires. This very
gesture—futile, even unsuitable in itself—indicates what he
was really longing for, the purifying balm of Confession.

He had sins to confess, even when still a child.

The sketch of little André as drawn by Gide in his
memoirs *(Si le Grain ne meurt)* is indeed appalling. "At
an age when you would expect every soul to be all trans-
parency, innocence, and affection, I find in myself nothing
but darkness, ugliness, and stealth."

A photograph taken at that time shows him in a ridiculous outfit, a kind of chequered crinoline, clinging to the
skirts of his mother; a sickly and nasty youngster with a
sidewise look in a sallow and twisted face.

This is, indeed, the problematical infant who indulged

in "evil habits" when he was not more than five or six years old. He was lonely and always haunted by a feeling of guilt. At times an indescribable apprehension would overwhelm him, without any visible reason. It happened that he came home from school and suddenly burst into tears at the dinner table. His horrified mother tried to comfort him, but in vain; he would not even disclose what caused his abrupt distress. His sole explanation were these terrifying words he repeated, convulsed with sobs, "*Je ne suis pas pareil aux autres! Je ne suis pas pareil aux autres!*"

"I am not like the others . . ." What an alarming wail to be hurled by a lad of eleven!

This incident took place about the time when André lost his father. From that point on, the climate of his youth seems imbued even more intensely with that extraordinary flavor of sorrow and moral struggle.

The boy's entourage consisted of three aging women, all of them dressed in black: his mourning mother; Anna Shackleton, a wretched spinster kept by charity; and the bigoted, bourgeois Aunt Clara. It was she, Aunt Clara— the embodiment of Puritan strictness—who watched jealously over the dignity of the house. She decided upon what was "done," and what not. Hers was the last word in all matters of virtue and etiquette.

Is it surprising, then, that a sensitive boy should have reacted against such a rigid and arbitrary ruler? Can we blame him for having subsequently developed a bitter resentment against the institution and authority of the Family as such?

Yet we must not forget that this very resentment, with

all its stimulating implications, is one of the precious things Gide owes to his austere upbringing. His sense of independence was aroused and sharpened by the oppressive tutelage he endured. The signal perspicacity of his ethical evaluations may in part be due to his early experience. By watching and criticizing his difficult relatives and unctuous pedagogues, he became familiar with many shades of furtive viciousness and ostentatious virtue.

But the advantages of Gide's Puritan education were not only of this indirect nature. For if it is true that they were stingy and narrow-minded, those demure females and smug gentlemen by whom young André was surrounded, it is also true that their way of life was determined by certain tenets of indisputable validity. The moral code they adhered to—if only for conventional reasons, in order to be *comme il faut*—consisted by no means solely of obsolete clichés. The Huguenot gentry, to which the Gides belonged, considered themselves the last trustees of moral traditions glaringly disregarded by most other sectors of society. Presuming even that their righteousness was not always genuine but primarily meant to impress or to dupe the world, the fact remains, and is significant, that those well-to-do Calvinist families deemed virtue indispensable enough to feign obedience to its rules at least, if not to obey them in earnest. The cant of the Pharisees implies the acceptance of certain basic moral principles. And La Rochefoucauld is right when he says that hypocrisy is the homage vice renders to morality.

Thanks to his Protestant education, Gide learned as a child to appreciate and exercise such qualities as self-control, pride, patience, and truthfulness. The moral climate in his mother's house was apt to teach him the painstaking conscientiousness typical of his style. In the peculiar milieu in which young André grew up, the rank of an individual did not depend completely on the size of his bank account, nor was money believed to be the only value worth aspiring to. Idealistic notions like honor, loyalty, and rectitude were still taken seriously—if not always followed—by the pastors and lawyers of which the Gide clan consisted.

Even the concept of culture maintained a definite meaning in this orderly, bourgeois world. Not that Aunt Clara or the *née* Rondeaux were connoisseurs of art and literature, naturally not. But they considered it *comme il faut* to be familiar, in some degree at least, with the works of French classical writers, German composers, Dutch and Italian painters. Needless to say that anything unusual or frivolous was strictly out of the question. As long, however, as the genius respected the taboos of prudishness, his work was tolerated, even enjoyed at times, by the civilized Puritans.

Madame Gide was in the habit of taking her son to all art exhibitions recommended by the conservative paper, *Le Temps*. Conscientious as she was, she would cut out, and carry along to the show, the article in which *Le Temps* appraised the paintings in question. Instead of looking at the canvases, Madame would reread, in front of them, the verdicts of the critic, as if she feared to be impressed by the wrong things otherwise, or to be not impressed at all.

As for music, the widow preferred Mozart and Beethoven, but did not really object to her boy's fancy for Schumann. Chopin, however, was disapproved of because of his "morbidity." When the great Rubinstein gave a series of piano recitals, in 1883, André was not allowed to attend the evening devoted to Chopin's work. It may be that his subsequent passion for the Polish romanticist results from such memories. Several decades later, in his *Notes sur Chopin* (1931), Gide speaks derisively of certain reproaches to which Chopin and Baudelaire were equally subjected. *"Unsound music,* one said about Chopin; *unsound poetry,* about Baudelaire . . ."* Characteristically, Baudelaire was long Gide's favorite poet, and the love for Chopin accompanied him throughout life. Not only did he never tire of listening to his *Etudes* and *Préludes,* but it remained one of his dearest pastimes to play them at the piano himself.

During a certain period of Gide's youth the spell of the theater almost superseded that of art, books, and music. The *Odéon,* the *Comédie Française,* the *Opéra Comique,* became the focus of his imagination, the temporary center of his life. But this fervent hobby did not last nor did it have significant consequences for André's further development. The same dramatic devices that once captivated and enchanted him, became later unbearable to his taste. "Maybe I had too much of it, at the time?" the former theater fan wonders, in *Si le Grain ne meurt.* "Everything in the theater now strikes me as prearranged, conventional, exaggerated, and dull."

Be this as it may, what counts is that Gide's tutors and relatives, and above all his mother, considered artistic impressions a vital part of their educational scheme. No matter how cautiously and arbitrarily selected these impressions may have been, the stimulus due to them is still important enough.

It was from his family that Gide received a first inkling of science and literature. The contact with his uncle, Charles Gide, an economist of international reputation, could not but enrich his young mind. Even more valuable is, perhaps, what he owes to the humble spinster, Anna Shackleton. A remarkable linguist, the penniless *mademoiselle* spent her time translating the masterpieces of foreign literatures into the French language. Gide dwells in his memoirs on the merits of her adaptations—praising especially the fine job she did in the case of Goethe's hexameter epos, *Reinecke Fuchs*. Thanks to the meek old lady, he became first acquainted with Goethe and also with the delights of botany. For Mademoiselle Anna was at least as interested in plants as in poetry—an amiable ambivalence of interest which greatly appealed to her young friend and pupil. In fact, botanic studies were to remain, like music, one of the occupations he could always have recourse to when his mind rebelled against the too long strain of creative thought.

It was within the circle of his family that André found the girl whom he never ceased to love, nay, to worship with a chivalrous, almost religious devotion. His future wife, Emmanuèle, was his cousin on the maternal side. Emmanuèle and André were children when they met, in Emmanuèle's home at Rouen. She was pious and sensitive. Her cousin and admirer later described the mysterious melancholy in her look and smile. "Not that I knew she was sad; for she never told me. But between my cousin and me there already was that conscious affinity of all thoughts and feelings, which I wholeheartedly wanted to develop and to deepen."

They played and they prayed together. Together, they explored and relished the miracles of nature. And, some years later, they embarked together, two congenial wanderers, on the infinite excursions into the realm of letters. "The extreme interest I now took in everything chiefly sprang from the fact that Emmanuèle accompanied me everywhere," Gide said when reviewing this period of his spiritual awakening. "I would presently inform her of any new discovery, and my joy was not perfect unless she shared in it."

The three crucial discoveries of his youth were the Bible, Greek mythology, and the *Arabian Nights*. The complicated structure of his intellectual organism is entirely based upon this triune revelation.

Of course, intimate and thorough knowledge of the Scripture was taken for granted in the Gide ménage. But André's religious obsession had nothing to do with the obligatory routine. At a time when other lads busy themselves with football or stamp collections, he was absorbed in a fervent and meticulous exegesis of the Gospels. "I read the Bible avidly, gluttonously, but methodically," he reports, in *Si le Grain ne meurt*. He perused the sacred text with the searching enthusiasm a scientist may experience in deciphering the traces of ancient civilizations. As a boy of fifteen, Gide tasted the double ecstasy of faith and criticism. He studied the Holy Word like a great work of art, but at the same time conceived it as what it is—namely, the revealed essence of Divinity.

The Book of Books disclosed graciously its intrinsic balm

to the eagerness of this precocious youth. So powerful, indeed, was the flame of this early ecstasy that it shed its light throughout a long and eventful life. The prayers cried out by the aging man will resound his juvenile impetrations. Fifty years after his First Communion he will not have to discover Christ any more: he will rediscover Him. By remembering his own childhood he will remember the Lord.

"*Je reviens à vous, Seigneur Christ, comme à Dieu dont vous êtes la forme vivante. Je suis las de mentir à mon cœur. C'est vous que je retrouve partout, alors que je croyais vous fuir, ami divin de mon enfance.*"

This candid invocation appears in one of Gide's more recent works—one of the finest testimonies of his mature thought and faith, *Les Nouvelles Nourritures* (1935). In the same volume, however, we find also the reaffirmation of his belief in Hellas and in the immortality of her gods. "Who dares say that the Great Pan is dead?" exclaims Gide, at the age of almost seventy. "Through the haze of my own breath I have seen him. My lips are longing for his caress . . ."

"The first condition to understand the Greek myths is to believe in them." With these words opens a brilliant essay about Greek Mythology which Gide composed in the prime of his manhood.

He never betrayed the Olympus which comforted and elated him when he was hardly more than a child. Early versed in all kinds of darkness and entanglement, he responded gratefully to the serene persuasion of Hellenic beauty. Man's errors and sufferings appear less bitter, easier to bear, when accompanied by the majestic smile of Apollo and Aphrodite. The lonesome, sensitive child, André, cloistered with his mourning *maman*, recognized in Ulysses the hero-wanderer he would have wished to be. Oh, to join this illustrious brother in his wondrous adventures! To share the hardships of his pilgrimage would also mean to enjoy—bound with him at the mast—the inconceivable sweetness of the siren songs; it would mean to participate in his wiles and pranks; would mean freedom and danger, pride and happiness.

Or would it be even more wonderful to be the companion of Sindbad the Sailor or of the disguised caliph when he loitered, incognito, in the midst of his gaudy subjects?

The *Arabian Nights* was the first book, after the Bible, that Gide read and loved. Twenty years afterwards he said that "the prodigious inventions" of these tales had never ceased to appeal to his *curiosity* (the italics are Gide's), that he remained captivated by the sensual flavor of the Oriental world.

It is the rampant avidity of both spirit and senses which enthralls him in the *Arabian Nights*. In comparison, all Occidental vagaries and romances appear cautious and lusterless. "How far are we from Greece!" exclaims Gide, and then quotes Ulysses, whose figure and destiny seems relatively akin to the Oriental pattern. But even he, the most daring, most cunning one among the Hellenic heroes, cannot cope with Sindbad the Sailor. For Sindbad has no Ithaca awaiting him, no wife, no son, no dog. Nor are there any feelings to restrain his fervor. No being could be freer, more vagrant, more detached. It even seems that Sindbad has no face—just new masquerades for every new adventure. His character consists but of one sole impulse, which is precisely the one impelling him to ever new risks —that is, an insatiable and inordinate curiosity.

Curiosity—an unquenchable thirst for action and suspense—is the one motive power behind all horrors and splendors of the *Arabian Nights*. There are no divine restrictions, none of the threats or promises so lavishly used by Jehovah. In the bedeviling maze of Oriental cities, instinct alone decides upon what Allah allows, what not.

Yet Gide goes so far as to compare the *Arabian Nights* to the Bible. Those who fail to understand and love, either the one or the other, are equally strange to him. He might have added the Hellenic myth as the third component without which he could not have become what he is and we could not understand him.

"How I envied him and his Protestant childhood!" Jean Cocteau said, referring to André Gide. "I visualized him skating with singular grace on the waters of Russia, with a Bible in his hand. In beautiful English style he wrote his name on the ice . . ."

He forgot to mention the grand setting in the classical French style in front of which the daring pirouettes were executed, and the thunderous German orchestra that accompanied the performance.

The scion of Puritan pastors, peasants, and lawyers—the heir of a ripe bourgeois civilization and of an agreeable bank account—was keen and resilient enough to absorb and integrate the most incongruous elements of the Occidental genius. Diligent and methodic, for all his erratic moods, he delved into the treasure-laden labyrinth of European thought, exploring the cosmic grandeur of Dante, Shake-speare, and Goethe; Racine's noble perfection and Molière's revealing drolleries; the baroque secrets of German Roman-ticism; the bountiful wisdom and wit of the English nar-rators; the divine confusions of Russian mysticism, and the transparent depth of Stendhal and Baudelaire.

Gide's idea of culture has never been limited by frontiers or prejudices. It comprises Dickens and Montaigne, Push-kin and La Fontaine, Rimbaud and Hölderlin, Whitman and Verlaine. Goethe meant almost as much to him as Racine; Nietzsche, more than Pascal. The acquaintance with Dostoevski was one of the turning points in his de-velopment. The frantic struggle of the Russian visionary seems more moving and significant to him than Balzac's royal self-assurance and "generous imperfection." Also, he plays Dostoevski off against Tolstoi—the inspired agonies of the epileptic against the Homeric equilibrium of the amazing squire who composed the saga of *War and Peace.*

For Gide's enthusiasm was at no point indiscriminate. Even in the days of youthful receptivity, he felt it neces-sary to make his choice among the manifold riches offered to him, to select whatever he deemed most wholesome and adequate. True, he was disposed to accept too many influ-ences, rather than reject a single one that promised a new stimulus. In a brilliant address, *De l'influence en littérature* (1900), he ventured to defend all influences *as such*—no matter if "good" or "evil." A strong and flexible nature, Gide holds, may succeed in transforming pebbles into bread, dubious advices into real inspiration. Did not Goethe pride himself on devouring everything recommended to him by Herder?

But in this particular case a selection was made all the same (as Gide must have realized but failed to mention), if not by Goethe himself, then by his trusted mentor. As for Gide, he had no experienced friend whose guidance he could have followed without questioning. In fact, he was not the man to follow blindly any kind of advice. Notwithstanding his unconditional eulogy of *all* influences, he knew very well how to pick out the right ones—that is to say, all those that could help him to recognize and fulfill another potentiality of his own being.

For this has always been, and still is, the essential purpose of his roving curiosity—to scrutinize and clarify himself by penetrating the spiritual substance and experience of others. Self-identification is the ultimate goal of all his intellectual adventures and transformations. Those who are afraid to jeopardize their personality by the contact with others are likely to be of rather tenuous substance themselves. How absurd and how undignified are their fears! They mean to protect their "original character," while in reality they prevent it from deepening and growing.

Gide believes in and reaffirms the old saying, that nobody can be taught from without what he does not have within, if only latently and subconsciously. The admiration one creative individual feels for another will not change his own intrinsic being. Quite the contrary, it will awaken and legitimatize what might have remained, otherwise, in a state of uncertainty and repression.

Later, in the days of his maturity, Gide was inclined to modify even more drastically the significance of outside influences. "It may be pretty hazardous to assert," he wrote in 1924, "that one would have had certain ideas, even without having read the authors from whom these ideas seem to be derived. And still I cannot help feeling that my views would be about the same if I had known neither Dostoevski nor Freud nor Nietzsche nor X nor Y, and that what I found in them was a confirmation rather than an awakening call (*plutôt une autorisation qu'un éveil*). Above all, they taught me no longer to doubt myself, not to be afraid of my own thought but to accept its guidance, as it turned out to be *their* guidance too."

The young Gide, however, had not yet attained such a high degree of spiritual independence. To him, influences meant something more decisive than "encouragement." His impressionable mind was easily touched and seized by any appeal that carried a congenial tune, a welcome stimulus.

He, who was destined to revive and reaffirm the classical French tradition, first abandoned himself to the sweet narcotic of extreme romanticism. It was not the romantic poets of France by whom he felt attracted—not Chateaubriand or Musset. Reading the works of Browning, he thought, with patriotic pride, "But we have Victor Hugo!" But a new occupation with Hugo's pompous oratory was rather embarrassing. "Nothing could be more magnificent, nothing more absurd," the young reader observed in his diary. And when he was asked, some time afterwards, whom he deemed the outstanding French poet, his succinct answer was, "Victor Hugo, alas."

His heroes, at that point, were mostly English or German. He deeply admired Keats and Hölderlin, Coleridge and Novalis, Shelley and Heinrich Heine. Byron cast his saturnine spell on him, as did Arthur Schopenhauer, in a different, more cerebral, fashion. He reveled in Schumann's floating melancholy, so well in keeping with Manfred's bombastic gloom. It was his ambition to translate the fragmentary novel of Novalis, *Heinrich von Ofterdingen*, and Chamisso's lovely fairy-tale, *Peter Schlemihl*. But later, when he really adapted foreign masterworks, the originals he chose were mostly written in English. He preferred Shakespeare and Whitman, Conrad and Tagore to the German romanticists.

This gradual shift from the Germanic sphere to the English is characteristic and significant. In his later years, Gide rather distrusted the Teutonic attraction, to which he had hitherto been only too sensible. True, he had no passion for Wagner to overcome; this typical disease of his epoch and generation was entirely spared him. Gide had alawys been impervious to the massive seduction of the Sorcerer of Bayreuth. He did not need to "overcome" the sirens of Tristan and Parsifal.

This complete immunity to the Wagnerian bacillus is indeed a striking proof of Gide's extreme independence in all matters concerning taste and style. While *tout Paris* was smitten with the portly heroes and heroines of the *drame musicale*, he remained glacially unmoved.

His language is as blunt as could be when he answers an inquiry of the *Berliner Tageblatt* concerning Richard Wagner's influence in France: "I have a horror of Wagner's work and personality; my passionate aversion has constantly increased since my childhood. This prodigious genius is crushing rather than exalting. He has encouraged scores of snobs, scribblers, and half-wits to think that they are fond of music, and has made some artists believe that genius is something that could be learned. Germany has never produced, perhaps, anything so great and so barbaric."

Did Gide deem Wagner typically German? It may be, alas, that he thought him more characteristic than, for instance, Goethe, whom he always admired and at times nearly worshiped. But while he never denied his vast indebtedness to the author of *Faust* and *Tasso*, he questioned occasionally what Goethe owes to Germany. In Gide's "Reflections about Germany" (1919) we find the following eloquent passage:

"Who could be more Spanish than Cervantes? More English than Shakespeare? More Italian than Dante? More French than Voltaire or Montaigne, than Descartes or Pascal? Who could be more Russian than Dostoevski, and still more universally human than all these men? But I hardly dare ask: Who could be more German than Goethe? For, in Germany's case, Prussia is responsible for a terrible misconception. Prussia has subjugated Germany so completely that we are forced to think: *Goethe was the most un-German one of all Germans.*"

It may be true—in fact, it seems certain to me—that the German vein in the compound of Gide's vision has been greatly exaggerated: partly by his German admirers who claimed him as a disciple of their native masters; partly by the French nationalists who took him to task for his sympathy with the Teutonic Antichrist. But it is also true that Gide at times unduly belittled what he owes to German genius. It sounds somewhat surprising to hear from him this reply to an inquiry about the influence of German culture: "I can hardly formulate an opinion about 'German influence'; for I have no opinion in this particular matter.

True, in my youth I was considerably impressed by Germany; but, after all, the best thing I learned from Goethe, Heine, Schopenhauer, Nietzsche is, perhaps, their admiration for France."

This he wrote in 1903, twelve years after the publication of his first book, *Les Cahiers d'André Walter*. The anti-German reaction was perhaps inevitable, according to the dialectic law inherent in his mental structure. He had gone very far—as far as possible—in the direction of musical pessimism, which is precisely the mood he confounded with the notion of *German*. What he had most deeply loved in German romanticism, and what he subsequently tried to eliminate, was the melancholy estrangement from reality, the Hamlet complex, of German genius.

Julian Green reports on a most illuminating conversation about Hamlet he once had with Gide. Hamlet's question—"And what make you from Wittenberg, Horatio?"—suggests, according to Gide, that the Prince of Denmark feels like an exile outside Germany. This nostalgia for Wittenberg may be understood as an additional hint at the essentially German character of Hamlet's problem and tragedy. *To be or not to be*, says Gide, could have been coined, almost, by Arthur Schopenhauer. This constant hesitation, this inability to act, this infirmity of purpose is neither English nor French, but typically German.

The young André Gide, and his first hero, André Walter, indulge—indeed, revel—in Hamlet-like dilemmas and inhibitions. Hypersensitive and hypervulnerable, they belong to those who have "thought themselves weary"—to use Goethe's formula. André (Gide or Walter) is paralyzed by introspection, incapable of coping with reality.

Thus conscience does make cowards of us all;
And thus the native hue of resolution
Is sicklied o'er with the pale cast of thought;
And enterprises of great pith and moment,
With this regard, their currents turn awry,
And lose the name of action . . .

Hamlet's wail might be set as a motto at the beginning of *Les Cahiers d'André Walter*.

The book is neither a novel nor a treatise nor a prose poem, but a loose compilation of lyric and philosophic *aperçus*, the posthumous confession, allegedly, of a young man who was destroyed by an overdose of music, madness, and meditation.

He enjoys life in his own way, which is a highly morbid and complicated way, to be sure. While fighting his carnal appetites, he relishes the more delicate sensations—perfumes and sounds and tints; tears and smiles and grand, wasted gestures; white blooms, and music—music above all. *"De la musique avant toute chose . . . de la musique encore et toujours . . ."*

He also loves a girl. The imaginary André Walter pays homage, ecstatically, to the quasi-imaginary sweetheart, Emmanuèle, of the real André Gide. But his love is as airy, as floating and noncommittal, as everything in this book. How could he love anyone, really and completely, since he is in love with his solitude, and wants to remain pure, to overcome the coarse temptations of the flesh? *"Les corps me gênent,"* admits this ascetic fiancé. Surely he desires the ultimate and perfect communion with Emmanuèle; but it is only in another world that he hopes to attain it. Here below, he would have to sacrifice his chastity—too high a price for a happiness that could not but be imperfect and illusionary. Leaving poor Emmanuèle to her own silvery reveries, he spends the summer nights with Chopin and Baudelaire—intoxicated by sterile subtleties and by his morbid pride. "*Oh Seigneur! je suis pur! je suis pur! je suis pur!*"

What an odd, disquieting prelude is this hallucinatory confession! Gide himself was pretty hard on it, in a preface he added to a new edition of *Les Cahiers*, in 1930, almost forty years after the first publication. He sharply disapproved, from the point of view of his maturity, of both the style and the moral attitude manifest in his juvenile outburst. "What embarrasses me most in rereading my *Cahiers*," he says, "is the self-indulgence with which every page is tainted."

Yes, the young man, high-minded but callow, who appears in the sentimental masquerade of an André Walter, certainly indulged in all kinds of vagaries and eccentric poses. His rhapsodic prose is rather shapeless and turgid, teeming with stylistic mannerisms and incongruities. But it is also full of superb and arresting things, inspired images and persuasive accents. *Les Cahiers* are, in their own fashion, as stirring and authentic as anything Gide has written. In fact, this opening song is indispensable to an understanding of the symphony of Gide's work, which is now on the point of unfolding.

* * *

"In order to oppose myself I first had to scrutinize my own being," Gide says in his retrospective remarks about *Les Cahiers d'André Walter*.

The first period of his creative writing is completely devoted to this painstaking effort of self-analysis. After having
abandoned himself, in the *Cahiers*, to his rampant emotions,
he found a more restrained approach to the mysteries of
his ego. The new pattern was a kind of poetic treatise, or
dialectic sermon, in which he exposed certain aspects of his
inner drama.

Le Traité du Narcisse (1892), the first and most significant achievement in that line, presents the artist in the
mythic disguise of the antique youth who was too perfectly handsome to fall in love with anybody but himself.
Absorbed in the reflection of his own immaculate image,
he despises the flattering propositions of the nymphs, who
are rightly shocked by such grossness. Poor Narcissus! Enviable, deplorable lad! How can he know that he has hurt
those nymphs, as he does not even perceive their existence?
"The poet is the one who contemplates," says Gide in
Narcissus. "What does he contemplate? Paradise."

Paradise is perfection—the original pattern of which all
things are but inadequate copies. Paradise is the archetype
of this imperfect creation, the Idea inherent in all palpable
and perishable forms.

Every artist keeps his memory of Paradise. His incurable
nostalgia for the *idea* behind the thing is his innate curse,
his permanent affliction, and also the source of his genius,
the heart and life of his vision.

Where can he hope to find it—his Paradise Lost, his idea,
his perfection? Not in reality, to be sure. Reality is impure
and distorted. Only the reflection of his own nostalgia,
only the images of his dream contain the memory of the
"pure Eden," the "Garden of Ideas."

Reality is unreal. Only the symbol has reality.

Gide's juvenile treatise bears the subtitle, *Théorie du symbole*. It is an eloquent and candid testimony of the Symbolist movement to which Gide adhered at the time.

The same may be said of the other products typical of that phase—*La Tentative amoureuse* (1893), *Le Voyage d'Urien* (1893), and *Paludes* (1895).

As for the last, it already marks, or at least foreshadows, a turning point and liberating crisis. For in *Paludes*, the "Hamlet complex" is subjected, for the first time, to a satiric treatment. Here Gide pokes fun at his own double— a Parisian *décadent* who has lost the ability to do anything, to make any decision—all entangled in the labyrinth of his psychological complications. The neurotic æsthete, whose follies and tribulations are dramatized and mocked in *Paludes*, is indeed the same who formerly described his obsessions, without any self-irony, in such essays, at once brittle and ponderous, as *La Tentative amoureuse*.

This "Tractate of Idle Desires," as Gide himself subtitles his work, exhales the same pathos of renunciation and solitude which resounds throughout the desperate monologues of the miserable, lovable André Walter. The hero of *La Tentative*, a pensive young gentleman named Luc, is no less harassed and disconnected, notwithstanding the philosophical serenity he displays. If André Walter clamored for purity and struggled against temptation, Luc placidly recognizes the vanity of desire. A scholarly ascetic, he quotes Calderon's word to the effect that "desire is like a flame: whatever it touches falls to ashes; nothing remains but a weightless dust which a breath can disperse. Let us think, then, of what is pure and lasting!"

"Things are not worth-while to go out of one's way for their sake." With these words Luc begins his credo. "We may embrace them as we pass by; but our ultimate goal is infinitely beyond all things. Why should we delude ourselves? Things are fleet and evasive. Our goal has to be immovable, and we will wander to reach it. Our sole goal is God; we will not lose Him from sight, as we perceive Him through all things."

Does one recognize the double impact of this philosophy? It echoes the Platonic concept of the Idea which is more real than reality, and at the same time the Christian doctrine which warns us not to overrate the importance of mortal stuff. The ultimate truth is transcendental; everything here below, only illusion and symbol. Luc, an inspired pilgrim, at once ascetic and hedonistic, continues his march toward God. His path is lined by works of art to his right, by beautiful landscapes to his left. But in front of him is always the open road.

We will wander to reach Him . . . This leitmotiv, voiced first in *La Tentative*, anticipates one of the leading thoughts woven to and fro throughout the texture of Gide's entire work. With this announcement—that he will have to wander—Luc refutes and overcomes, at least in principle, his narcissistic isolation. André Walter was ecstatic but motionless, all absorbed in his own image, like Narcissus. Both André and Narcissus avoided reality. Luc, however, one degree more mature and more virile, already attempts to perceive God *without* his ego—no longer exclusively *within*. At this point his quest begins.

It begins timidly and reluctantly, to be sure. *Le Voyage d'Urien* shows us how difficult it must be to break out of an ivory tower. The will to escape, to rove, to take chances, may precede the actual ability to do so. Gide made up his adventures before he dared to face them in reality. How blurred and pallid are the baroque tales of his invented travelers! How playful and precious, compared with the striking simplicity of his later accounts! The skies that witness the fights and romances of these errant knights seem illuminated by hectic suns and artificial stars. The fruits they eat are dream fruits; the oceans they cross do not exist in reality. In the end, the author has to admit, to the woman to whom his fantasy is dedicated, "I have fooled you, Madame. We have never made this journey. I beg your pardon for having lied to you. All these adventures took place in my imagination. I did not leave the cave of my reveries. I passed through life without seeing it. I spent my life reading books."

He might as well have said that he remained cloistered in the solitude of his dreams, even when traveling. For at that time, about 1890, Gide began to travel, or rather, he began to move from one place to another, not so much because he was avid for new impressions as, rather, because he was impelled by disgust with the things and faces surrounding him.

The occasional notes he took during these early trips sound indeed rather dreary. In Belgium our weary tourist confides to his diary: "Saw Brugge and Ostende, yesterday. Such boredom, such lugubrious languidness, overwhelms me as soon as I am in a new city, that my sole desire is to leave immediately. I have been strolling along the avenues in a state of veritable distress. Even if these things are admirable, the mere idea that I should look at them appalls me."

And, again, on the last day of the same journey: "*Grottes de Han.* August 7, 1891: Just finished *War and Peace.* Began to read it the first day of this trip; ended, the last day. Never before, I believe, have I lived so completely in and with a book. Really, I did not travel. The other day, in the famous grottos, I could hardly concentrate. I kept thinking of Tolstoi who awaited me in the car, and it irked me that I had had to stop reading."

The only reality he recognized as such, the only sphere where he felt at ease and not in exile, the only dimension he actually knew and loved, was *art*—art as an aim in itself, for its own sake, *l'art pour l'art;* at once the essence of life and the balm that makes its bitterness endurable. "The work of art," Gide said, in one of his early essays, *Littérature et morale,* "has an equilibrium beyond time, an artificial soundness." And he loved Delacroix for saying, "There is a sort of validity in art which is lacking in man."

It was not an artist's fame that attracted the shy and haughty young man. Quite the contrary. Again and again he insisted on his indifference to, even his contempt of, quick and noisy success. The author of *Les Cahiers d'André Walter* not only did not run after popularity but actually avoided and spurned it. He tried to hide behind the character he created; his first book was published anonymously, as though it were really the legacy of a defunct vagabond. The volume was brought out at Gide's own expense and read (not always bought!) by a few hundred people.

Decades afterwards, at the peak of his fame, Gide remembered, with sincere nostalgia, the peaceful days of darkness. "Oh! happy time when I was not yet heard! And how well one speaks as long as one speaks in the desert!"

"Of course, I spoke in order to be heard," he added, "but by no means in order to be heard at once."

He spoke, he wrote, he sang, and he lamented in order to be heard by other artists—by his peers, his colleagues, his friends. For there is no such thing as art for its own sake. But there is such a thing as art for artists. And that is precisely what flourished in the Paris of 1890—the intellectual center of the *fin de siècle*, the artistic capital of the world.

Life was gregarious, in the Ivory Tower. The eremites stuck together, sneering collectively at the Philistines and at those fellow-artists who fawned upon the Philistines— namely, the outdated, tiresome, clumsy, plebeian Naturalists.

The embittered reaction against Zola and Taine, Renan and the Goncourts, was the motive power behind all Parnassian and Symbolist devices. The naturalistic school had degraded art to a parrot or propagandist of scientific theories or political programs. The Symbolists, clustering around their poet, Stéphane Mallarmé, despised as trivial and journalistic the faintest trace of social criticism, the most casual allusion to any topical issues that crept into the work of art. Only "the Absolute" counted, only the form, the disinterested play of rhythms, colors, and sounds.

They were not cynics or sybarites, those intense young men of Montmartre and the Latin Quarter. They took their métier and mission as seriously as saints or strategists take theirs. At once blasé and exacting, they criticized and analyzed each other, exclusively concerned with their own problems, their own evaluations, their own hierarchy. The heirs of a mellow and secure civilization, they commanded plenty of leisure and, in most cases, sufficient funds to indulge in their caprices and intuitions, regardless of the tastes and the requirements of the public. The painters portrayed the poets, the poets wrote lyrics for the musicians, the writers dedicated their books to each other. Gide dedicated every new work to another friend—*La Tentative amoureuse* to Francis Jammes; *Le Traité du Narcisse* to Paul Valéry, and so on.

The time when terms like "solitude," "estrangement," "isolation," occurred most frequently in Gide's writings was, paradoxically, the most social time in his life. He was one of the Symbolist clique. He belonged to a coterie.

On Tuesday afternoons, Mallarmé received his disciples, including the young André Gide, in his modest apartment. While the men discussed the highest and finest things, Madame Mallarmé concentrated on her embroidery, and Mademoiselle Geneviève, her daughter, prepared a grog for the poets. Sometimes a painter would join the literary gathering—Gauguin, for instance, or Whistler. Or one of the high priests of the slightly outdated Parnassus would drop in and display the most affable suavity towards the young colleagues. The celebrated Parnassians, Leconte de Lisle and Herédia, were frequently seen among Mallarmé's Tuesday guests, while many of the Symbolist crowd showed up at Herédia's Saturday receptions.

Herédia's home, in the *rue Balzac*, was more worldly and sumptuous than Mallarmé's austere dwelling in the *rue de Rome*. Not only the poets flocked to his "Saturdays," but also diplomats, journalists, and society women. As for André Gide, he felt awkward and inhibited in the midst of these brilliant assemblies. "I would have died with embarrassment," he confesses in *Si le Grain ne meurt*, "if it had not been for Pierre Louÿs."

His diaries of that time are full of references to this rakish, amiable pal—Pierre Louÿs (or Louis), who played the rôle of a mundane mentor in his relation to the grave and bashful young Gide. They had met at the *Ecole Alsacienne*, where they were classmates and rivals. André and Pierre were the two brightest boys of the lot, and both wrote poetry, as Louÿs found out when he surprised Gide absorbed in a volume of Heinrich Heine. "You're fond of that kind of stuff?" Louÿs grinned. "I bet you try to write verse yourself."

The two had the time of their lives, later, when they sauntered together through the narrow streets of the Latin Quarter, provoking the bourgeois and evaluating the cosmos. Pierre read poetry to André. André played Schumann and Chopin to Pierre. They needed no other audience. To woo popularity, to become professional, would have meant to betray the intrinsic rules of this friendship.

Louÿs made himself guilty of this unpardonable trespass when he condescended to the cheap taste of the masses and produced a novel, *Aphrodite*, that appealed to the "Boulevard." It was a success, and success was tantamount to betrayal.

Others remained faithful to the romantic innocence of the vanguard, the exclusiveness of a high-minded dilettantism. Paul Valéry, for one, never acquiesced in the requirements of vulgarity. His friendship with André Gide was destined to survive all other comradeships of that period. Long before Valéry had written any of the things to which his glory is due, Gide sensed the aura of his coming greatness. Effusively young, each one was fascinated by the promise emanating from the other's yet unproved genius. Forty years afterwards Gide could assert, in an article appraising the work of a third writer, that, in his opinion, that novelist's art was "one of the most admirable accomplishments in our time. I would indeed say, *the* most admirable one, if Paul Valéry did not exist."

The novelist in question was Marcel Proust, who, in the early nineties, made his timid entrance in the literary salons, under the auspices of Anatole France. But Gide, whose attitude towards the grand old man of French letters was always rather chilly, was scarcely interested in France's protégé, a coy and sickly young snob. The story has often been told—also by Gide himself—how the *Nouvelle Revue Française* turned down the opening volume of Proust's *A la Recherche du temps perdu*, thanks to, or rather, by the fault of, its reader of that time, namely André Gide.

In 1890 and 1895, however, there was no *Nouvelle Revue Française* as yet, and Gide was by no means in a position to decide upon the policy of any major publishing house. There were only little magazines springing up like mushrooms and mostly disappearing with equal swiftness. Gide was involved in many of these ventures. First he founded the little *Potache Revue* (Schoolboy's Magazine), together with Louÿs and a number of other companions. Then it was *La Conque* (The Shell)—about as short-lived and as amateurish as its predecessor. As for *Le Centaure*—following *La Conque*—it could pride itself on original illustrations by Odilon Redon and Puvis de Chavannes. At the *Revue Blanche*, Gide succeeded Léon Blum as literary critic. At *L'Ermitage*, he was a fellow-contributor of Rémy de Gourmont, whose cultural chauvinism he was to oppose so violently in later times. It was from *L'Ermitage* that the *Nouvelle Revue Française* emerged, in 1908, after a good many inside intrigues and quarrels.

But we are not yet at this point of our report, so far. Frankly, we enjoy lingering, for a little while, on those vernal years of expectation and obscurity. How curious, how stimulating, to imagine the savage pranks Gide performed together with Henri Ghéon—a young writer of overflowing vitality, and André's most intimate companion when the friendship with Pierre Louÿs cooled off. How amusing to visualize Gide chatting with Henri de Régnier, one of the most colorful Parnassians and a brilliant man of the world. Gide was heartily devoted to him. "*Je l'aime énormément*," he exclaims in his journal.

One evening Gide found Régnier downhearted and despondent.

"What's the matter?" asked Gide.

"*Ah! mon ami!*" sighed the poet, shrugging his shoulders and dropping his monocle. "I'm getting old, that's all. Almost thirty already . . ."

"How long ago all this seems!" the aging Gide muses in his memoirs.

Long ago . . . It was the time when Gide, after the publication of *Les Cahiers d'André Walter*, received an enthusiastic note from Maeterlinck and a scathing judgment from Huysmans, who described Gide's work as a "product of hideous vulgarities." It was the time when the eager beginner could jot down in his diary these three laconic, suggestive words: "*Visite à Verlaine.*"

Or, in Bruxelles, under the date of July 23, 1891: "Bade farewell to Maeterlinck" (who had read to him, the preceding day, *The Seven Princesses*). "We just began to chat. I regret all the things we might have told each other. I would like to write to him. The desire to work in solitude possesses me again. Maeterlinck is of admirable energy."

There were congenial minds scattered all over Europe. The creative élite, entirely cosmopolitan, formed something like a masonic order, whose members recognized each other, everywhere, by certain rites and gestures. From St. Petersburg to Lisbon a set of people were occupied with the same issues: the antagonism between Nietzsche and Wagner, Ruskin's style, the Pre-Raphaelites, the Lake Poets, the chances of the poetic drama, Debussy's musical impressionism, the epigrams of Oscar Wilde, the revolutionary impact in the works of Ibsen, Hauptmann, and Shaw.

Gide—the timid and touchy Gide of 1890—maintained personal contacts with the whole pantheon of the *fin de siècle*. He knew Verhaeren and Rodin, D'Annunzio and Hofmannsthal.

As for the last, he might have had more to give than Gide was willing to accept at that time. No doubt, there are signal affinities between Hofmannsthal's early style and André Gide's beginnings: the same blend of fastidious sensitivity and melancholy reserve in their approach to life; the same juvenile grace; the same solemn elegance of expression. Yet it seems that Gide was unaware of this similarity, or that this rapport had already ceased to exist when the two writers met in 1905. At any rate, Gide's remarks about the Viennese poet convey only a somewhat desultory interest on his part. "It is rather strange," he says, "that I find nothing worth-while to repeat, after a conversation of two hours with him. And still I like him a lot. But there seems not quite enough darkness in his character, nor does he have great mysteries to conceal. I enjoy chatting with him all the more as it is he who does most of the talking. It would be very pleasant to see more of him."

They did not see a great deal of each other, though, during the years to come.

Yet it was in part thanks to Hofmannsthal that Gide came to know a number of the Austrian and German æsthetes, who, in their turn, were instrumental in introducing Gide's early books to the esoteric *avant-garde* of the Germanic countries. Franz Blei and Hermann Bahr, two leaders of the æsthetic renaissance in Vienna, spread Gide's reputation through the many little magazines they controlled. In Munich he made the acquaintance of Rudolf Kassner, one of the most sagacious German critics and connoisseurs, and the first to speak to him of Kierkegaard, the religious thinker of Denmark. This was indeed a valuable tip. Gide used it presently, in a speech he delivered on the occasion of a French art exhibition which had just opened in Weimar, under the auspices of the Grand-Ducal court. Gide's host in the Goethe-town was Count Harry Kessler, cosmopolitan man of letters and of the world, and one of Hofmannsthal's lifelong intimates.

The finest translation, probably, ever made of any of André Gide's works into any foreign language, is the German version of *Le Retour de l'enfant prodigue,* by Rainer Maria Rilke.

The contact with Rilke was more lively and, above all,

more lasting than the transient rapports with the two other great German poets—Hofmannsthal and Stefan George. The latter crossed Gide's path but once, in 1908—at a time, that is, when George was already the idolized center of a mystic cult. Gide, according to his own account, was looking forward to shaking hands with the man whose work he greatly admired—"that is to say, whatever I am able to understand of it," as he adds with a queer mixture of modesty and malice. For Gide realized, of course, that George's ornate auguries were considered utterly obscure, even by German readers.

What Gide and George have in common, among other things, is their enthusiasm for Mallarmé. There was a period in George's life when he was closer to the Parisian Symbolists than to the Teutonic professors, who later usurped his legend and tried to corrupt his style. When he met André Gide, he was just at the juncture between the æstheticist phase of his development and his subsequent rôle of a hero and herald of sublime Nationalism.

The conversation at the luncheon table may have been interesting enough. However, Gide contents himself in his journal with registering all the details of George's appearance—including the shape of his hands, the color of his complexion, and the material of which his clothes were made. The result of this effort is a nervous sketch showing an impressive figure of sacerdotal beauty and dignity. But, alas, the august apparition is mute.

Gide's D'Annunzio is more eloquent. He talks not only literature but also hygienics; in fact, we hear him outline a complete strategy of wholesome life, with plenty of horseback riding, extensive walks, and all kinds of tonic exercises. As for literature, the Italian genius announced his dislike of Maeterlinck, whose style he deemed "too simple," and also of Henrik Ibsen, in whose works he missed "beauty." His inquiries about French writers indicate knowledge rather than curiosity. So stupendous is the great man's familiarity with literary goings-on in Paris that Gide exclaimed at last, "But you've read everything!"

"Everything," D'Annunzio confirmed gravely. "I believe in reading everything." After a while he added, "We read everything as we don't cease to hope that we may find, eventually, the true masterpiece awaited by all of us."

The true masterpiece . . . : One might find it by reading everything, but one is not likely to create it as long as one reads too much.

The young Gide became frightened by the perfumed narrowness surrounding him. The atmosphere in all these drawing rooms was at once stale and hectic, unwholesome to breathe. Was it a bedlam's climate? Or the sultry mist of a hothouse? Or was it simply the stifling air of jail?

No matter what kind of air, this young man was sick and tired of it. At one point he had already thought of suicide —disgraceful, craven idea! He thought himself gravely ill (tuberculosis had killed his father). He feared also that he might lose his mind.

He had to overcome his ascetic ideals and fastidious vagaries, his depressions and inhibitions. He had to forget all about his Puritan past and his Symbolist present, or else he would go to pieces.

He was doomed, mercilessly, if he could not forget about his being an heir—the heir of Protestant ministers and of

Stéphane Mallarmé, of wealthy industrialists and of the Parnassians, of Mademoiselle Shackleton and Uncle Charles Gide and of the *Ecóle Alsacienne*.

To forget Chopin and Baudelaire and Pushkin and even the Holy Bible! To abandon the heritage!

To forget what other men have ever written, and what they have loved and thought! To forget what you have thought and loved yourself!

To be born anew . . .

III. THE PRODIGAL SON

I believe in the flesh and the appetites;
Seeing, hearing, feeling, are miracles, and
each part and tag of me is a miracle.
WALT WHITMAN

Ne souhaite pas, Nathanaël, de trouver Dieu que partout.
ANDRÉ GIDE

T H E exemplary sinner—according to pious legends —inevitably reaches the point where he feels fed up with sin; whereupon he withdraws presently to the desert, to atone for the fun he had. There, surrounded by sand, the penitent lives on grasshoppers and keeps striving for sanctity.

Our story, then, is a reversed legend: namely, the truthful account of a man who went to the desert, not to gain sanctity, but to get rid of it. Besides, this tale contains the unmistakable ingredients of an edifying parable, including a wicked tempter who is eventually punished. As for the Devil's victim, we are sorry to say that he does not feel remorseful at all, but rather regrets the irretrievable years wasted with sanctity. A typical convert, he overdoes his new creed and makes a little too much fuss about the vices he has just acquired.

The tempter has neither horns nor a club-foot, but looks quite alert and jolly—an enterprising colossus with wide, lustrous eyes and a proud, sensual mouth in a pale, rather flabby face. His pure, beautiful forehead is framed by rich, perfumed hair. His gait has a voluptuous, heaving quality. He wears too much jewelry and smokes too many gold-tipped cigarettes.

As for the victim, he is young and shy, almost priest-like in his dark clothes. The pallor of his face is all the more conspicuous as it contrasts with a black beard and mustache, a paradoxical adornment of this delicate physiognomy.

On a gloomy day in January, 1894, our traveler arrived in Algeria, where he hoped to find sunshine and laughter and the perfumed breath of spring. But Algeria looked as bleak and murky as could be, utterly devoid of any exotic charm. So the traveler, disappointed, packed up his belongings—a heavy, cumbersome burden consisting mostly of books. The works of English novelists and German thinkers had accompanied him from France to Switzerland, and then down to and across the Mediterranean. He carried Dickens and Fichte along as he now made for the desert.

He stopped at a place named Blidah—nearer his goal, the Sahara, but not yet quite near enough.

He was disillusioned again. Where were the cloudless horizons, the glowing colors and sweet fragrances he had longed for, back there in Paris and in the dreary mountain resorts of Switzerland? In Blidah, a low, rainy sky hung over freezing palm trees. For three long and depressing days the young man kept roving through squalid streets— aimless, joyless, and lonely.

At the end of the third day he decided to leave.

Waiting for his hotel bill, he loitered in the lobby, while his book-charged luggage was already piled up in the omnibus. Automatically—out of boredom, rather than induced by curiosity—he studied the blackboard on which the hotel displayed the names of its current guests. The two last names of the list startled him: Oscar Wilde and Lord Alfred Douglas, from London.

Gide's first reaction was to wipe out his own name, inscribed on the board not far from the names of the English visitors.

What prompted him to make such a futile and impolite gesture?

In the first place, he did not feel like seeing anybody. Besides, the idea of seeing Oscar Wilde embarrassed him particularly. For our somber young wanderer was not yet, at that point, quite free of conventional inhibitions, and people had begun to say peculiar things about Wilde. While London society grew indignant at his provocative conduct, the literary world of Paris was rather inclined to ridicule his forced and fatuous eccentricities. *"On se scandalisait un peu,"* according to Gide's report, *"mais surtout on le prenait à la blague."*

Gide erased his name because he feared Wilde might discover it, at the last moment, and follow him to the station. A meeting with Wilde seemed undesirable, first, because Gide wanted to be alone; secondly, because of Wilde's scandalous reputation; thirdly . . . But the third point is vague—a matter of conjecture, rather than of knowledge. It may be that the priest-like tourist was simply scared in face of the unexpected proximity of the tempter. He sensed danger. He wanted to escape. He ran away, or rather, he tried to do so.

Of course, he did not succeed. Too chivalrous to dodge risks and insult old acquaintances, he changed his mind as soon as he reached the railway station. Before it was too late, he recognized, blushingly, the foolishness of what he was doing. How silly and ungrateful, he thought, to cut a man to whom he owed so much delight and instruction. After all, he used to see a good deal of Wilde, three years ago, in Paris—and how intensely he had enjoyed seeing him, at the time! Then the *enfant terrible* of English literature was at the peak of his dazzling career: he possessed and emanated what Thackeray calls "the principal gift of great men"—*success.*

"His gestures and looks were triumphant." Thus Gide described subsequently the effulgent Wilde of 1890. "His books startled and charmed. His plays drew jammed houses in London. He was rich; he was grand; he was handsome, pampered, celebrated. Some of his admirers compared him to an Asiatic Bacchus; others, to a Roman emperor; others again, to Apollo himself. And, in fact, he radiated."

This is the kind of thing Gide remembered, lingering in the dreary waiting room. What would Oscar think of him when he noticed that he had effaced his name from the blackboard? He could not but feel bitterly hurt, betrayed by another friend. "I have always been looking for friends," he had said to Pierre Louÿs, a few months ago. "And all I found were lovers."

Half because the danger tempted him, half out of pity for the endangered tempter, Gide walked back to the hotel and shook hands with the Devil.

He found Wilde considerably changed, not so much in appearance as in spirit and attitude. His epigrams and motions, his mannerisms and puns—his whole behavior had assumed a desperate violence, something savage, almost frightening. His laughter sounded forced when he told André Gide, "I am in Algeria because I am bored with art. From now on I refuse to adore anything but the sun. Haven't you noticed that the sun abominates and paralyzes thought?"

And, again: "Do you know my real tragedy? I have put my genius in my life; in my work, just my talent."

What ominous undertones in his mirth as he ranted: "My cardinal duty is to have a tremendous lot of fun. Fun—not happiness! Happiness doesn't count. I don't want it. We must always aspire to the more tragic solution . . ."

Haunted by his lust for fun and tragedy, he paraded his vices in the streets of Blidah and Algeria, prodded and provoked by Lord Alfred, who relished scandal as a child relishes candy. Surrounded by the scum of the Arabian underworld, Oscar, the "King of Life," strutted in front of the shocked tourists from London, New York, and Paris. Indiscriminately, he distributed money among the attractive rascals tagging him wherever he went. "I hope to demoralize the whole place," he would boast, cheerfully.

It may be doubtful whether there was much to demoralize, in the case of the native prostitutes and procurers. At any rate, the tempter did a remarkable job in demoralizing one young Puritan.

A few years before, in Paris, Wilde had said, when he first met André Gide, "I don't like your lips. They are straight like the lips of those who have never lied. I will teach you the art of lying to the end that your lips become beautiful and voluptuous like the lips of an antique mask."

Evidently, the tempter did not follow a sudden whim when he corrupted his inexperienced companion; it was an old favorite plan that he could now carry out at last.

His bait was the svelte, dark-skinned body of an Arabian youth.

The great pleasure of the debauchee is to debauch others. Wilde had the time of his life when he revealed to his timid friend certain penchants inherent in his nature but repressed hitherto, and also the appropriate methods to satisfy such desires. Gleeful, "like a child and a devil," the seducer watched the struggle taking place in his victim's soul and reflected in his twisted face.

The setting of André's fall was a sordid café in Algeria. The instrument of corruption was a handsome flutist named Mohammed, sweet and slender, only fourteen years of age. Gide gazed at him, spellbound, bewitched. Suddenly he felt on his shoulder the blandishing touch of Wilde's soft and enormous hand.

Whispered the tempter, "My dear, *vous voulez le petit musicien?*"

And the victim, in a strangled voice, almost soundless, produced his pivotal "*Yes.*"

Satan burst out laughing. He shrieked, bellowed, almost suffocated—overwhelmed by a veritable tempest of hilarity. "I beg your pardon," he panted. "But you're too funny for words . . ."

The Devil had plenty of fun; and so had, indeed, the victim.

The significance of the Algerian episode in Gide's biography can be gauged only when we fully consider the force of the qualms and scruples accompanying and preceding it. There is nothing reckless or cynical about this ultimate submission to long-suppressed appetites. The new experience did not seem an aberration to him; rather, a liberation. He rejoiced at having found his predestined form of eros, or what he called his own inborn normality.

"*Ah! de quel enfer je sortais!*" he exclaimed, by no means in reference to his present depravity but alluding to his past privations. What he had passed through was hell; what he now experienced was heaven.

"O happy earth! reality of Heaven!" Gide's heart echoed Shelley's jubilation as he wandered and ran through the desert—alone but no longer lonesome; elated, intoxicated, in raptures, his heart winged and weightless like a bird rising to the sky.

Where to, flying heart? To what dazzling heights do you soar, daring bird? Be careful! Those who go up too high are likely to fall the farthest. Look at your master-flier, your arch-hedonist, your glamorous prince of sin! Look how he provokes and precipitates his undoing!

Did Wilde not realize what he risked when he returned to London to challenge Lord Alfred's father, the quarrelsome Marquis of Queensberry? It was his fate he challenged, and he knew what he did.

Gide remained in touch with him throughout the tragedy, if only at intervals. He saw Oscar, the King of Life, transformed into an ex-convict called Sebastian Melmoth, hiding in a humble village, Berneval near Dieppe. What saddening contrast between that dreary hole and the colorful settings of Wilde's former adventures! What anticlimactic epilogue to a fine and hazardous drama! He who had once sparkled with wit, now just lied and lamented like any broken-down adventurer, any stranded impostor.

"Don't be hard on me!" Sebastian Melmoth whimpered. "Don't be hard on a man who has been beaten!"

Was this the inevitable result of "living dangerously"? Humiliation and wretchedness—was that the end of the flight? The intrigues and treacheries of "Bosie," the once beloved friend; the harassing want of money; the inability to work; the loneliness of an outcast; finally the collapse, the squalid and trivial end—was all this the price that had to be paid, inexorably, for defying society? But no warning example could mar or moderate the new ecstasy kindled in Gide's heart. If there were risks involved, he had to accept them. There was no choice. Besides, he knew that the dangers confronting him were not the same as those by which Oscar Wilde was crushed. For Wilde was a genius of life: which means that his inward drama had to become manifest entirely in his actual biography. Gide, however, is a genius of thought. His crucial adventures take place within himself, occasioned or illustrated by the vicissitudes of his empirical life. The polarities and tensions of his cerebral quest do not need to be punctuated or verified by any extraneous triumphs or tribulations.

When André Gide read in the papers, in December, 1900, the news of Wilde's pitiful end in Paris, he must have been moved and grieved. For the life just extinguished had crossed and influenced his own at a juncture of extreme significance. Oscar Wilde, purified at last of all distortions and mannerisms, had fulfilled his fate according to the law inherent in his being. André Gide, deprived of a friend, continued his pilgrimage.

There is no reason to question the sincerity of the grief with which he stated in his pamphlet, *In Memoriam Oscar Wilde* (1910), that technical circumstances prevented him from joining the meager cortège behind Oscar Wilde's coffin.

André Gide, at the time, was sojourning in Biskra again.

Algeria, Tunisia, and Morocco meant to him what Italy meant to Goethe—a vital turning-point and joyful revelation. Gide was wont to quote an enthusiastic word he attributed to Goethe—erroneously, as he was to find out. In Gide's version, Goethe expressed his gratitude to Rome and the Southern skies by exclaiming, *"Endlich bin ich geboren!"* (Finally I am born!). His actual wording—more moderate and less beautiful—was, *"Endlich bin ich geborgen!"* (Finally I am secure!). Gide's misquotation—discovered and rectified by himself—rather improves the original, or at least renders the citation more applicable to his own frame of mind.

For it was indeed a psychological rebirth he experienced in the oases of Biskra and Touggourt, in Blidah and Kairouan. Suddenly, as by magic, he saw, felt, understood *life*. The pallid cult of pure ideas faded away, superseded by this rampant sensation. Nothing seemed valid and relevant but the palpable, perishable, adorable stuff of which earthly things are made.

Of course, this ecstasy infinitely transcended the sexual impulse from which it originated. Nor can this erotic-pantheistic credo be reduced to the cynical hedonism preached and demonstrated by Wilde. Gide's emotion is no longer fastidious, but it has become cosmic, comprehensive, billow-like. Its sweeping embrace includes flowers and clouds, fruits and rivers, statues and stars and streams. All things ever created—this exuberant credo proclaims—all fleet formations and mortal phenomena indicate God, but none of them can reveal Him. Therefore, who contents himself with one love inevitably misses divinity in millions of other forms. The most vagrant tenderness, the most unfixed delight, is the nearest to the Supreme Being.

I call God everything I love, and I love everything: This is the idiom of the indiscriminate, universal lover—the rhapsodic, embracing style of *Les Nourritures terrestres.*

This dithyrambic outburst of sensual gratitude is the main product of the new phase of Gide's development. Published in 1897, it marks the end of Symbolist æstheticism, in Gide's personal career and, less conspicuously, in French letters at large. Not that the Symbolist school as such disintegrated; but it stagnated, lost momentum. The death of Stéphane Mallarmé, in 1898, seemed to seal a decline which had begun with Gide's apostasy.

For there can be no doubt that the streaming eloquence of *Les Nourritures* deviates entirely from the Symbolist pattern and disregards the basic principles of the movement —namely, the supremacy of idea and symbol, in brief, of the absolute, over reality. The same Gide who had hitherto preached the vanity of desire, now cried out his powerful song-of-songs glorifying all forms of passion and joy. Narcissus gave up his splendid isolation, attracted by more palpable splendors than his own beauty mirrored in water. He began seeking other beauties, other kisses, other waters. Narcissus became thirsty, burning with unquenchable thirst.

Les Nourritures terrestres is the song-of-songs of all thirsts. It extols the thirst even more rhapsodically than the satisfaction of drinking or the fruits that give the refreshing juice. Insatiably, the vagabond-lover keeps searching for new liquids, whose irretrievable flavors would make for even more thirst.

> *Où sont, Nathanaël, dans nos voyages*
> *De nouveaux fruits pour nous donner d'autres désirs?*

Nathanaël is the imaginary disciple to whom Gide addresses his sermon. The whole abundance of praises and auguries is meant to instruct, to liberate, to awaken him, the imagined youth and ideal listener—"*toi, mon Nathanaël, que je n'ai pas encore trouvé.*"

Gide teaches Nathanaël what he, in his turn, has been taught by Ménalque. Ménalque is as unreal as Nathanaël, or as real, perhaps, as is Gide's passion for both. He, who is teacher and disciple in one, is in love with his teacher and with his disciple. He tells the latter what the former so often impressed on him: that only love counts. "*Love, not serenity pure, but strong from weakness*" (to use Robert Browning's words); not compassion but passion; ("*Non point la sympathie, Nathanaël—l'amour!*"); not wisdom, not wealth, not security—only love.

Ménalque has taught André Gide, who repeats it to Nathanaël, that the more things and faces we know the more we can desire, and the more we desire the better. We ought to know indeed all things and faces to love all of them with all our love, always.

Oh! my Nathanaël, I will teach you fervor!

Nathanaël is urged to keep moving, changing, seeking. A strenuous, uprooted life is preferable to tranquillity. André Gide contradicts, refutes André Walter. The fear of risks and of action is now considered disgraceful. Gide-Ménalque glorifies action as such—quite regardless of its ethical implications. "To act without judging whether the action is good or evil! To love without worrying whether it's right or wrong!"

The Hamlet complex seems infinitely remote. Nathanaël is told that act he must; for every perfect action results in lust, and lust is what we should aspire to, always and above all. "Oh! Nathanaël, do not distinguish between God and your happiness!"

The message of *Les Nourritures terrestres* is anti-intellectual and anti-historical—free of all moral ballast, opposed to all traditions and principles. Nathanaël is warned against memories and against affiliations. He must not stay anywhere. Nothing is more pernicious to him than his home, his family, his past. He is to forget his past, to burn the bridges behind him.

Gide wants Nathanaël to throw all books away, even *Les Nourritures terrestres*. "*Nathanaël, à present, jette mon livre! Emancipe-t-en! Quitte moi!*"

This is the master's farewell to his beloved, nonexistent pupil: "Emancipate yourself! Abandon me! Distrust this book! Realize that it expresses just one possible attitude towards life—just *one* among a thousand others. Seek yours! Don't waste your time by doing things which anybody else could do as well as you! Develop those qualities that are unique, that nobody else commands! Make of yourself, patiently or impatiently, the most irreplaceable being!"

Does one recognize the grand, rousing accents? Gide-Ménalque echoes Nietzsche. *Les Nourritures terrestres* reads in parts like a French version of *Thus Spake Zara-thustra.*

André Gide later disclosed that he was not yet familiar with that particular work when he composed his book. Moreover, he likes *Zarathustra* less than anything else by Nietzsche. "Tried for the seventh or eighth time (at least) to read *Also sprach Zarathustra,*" he says in his diary. "IMPOSSIBLE. The very tone of this book is unbearable to me. And all my admiration for Nietzsche will never make me bear it."

But this was in 1930, when Gide no longer approved of his own early style, either. True, he never was quite so hard on *Les Nourritures* as he was on *Les Cahiers d'André Walter.* Yet what he has to say about the former, in a preface to a later edition (1926), sounds reserved and even somewhat apologetic. He explains the lyrical mannerisms partly as a natural and necessary reaction against Symbolist artificiality; partly, out of his personal state of mind and *health,* at the time.

"*Les Nourritures terrestres,*" we read, "is the product, if not of an invalid, at least of a convalescent, of some-body just recuperating from a long disease. There is, in its lyricism, the excess of one who embraces life as if it were something he had already thought lost."

But this is Nietzsche again—unwittingly so, perhaps; out of a natural affinity, rather than by direct influence; yet the resemblance is striking, unmistakable. The stimulus in-herent in the state of convalescence, both spiritual and physi-cal, is indeed a leitmotiv throughout the second half of

Nietzsche's lifework. Again and again he dwells on what he owes to his suffering, and describes, in dozens of suggestive variations, the exuberant joy succeeding long periods of darkness and apathy. In his amazing introduction to *The Joyful Science*—to take one example at random —he deduces the origin of his entire vision from this one central, indivisible experience, malady and recuperation.

According to Nietzsche's reports, the state of convalescence can be tantamount to an ecstatic awakening, a shock-like revelation. "A joy, strained to a tremendous pitch which sometimes seeks relief in a flood of tears,"— thus he describes the divine hour when he conceived—or rather, received, all ready-made—the complete structure of *Zarathustra*. "A perfect ecstasy, with the most distinct consciousness of an endless number of delicate shocks and thrills to one's very toes; a feeling of happiness, in which the most gloomy and painful feelings act, not as a contrast, but as something expected and inevitable, as an essential coloring within such an overflow of light. . . . This is my experience of inspiration. I have no doubt that we should have to go back many thousands of years before we could find anyone who would dare say to me, 'It is mine as well.'"

Was André Gide the one, perhaps, who might have dared say, "It is mine as well!"—who passed through the same adventure, not thousands of years before Nietzsche but hardly one decade after him? Nietzsche's boastful and glorious account of Zarathustra's not quite immaculate conception dates from 1888, just nine years before the appearance of *Les Nourritures terrestres*.

It hardly matters whether Gide was directly inspired by

the German poet-philosopher when he composed his glowing eulogy of desire. Suffice it to say that *Les Nourritures* is saturated with Nietzsche's spirit and rhythm. The emotional approach of Zarathustra and of the Gide of that period is basically the same. Both deny and disparage the ascetic ideals; both stress the supremacy of biological values over ethical virtues; both challenge Christian morality and preach a transvaluation of all values. Gide's exaltation of energy and action, his vision of Dionysiac love played off against Christian charity, his whole idolatry of life, even the cadence of his style, the fusion of sacerdotal and iconoclastic gestures—all this is typically Nietzschean.

Of course, that is not to say that Gide embraced Nietzsche's ideas altogether. The Will-to-Power philosophy, the rabid denouncements of both Reformation and Revolution, the cult of the Superman, and many another ingredient of that arbitrary prophecy is essentially strange or even inimical to André Gide's vision. Nor do I mean to suggest that Nietzsche's influence, predominant as it may be, is the only one, or the only important one, traceable in the texture of *Les Nourritures terrestres*. Evidently, there are other currents, other overtones. We might go back to Jean-Jacques Rousseau's *Retour à la nature* to locate the spiritual sources of this sentimental paganism.

The irrationalism of Gide's attitude suggests the influence of Henri Bergson, whose first books came out shortly before the publication of *Les Nourritures*. True, his most famous work, *Creative Evolution*, did not appear until ten years afterwards, in 1907. But Bergson's new approach to physics and metaphysics, his exaltation of motion and intuition, were already perceptible in the air, if only as a promise, an indistinct hope and challenge. Gide's youthful enthusiasm anticipated the philosophy of the *élan vital*, years before Bergson established it as a system.

Also, certain fragments of Rimbaud's savage and tragic song are interwoven in the milder symphony of *Les Nourritures*. Arthur's *Bateau ivre* was one of the vehicles André used to reach his African dream land. But he stopped in the lush oases of Morocco and Tunisia, while his desperate brother and predecessor had ventured on into the gruesome solitudes of the interior.

Rimbaud went farther than Gide. That is why Gide had to write, in 1905, "The reading of Rimbaud . . . makes me feel ashamed of my own work."

But Rimbaud perished. His romanticism has the compelling grandeur of cosmic catastrophes. Whatever he wrote foreshadows and extols his own doom.

Gide, less violent, more tenacious, continued to live. He resisted. His dithyrambs do not sing disaster; they sing life. "Oh my Nathanaël! I will sing you the evening song and the morning song; the songs of departure and the songs of sleep; songs about highways and parks, about children and diseases; songs of cities and of solitudes, of figs, grapes, and pomegranates; songs about fountains and butterflies, tempests and prostitutes. Have I already told you about the various flavors of coffee? Did I duly praise the many sorts of Arabian candy? Did I enumerate the innumerable ways of making love, playing with animals, praying to our God? Did I indicate at least the millionth part of the billions of miracles of which our life consists? *As for me, I know of nothing else but miracles.*"

Does the last line differ in any respect from the preceding text? It is neither Gide's nor my own, but Walt Whitman's.

The great American's grip of Gide's thought and feeling is as powerful, and not so ambivalent, as the authority Nietzsche wielded on him. Free of hysteria and aggressiveness, Whitman's mighty appeal transmits confidence and creative passion. His approach to things is sturdy and realistic, despite all the mystic exuberance involved. Whitman is an excellent master for an impressionable and yet independent disciple like the young André Gide. Throughout the *Nourritures* we recognize the tonic enthusiasm of his transAtlantic inspirer. *Afoot and lighthearted, I take to the open road,—Healthy, free, the world before me* . . . Whitman's effulgent carol might be a part of Gide's joyful sermon to Nathanaël.

It is in this spirit of joy that Whitman and Gide resemble and find each other. *Joy! Joy! all over Joy!*—this is the message of both the *Leaves of Grass* and *Les Nourritures terrestres*. Without jeopardizing his originality, Gide was free to employ, in this particular context, Whitman's technique of sweeping enumerations, his famous way of cataloguing the splendors of this world. The grandiose pedantry of Whitman's cosmic inventories is an element also of Gide's style at that point. Whitman and Gide agree that "all forms are lovable as all of them express God," and both —remarkably conscientious in all their ecstasy—are therefore anxious not to omit any phenomenon.

"Nathanaël, I will teach you that all things are divinely natural." Whitman could have addressed himself with these

words to one of his unknown brothers: "Camerado! Whoever you are; wherever you are, I wish to talk to you about
all divinely natural things . . ."

"*Nathanaël*," says Gide, "*je te parlerai de tout.*"

Of course, *Leaves of Grass* is a greater book than *Les
Nourritures terrestres*. Whitman delivered his complete
message in this cataractic hymn, which remains his definitive and glorious testimony. The *Leaves of Grass* is Whitman.

As for André Gide, he must not be identified with any of
his books. As a complex whole and an organic entirety, his
writings express his being; but each individual work discloses only aspects and potentialities of his character and
his message.

In the case of *Les Nourritures* it would be particularly
dangerous to take this document of one Gidean vein for the
expression of his totality. Gide himself has warned against
such a misconception.

"I am judged too often by this work of my youth," he
complains in his introduction to a later edition, "as if the
ethics of the *Nourritures* were that of my entire life; as if
I had not been the first to follow the advice I give to my
young reader: 'Throw my book away and abandon me!'
Yes, I abandoned presently the being I used to be when
writing *Les Nourritures*. In fact, when I examine my life,
the predominant feature I find is by no means unsteadiness
but, quite the contrary, loyalty."

A critical reader might object, at this point, that Gide,
by revoking the doctrines of his vernal panegyric, para-

doxically adhered to them: he recommended inconsistency in *Les Nourritures* and behaved accordingly—namely, inconsistently. His own statement, that he followed the advice of his early sermon, does not quite jibe, apparently, with his subsequent assertion that his prevailing quality is loyalty—not the unsteadiness he praised in his callow youth.

The solution of this seeming paradox is, perhaps, that Gide can be loyal only by giving the impression of disloyalty. He would betray the inmost law of his nature if he became consistent—that is, limited.

Les Nourritures reveals the immaturity of its author, not by preaching inconsistency, but by being unduly consistent. In none of his later works has Gide been as one-sided as he appears in *Les Cahiers d'André Walter* and in *Les Nourritures*. In all his subsequent books there is—dialectically inherent—an antithesis to the central thesis, a counter-tendency which at once modifies and strengthens the predominant theme. But the two early works, while balancing one another, are unbalanced in themselves. The Dionysiac hedonism of *Les Nourritures* is as un-Gidean as was André Walter's hysteric sanctity. One has to visualize the two extremes together to find the human face behind the Janus mask.

"They want to know my secret," King Saul says in André Gide's drama. "But do I know it myself? I have many secrets."

The holder of many secrets has to employ many idioms to express himself, to unload his woeful and joyful heart. Not always—or rather, not more than once—can he indulge in the redundant vocabulary of Gide's early work. After *Les Nourritures terrestres* his style suddenly hardens and

contracts, becomes almost rigid, as if fearing too much melody. King Saul, of whom I have just quoted a suggestive
word, appears at times almost inarticulate. Harassed by his
demons, torn by his fears and desires, he cannot formulate
his tragedy but can only cry out his anguish. The intolerable strain of suffering has reduced his royal eloquence to
rugged wails and frenzied outbursts. David has his voice
and beauty; young Jonathan has youth and also the love of
David; but the King has nothing except his demons. Whatever he touches becomes terrible. Those he loves turn
against him. *"Tout ce qui t'est charmant t'est hostile,"* says
the sorceress to the tormented King.

Gruesome words, these!—a scathing, merciless verdict.
It seems almost incredible that it should originate from the
same author who announced, about the same time, that he
did not want to miss "any sweetness on earth."

Saül, a drama in five acts, was not released until 1903,
although written shortly after *Les Nourritures*. Gide with-
held the book edition as he hoped to see his play on the
stage and thought a premature publication might hamper
its theatrical chances. Yet the production which Antoine
had been planning was prevented by circumstance. A play
by Brieux that the famous director brought out was a complete failure, leaving the company without money for venture. Thanks to the disastrous *Outcome of the Race* (the
title of Brieux's work), Antoine could run no more risks,
and had to drop Gide's philosophical drama.

The disappointed author had better luck with another
dramatic effort, *Le Roi Candaule* (1901). This time the
plot is derived from Greek antiquity. The drama is based
on Herodotus' report on a generous king, Candaulus, who

permitted, or practically forced, a humble fisherman, Gyges, to have a good look at his, the king's, wife, Queen Nyssia, who was to appear, on the occasion, without anything on. There are other things involved—magic rings, and so forth. But the scandalous generosity of the monarch is the central theme, especially in Gide's interpretation. Gyges kills the king after having gloated on the nakedness of his wife. According to Friedrich Hebbel—a German playwright who used the same story fifty-five years before—the humiliated lady (who is called Rhodope, in the German version) commits suicide, notwithstanding the fact that her disgrace has been drastically revenged. Her French double, Nyssia, is more sensible. She gets married to Gyges, who had seen her anyhow. The first command of the new master is that the Queen veil her face in front of every man—except, of course, in front of him, who happens to be the murderer of her legitimate husband.

Le Roi Candaule was the first work of Gide to be seen on the stage. In Paris it was produced by Lugné-Poe, who played the part of the King, while the celebrated Max (to whom *Saül* is dedicated) was Gyges, with Madame Claude Farrère assisting him in the rôle of Queen Nyssia. The experiment was successful enough to be repeated in Prague, Vienna, and other cities. In Berlin, where the play came out in 1908, the whole press disapproved angrily of Gide's effrontery in competing with Hebbel. A living Frenchman who dares to rival a great old German master? It was too much for the critics of the Imperial capital. Gide quotes in his diary some of the one hundred and fifty-three newspaper clippings he received from Prussia—all of them "insulting, stupid, dishonest, and infamous." Said one of the augurs on the Spree River, "Hebbel's vision is, in our opinion, as infinitely superior to Gide's as is Kleist's presentation of the Amphytrion legend to that of Molière."

And the bilious gentleman did not even know as yet that another impudent Frenchman, Jean Giraudoux, was to add another Amphytrion, the thirty-eighth, to those by Kleist, Molière, and the thirty-five others.

Gide hardly aspired to the fame of a dramatist. His attitude towards the theater was always reserved, at times even inimical. The book edition of *Le Roi Candaule* is preceded by a preface in which the author reaffirms his skepticism as regards the validity of dramatic art. "Even if my play happens to be a success," Gide remarks, "it might be on account of a miscomprehension. The enthusiasm with which the plays of M. Rostand are received by the public makes it very plain that success and literary quality have nothing to do with each other as far as the theater is concerned."

Le Roi Candaule, like all other works of Gide, is conceived and composed, not for the sake of effects, but to express and clarify certain ideas. The issue at stake, this time, is the antagonism between generosity and discretion, frankness and shame—a problem most relevant to Gide's work and one most appropriate to be tackled by the author of *Les Nourritures terrestres*. For that book, published only four years before the Candaulus drama, is a striking manifestation of frankness and of generosity—"generous to the point of vice," as Nietzsche said in reference to the Candaulus-Gyges situation.

"It is a noteworthy fact," Nietzsche observes, in another context, "that excessive generosity involves, necessarily, the loss of shame."

A warning to artists! . . . That is what Nietzsche had in mind, and what André Gide meant by his Candaulus parable. The king who reveals the nakedness of his wife symbolizes the artist who wants the whole world to witness his most intimate, most delicate experiences. The artist, unduly expansive by nature and profession, prostitutes himself and also what he loves by making a show of his romance or tragedy. His exhibitionism shocks, and rightly so, the upright man who is Gyges. He kills the decadent aristocrat, Candaulus, who was generous and tactless enough to let him enter the sanctum of his royal existence.

Those who are invited to partake in the refined entertainments of the happy few prove sometimes less democratic than their hosts try to be. The masses may grow indignant when the élite becomes indiscreet and gives up its splendid isolation. Far from feeling flattered and obliged, the plain fellows may turn out to be hurt and angered by the unwished-for confidence of poets, royalties, and the like.

Candaulus was too happy, as was the Gide of *Les Nourritures*.

The happy King wanted to communicate his tremendous joy to others, as Gide wanted, when sharing his bliss and wisdom with Nathanaël, and with the world.

The priest who unveils the mystery of the temple profanes the gods: this is the meaning of Gide's play on King Candaulus.

Beware of profanation!

"Listen, my dear," Oscar Wilde said to Gide, in Berneval. "*Les Nourritures terrestres*—that's fine, that's excellent

. . . But now you must promise me something: from now on never write the word *I* again!"

And as Gide didn't quite understand, he added, "You see, there is no *first* person as far as art is concerned."

Gide, who quotes this bit of dialogue in his booklet on Oscar Wilde, does not comment upon it. But he followed the advice, in some degree, at least; that is, as far as seemed wholesome to him and compatible with the requirements of his genius.

He ventured on a regular novel—an objective narrative, with a plot and a hero. He wrote *L'Immoraliste* (1902). It is a confessional novel, couched in the first person singular. Wilde would have disapproved of it. The leading character, Michel, is the narrator, and the novel is his story and confession.

But Michel is not André Gide, or, rather, he is not the whole André Gide. The character in the novel embodies and exaggerates certain qualities of his author. He does not discuss or preach these qualities, but represents them, objectively. In other words, Gide, by writing *L'Immoraliste*, has not contented himself with exposing his own drama as he did in his previous works, but has created something new, an autonomous cosmos, a miniature world with its own equilibrium, its own justice and beauty.

The affinities between Michel and André are evident enough, to be sure. Many elements of Gide's own biography and Gide's own dilemma are interwoven in the Immoralist's confession. Michel's youth, like Gide's, has been darkened by Puritanism and constant intellectual strain. Michel's wife, Marceline, bears obviously the angelic features which Gide loved in Emmanuèle.

The man who wrote *L'Immoraliste* was married to his pious cousin, on October 8, 1895. Emmanuèle did not mind his erratic habits, or at any rate did not prevent him from indulging in them. Gide, the husband, roved through the world—no less unbound than did Gide, the bachelor.

As for Michel, he takes his wife to the very spots in North Africa where his author made the acquaintance of Mohammed and Athman (Gide's Algerian guide and favorite companion for a number of years) and of many others.

Michel falls sick with tuberculosis, the disease with which Gide feared to be stricken. He recovers, and experiences the exuberant euphoria described in *Les Nourritures*. The well-being of convalescence assumes the character of a true paroxysm—slightly disquieting for poor Marceline, particularly since her husband appears only too sensible to the rakish charm of Arabian youth.

In Italy he is bored, as was Gide when he stopped there on his way home from Tunisia. Here the novel takes up and reaffirms another theme present in *Les Nourritures terrestres:* the disgust with knowledge and civilization. The Immoralist, intoxicated with life, becomes irreverent, antihistoric. Abandoning himself to every fleeting moment, to every sensation, he comes to scorn and disregard the legacy of past generations.

The country house in Normandy, where Marceline and Michel settle down for a while, is called La Morinière and is a meticulous reconstruction of Gide's estate, La Roque, which he inherited from his mother. Madame Gide, née Rondeaux, died shortly before her son married. In fact, André's engagement to Emmanuèle was decided upon in front of the mother's bier. Michel marries Marceline to make good a promise he gave to his dying father.

Michel's conduct in La Morinière is at least as unsavory as it was in the African oases; if anything, it deteriorates. He loses all sense of discipline and duty; experiments promiscuously with peasants and vagabonds; worships the Great Pan and neglects his wife. The last is all the more objectionable as Marceline, at this point, is very ill. She has contracted the tuberculosis infection which her husband had suffered from in North Africa. It seems only natural that the new patient should seek healing in the same tonic climate. The young couple leave for Algeria once again.

But Michel turns out to be a rather dangerous traveling companion for an invalid. The more her vitality dwindles, the more violent his becomes. He runs wild altogether. The renewal of his contact with Ménalque—you remember Ménalque, of course?—cannot but exacerbate his already critical state. This arrant adventurer and anarchist gives Michel the kind of talk Gide used to convey to Nathanaël: about the irretrievable seconds which have to be relished, regardless of past and future; about the cumbersome monotony of an orderly life, and the dreariness of moral principles, and other questionable ideas, all apt to undermine the last remnants of decency in Michel's character.

Marceline has to suffer from Ménalque's hazardous theories. Her husband—now completely reckless and cynical—drags her from place to place, from oasis to oasis—Touggourt, Kairouan, Biskra: the whole list so familiar to us from Gide's *Feuilles de route*. A native lad by the name of Moktir—a double, presumably, of the fabulous Athman—joins the curious ménage. This is more than Marceline can endure. She collapses. The description of her agony is one of the most cruel and most compelling things Gide has ever written.

What, then, is the meaning of this dismal tale? No doubt, Michel behaves in a criminal fashion. Marceline is as meek and patient as can be—a truly seraphic figure. Does that indicate that the purport of the book is a moral one, in a conventional sense? Does Gide take his hero to task? Does he arraign and condemn Michel? Or does he, quite to the contrary, approve of the young husband's abominable behavior? Does the author endorse Michel's irresponsible tenets? Is the tale meant, perhaps, to vilify virtue (i.e., Marceline) and to extol wickedness, in the person of a sadistic scoundrel?

According to Gide's own statement, his novel is neither an accusation nor an apology. The author does not intend to justify his hero nor does he care to indict him. He is neither "in favor" of Marceline and "against" Michel, nor the other way round. Is Shakespeare in favor of Hamlet or of Ophelia? Does Goethe side with Faust or with Margarete? Thus Gide questions. He answers in the negative. The writer, he asserts, is not the one who judges but the one who forms. He is inherent in all his characters: it does not behoove him, therefore, to come out for or against any of them. The artist is detached, disinterested, Godlike. Like the supreme Creator, he contents himself with demonstrating certain energies.

"In art," Gide proclaims, "there are no problems for which the work of art as such is not an adequate solution."

This is wholly true but by no means the whole truth.

Ibsen was not wrong, either, when he said that creative writing is tantamount to exposing and judging the devastating forces latently inherent in one's own self. How could the writer aspire to the aloofness of God? How is he in a position to know that God is indeed impartial? And is not *L'Immoraliste* in itself a striking and moving example for the subjectivity of all art? Evidently, it is a document of self-scrutiny and of self-indictment: in fact, the very effectiveness of the novel is due to its autobiographical impact.

But it is also due to its objectivity.

To say that *L'Immoraliste* is a great work of art—which it undoubtedly is—implies the twofold nature of its persuasion. The work of art is at once personal and detached. The real artist is confessor in the double sense of the term: he judges and confesses simultaneously; he is within and without his creations.

Yes, Gide *is* Michel. The Immoralist is derived from his author's innermost substance. But Gide is also Marceline; he shares in her martyrdom by describing its sinister details.

L'Immoraliste refutes and at the same time reaffirms the emotional philosophy of *Les Nourritures terrestres*. The analytical novel objectifies and pushes to the extreme what has hitherto been presented in a more nebulous manner— namely, the idea of radical hedonism. If Nathanaël took Gide's advice literally, he would become like the Immoralist; that is to say, he would ruin his life and that of his wife to boot.

Gide points out the dangers inherent in his own doctrines but he does not revoke what he has preached before. There is no contrast between *L'Immoraliste* and *Les Nourritures* which could be compared to the antagonism between the

latter and *Les Cahiers d'André Walter*. For while those two
early works dramatically contradict each other, the novel
dramatizes the abstractions of the Dionysiac credo. If it is
true that the story of the Immoralist demonstrates the im-
practicability of absolute liberty and rampant libido, it is
also true that it proves and praises the glorious appeal of a
lustful and dangerous life—a life beyond good and evil.

Certainly, the sinister Michel who destroys Marceline is
refuted, condemned, and doomed. But would the author
prefer a tame, virtuous hero? Would he like Michel more
if he had not abandoned his Calvinist home and past? A demure, Puritan Michel could hardly conceive the sort of
reveries and seekings for the sake of which André Gide
remains, in spite of everything, fond of his hero.

The murderous Michel muses: "I want to perform new
deeds. I am longing for unknown lands. Does man already
know everything? Has he scrutinized his own being? Has
he disclosed already his last, ultimate secrets? Will he have
to repeat himself from now on?

"Or are there still unprecedented issues to tackle? New
experiences to undergo? Unknown miracles to explore? No
doubt, there must be tremendous treasures yet undiscovered: with every new day I am more sure of it. There must
be splendors, somewhere, blocked and buried, for ages, by
a labyrinth of conventions and inhibitions . . ."

This is the Immoralist who is truly André Gide's brother.
He hymns a theme that will reverberate throughout Gide's
thought and work. He articulates the heart and the motive
power of Gide's creative effort: curiosity as ethical impulse; adventure as method and mission; the discovery of
man as the goal.

He who strives and struggles is neither right nor wrong. He may be judged only by the fervor and purity of his effort.

Is the Prodigal Son a sinner? He is, from a bourgeois, or rather from every social, viewpoint. For he gathered all his belongings, and took his journey into a far country, and there wasted his substance with riotous living. He is a parasite; any collective morale, whether conservative or revolutionary, must disapprove of him.

But he is objectionable to the immoralist as well. For he is weak and a failure. Unable to endure the hardships of dangerous life, he gives in, returns to his home, and prostrates himself. "Father, I have sinned against heaven, and before thee, and I am no more worthy to be called thy son . . ."

All of us know the story submitted by our Lord to explain his lenience towards the outcasts and sinners. The Pharisees, who were covetous, heard all these things, and they derided Him. But the poets and dreamers have always been especially sensible to the magnanimous message of Jesus' beautiful tale. The prospect of the fatted calf that would be killed to celebrate his return, was comforting and elating to many an errant youth. And what infinite solace emanates from Christ's generous paradox to the effect that he who has lost and devoured his living with harlots will be not only forgiven but even preferred to his brothers, who stayed at home, and served, and never transgressed a commandment.

To André Gide the lovable parable became a mine of profound allusions and meaningful contradictions. He had never quite ceased to visualize himself as the prodigal son—

the one who wastes his substance and leads a riotous life. He was not completely sincere when he proclaimed, "Nathanaël, I no longer believe in sin!" He wanted to impress Nathanaël and also to drown the soft but penetrating voice of his conscience. He always believed in sin, with one part, one central element of his being.

Gide's pose toward Nathanaël resembles the attitude of the Prodigal Son toward his younger brother. The dialogue of the two is the concluding and, perhaps, the most enchanting scene in that enchanting composition, *Le Retour de l'enfant prodigue* (1907).

This superb piece of chamber music is, in its minor, unassuming way, the finest, most nearly perfect thing, perhaps, which Gide has ever produced. With playful gravity and solemn grace the author resumes and fuses all emotional themes of his striving youth: the weariness of the heir; the rapture of his escape to freedom; the rebellion against obsolete conventions and limitations, but also the grandeur and validity of the heritage; the rousing appeal of the distant and undiscovered; and, again, the legitimate power of the familiar, indisputable hierarchy.

"Leaving diffused and yet entangled the double inspiration that kindled in my heart, I do not attempt to prove the victory of any god over me—nor mine." With these words the author presents the pious picture he has composed to his own "secret enjoyment."

No problems or antagonisms are solved in these dialogues, but they are purified and transfigured by the magic of art. There is nothing proven, save the inevitability of certain basic polarities which have to be accepted as intrinsic parts of our substance and of our quest.

The Prodigal Son was right when he ran away: he wanted to burn with a more glorious flame, he sought new passions, new inspirations. He was right also when he surrendered and renounced his rampant vagrancy. He was right to admit his defeat, to follow the voice of his conscience which was, too, the voice of his love. For the Prodigal Son loves his Father. He was right to go home.

His first dialogue is with the Father, who is all forbearance and kindness. The Father asks: "Son, why did you leave me?"

And the Prodigal Son: "Did I really leave you? Father! Are you not everywhere? I have never ceased to love you."

And as the Father inquires whether the son was happy, far away from him, the son says to him, truthfully: "I have never felt far from you."

The Father knows that his son does not lie to him. He knows his son; he has made him. There is no impulse or thought in the seditious child that does not come from the Father.

"I know what drove you away," says the Father. "I was always with you."

"Father!" exclaims the son. "Does that mean, Father, that I might have found you again, even if I had not come home?"

"You were right to come home, son, as you felt forlorn and weary."

He says also more severe, more frightful things—the mild, knowing Father. For he is not only the Father of the Prodigal Son, he is the Father of the virtuous son as well—the Prodigal Son's older brother, the one who remained at home and transgressed no commandments.

The older brother is right too, in his way, as the second dialogue demonstrates. He believes in hierarchy, law, and order. The Father's House is the only order, the sole reality he recognizes. Whoever betrays the House betrays the Father as well. The voice of the older brother is the voice of the Holy Church, more stringent and forbidding than the Father's word.

Not that the older brother rejects the Prodigal Son; he welcomes his final submission. But he is exacting and merciless. His ambition is to impress his own faith and form on the restive, depleted sinner.

"Brother," says the Prodigal Son. "We are hardly alike."

"It's your fault," says the brother.

"Why—my fault?"

"Because I am in order. In whatever you differ from me, it cannot be but heresy and transgression."

The older brother is right.

So is the mother—naturally she is. Mothers are always right. The conversation with her—the third one of the cycle—deals mostly with simple and solid things. She wants her boy to get married. She is glad to have him again. But she is also worried—not because of the Prodigal Son, to be sure; he is back, he will be all right. But there is another boy, the youngest. He seems restless, these days. Is it now his turn to toy with dangerous thoughts? Will he too run away and live riotously? In this case, he will have to fill his belly, eventually, with the husks that the swine do eat. Mother knows life, or doesn't she?

If she knows life, and if she knows her boys, why, then, does she ask the Prodigal Son to talk to his younger brother? How can she make such a blunder? Does she in all earnest expect that the stranded runaway will have a good influence on her new problem child?

Or does she want, at bottom, her youngest child to go off and take chances? Would she prefer, perhaps, to see him encouraged, rather than warned and frightened?

Mothers are often puzzling, but never entirely wrong. So the Prodigal Son has his fourth talk—with the youngster.

Does he corrupt the child? He only confirms what the other has already divined in his reveries: that there are other kingdoms to discover, outside the hierarchy of the House, and also lands without a king. The traveler, exhausted but still glowing with the seduction of foreign lands, offers the fruit of adventure—not the apple of wisdom which quenches the thirst, but the savage pomegranate whose bitter-sweet aroma makes for more thirst and makes the lover love his longing. It is the same fruit Ménalque offered to André; André, to Nathanaël.

"Leave your home and your dogmas!" says the Prodigal Son to his little brother. "Go! Be strong! Forget us! May you return no more . . ."

The younger brother runs away. He is right.

IV. STRAIT IS THE GATE...

The road of excess leads to the palace of wisdom.
WILLIAM BLAKE

Connaître Dieu, c'est le chercher.
ANDRÉ GIDE

T H E geometric pattern according to which life proceeds is neither a straight line nor a zigzag, but a spiral curve. The spiral seems to obey a double magnetism: its ascension is punctuated by an inherent backward tendency. The rising swing is more powerful than its opposite, to be sure. And yet the energy manifest in the moving line would betray its intrinsic law if it followed exclusively the appeal from above and disregarded its proclivity back to the ground whence it originated.

The curve of André Gide's biography is particularly apt to illustrate and dramatize this twofold trend. Evidently, his advance is constantly interrupted and modified by what may look like relapses into conflicts and conceptions long overcome. Every idea that has once been central in his philosophy will remain relevant to his thought; sooner or later he reverts to it and reaffirms its validity on a higher plane. The elements of which his vision consists—incongruous, divergent as they may appear—are not only interrelated among each other but also developed from a common basis.

One might almost say that Gide's entire work is organized around a very few leading thoughts, which we find constantly resumed, varied, and amplified.

Whenever he has assimilated a new ingredient to the organic compound of his identity, he is likely to return to a previous stage: to transpose, as it were, his older experience up to the newly attained level. Thus he succeeds in maintaining the spiritual continuity indispensable to a sound and creative growth.

Of course, this regular resumption of already familiar themes is less stimulating than to explore virgin zones and to walk on untrodden paths. What is really a steady, consistent progress might be felt, subjectively, as decline and self-repetition. It cannot be elating to take up, once more, the ascetic ideals of one's youth, after having forsworn and refuted them in glowing manifestoes. Was André Gide not through with the notions of "sacrifice," "sanctity," and the like? After all, the author of *L'Immoraliste* and *Les Nourritures terrestres* could hardly exalt purity and virtue again. Couldn't he? He could; in fact, he had to—compelled by the inmost law of his nature. The concepts of sanctity and renunciation are realities in his life, cogent and valid forever; he is not free to deny them. All he can and must do is to develop and deepen their purport.

Yet the formulas and demands of ascetic morality may have seemed stale and tedious to him, after his bold excursions into more breezy, more colorful spheres. He had gone daringly far in one direction; now the reverse tendency of the spiral line forced him to take a step backwards. He followed, but grudgingly.

There was a period of depression and uncertainty in

Gide's life, after the appearance of *The Immoralist*. Not that he was altogether despondent; *The Return of the Prodigal Son*, written in that time, does not look like a downhearted man's achievement. Still a gloomy vein prevails in most documents of that epoch. The euphoria of moral awakening and physical convalescence was superseded by darker and deeper moods. Gide, who had praised the rapture of amative potency, now dwelt on the profound stimulus inherent in suffering and disease. Characteristically, he quoted Pascal who besought God to let him make the right use of his malady. "Disease as source of restlessness," André Gide adds. "Nothing to expect from the satisfied ones. The value of Jean-Jacques Rousseau, just like Nietzsche's, is due to his malady. Without his illness, Rousseau would have been an unbearable orator in the line of Cicero."

And what would Gide have been without his insomnia and his constant headaches? His complaints about all kinds of physical disturbances multiply in that period. The herald of Joy appears moody, at times bilious and cranky. He seems rather lonely too, notwithstanding the comparative popularity of his novel. The public was fairly pleased with *The Immoralist*. A real novel at last!—something they could pigeonhole according to their accustomed patterns. But the vanguard's reaction was all the more chilly.

Gide had no "circle," no following, at that point. The group around the *Nouvelle Revue Française* was not yet established, while his former contacts had definitely ceased to exist. As for the Symbolists, Gide's judgments of them become increasingly derogatory. He blames them for their complete lack of curiosity and élan, their corrosive pessimism, their resignation. Even Henri de Régnier, hitherto

so warmly admired, is not exempted from this verdict—let
alone Pierre Louÿs, who degraded his gifts to the nether
world of trash.

The aversion was mutual, for that matter. The Symbolists, or what remained of their coterie, were, in their turn,
pretty hard on Gide. *L'Immoraliste* was a gross disappointment to them, even more naturalistic than *Les Nourritures*,
and, hence, even triter. Rumor had it that the great Herédia, briefly before he passed away, mumbled something to
the effect that "poor André Gide will never do anything."

Small wonder, then, that Gide avoided Paris, where even
the moribund seemed malicious. More haunted than ever,
he led his nomadic life between Marseille and Morocco,
Central Europe, North Africa, and Asia Minor. It was at
that time that he transcended the traditional scope of his
journeys, from Berlin to Biskra, and ventured on an expedition to Greece and Turkey. From this trip resulted a slim
collection of travel notes published under the title *La
Marche turque*. The Oriental diary—a rather flimsy piece
of writing, incidentally—carries a dedication to "Em."—
Madame Emmanuèle Gide. The young husband and solitary vagabond apologizes for the "inadequate letters" he
wrote to his wife from "down there," and offers her some
"even more inadequate pages" as a well-intended postscriptum.

What an odd ménage!—disorganized, eccentric, and yet
not without a certain respectability. Everything was done
on a large scale. For a while the Gides had three homes, in
none of which the master spent much time. Emmanuèle had
inherited an estate, Cuverville, in Normandy, whereas
André owned La Roque, which came to him from his

mother. Moreover, the young couple bought a villa in a fashionable suburb of Paris, with the intention of "making a home." But it was not a big success. Gide, who can be a charming host in the country, is scarcely equipped to face the intricate requirements of metropolitan social life.

Was he happy, with all his country seats and Oriental impressions? We are not entitled to ask this question. His diary is utterly discreet as far as his married life is concerned. All we know, or are allowed to guess, is that it meant a more essential and more predominant experience to him than he chose expressly to admit. As regards his romance and his engagement with Emmanuèle, Gide's memoirs are detailed and eloquent enough. But what follows, the marriage proper, seems shrouded in mystery. In the published version of the *Journal* everything in respect to Madame Gide is omitted, except a few references to *Em.*, all couched in the most noncommittal fashion. Even when he has lost her, as an aging man, he will content himself with one veiled allusion to "the secret drama of my life."

There can be no doubt, however, that this "secret drama" is of cardinal significance to Gide's development and production. To prove this, we have the stirring evidence of two master novels—after *The Immoralist*, a second work immortalizing *Em.*, namely, *La Porte étroite* (1909).

If the former is a dramatic exposure of the author's "wicked" impulses and doctrines, the latter was originally conceived as a satire on his—and, perhaps, on *Em.*'s—ascetic aspirations. *La Porte étroite* is the narrative pendant to *Les Cahiers d'André Walter* and to the works that followed it, just as *L'Immoraliste* illustrates the tenets of *Les Nourritures terrestres*.

L'Immoraliste is the story of a man who destroys his own happiness and the life of his wife by his immoderate avidity. *La Porte étroite* is the story of a woman who destroys her own happiness and her life, and the happiness of the man she loves, by her immoderate virtue. Originally it was Gide's idea to prove, even to ridicule, the futility of unwished-for sacrifices.

The first reference to this theme occurs as far back as 1894, shortly after the publication of *Les Cahiers d'André Walter*. "It is good for a soul to recognize, as long as it is still young, that we cannot lose sight of God, no matter to what direction we turn." And Gide adds, ominously, "Possibility of distress: A soul that believes it has served God in a fallacious way. (*The Death of Mlle. Claire.*)"

A footnote informs us that *The Death of Mlle. Claire* is to become, fifteen years afterwards, *Strait is the Gate* . . . Mademoiselle Claire, who serves God in a fallacious way and perishes, will be resurrected in the more effulgent shape of Alissa, the heroine of *La Porte étroite*. Even the faintest traces of irony are removed from the definitive version of her adventure.

And yet it is not too difficult to imagine the plot of *La Porte étroite* treated in a satirical manner, as Gide had first planned to do. Alissa's story would indeed yield material for a delicate, suggestive comedy—the melancholy farce of a high-minded but rather flighty young lady who makes a mess of things, impelled by her fixed idea that God wants her to do so.

Alissa loves her cousin Jerome (yes, the boy she loves is her cousin: just in order to stress, as it were, the autobiographic impact of the situation). Jerome, in his turn, loves nobody but Alissa. But she is not the only one who loves him. Alissa's sister, Juliette, falls in love with Jerome too. The incident is in itself not grave; for, in the first place, Juliette is rather on the frivolous side; besides, she will be taken care of by another admirer. Nobody expects Alissa to give Jerome up for the sake of Juliette; but that is what she does. In fact, she abides by her noble gesture, even when Juliette has already contented herself with another man. As for Alissa, she is now in love with her sacrifice rather than with Jerome. She does not want to renounce her renunciation. After having sent Jerome away, she dies in a state of ecstasy and frustration.

It would be feasible and also pardonable to tackle this affair in a diabolical fashion. Alissa's sacrifice might be judged with such sardonic skepticism as of La Rochefoucauld, that classical debunker of fine emotions and bombastic words. His *Maximes* offer a profusion of caustic wisdom revealing the petty motive powers behind our bumptious gestures. As for man's moral resistance to carnal passion, the irreverent psychologist suggests: "*Si nous resistons à nos passions, c'est plus par leur faiblesse que par notre force*,"—a truthful word, which is strikingly confirmed by William Blake. "Those who restrain desire, do so because theirs is weak enough to be restrained," he observes in *The Marriage of Heaven and Hell*. And since we have already referred to this astounding opus, the bearing of which on Gide's thought will have to be elucidated later on, we may as well quote another "Proverb of Hell" that might seem applicable to Alissa: "He who desires but acts not, breeds pestilence."

But renunciation too is action—perhaps, the most dramatic and dynamic action. For human impulses and gestures in general are corrupted and dislocated by interest—the interests of greed, vanity, lust. Only the disinterested, the gratuitous, act has the original grandeur inherent in all manifestations of nature and of genius. A sacrifice, therefore, is the more admirable the more futile it seems. Was not Nathanaël urged, in *Les Nourritures terrestres,* "to act without worrying whether the action is good or evil"? Alissa, on her part, follows this advice, in a somewhat modified, if not reversed, sense. She makes her sacrifice, regardless of its consequences. Thus *La Porte étroite* resumes another leitmotiv of Gide's work, the postulate of gratuitous energy, and fuses it, surprisingly, with the idea of renunciation and self-denial. Far from mocking or disparaging Alissa's useless gesture, the novel exalts her martyrdom precisely on account of its futility.

Besides, the question remains, and is greatly relevant, whether a disinterested action is necessarily a voluntary one. Maybe Alissa had to act the way she did? "Sanctity is not a choice but a compulsion," she discloses to her friend, underlining the word "compulsion" three times in the text of her letter. "If you are the one I have believed you to be, you will not let yourself be distracted from it, either."

Alissa renounces, in fact, refuses Jerome because she loves him too much. (*"Ah! sauras-tu jamais combien je t'aime . . ."*) She is afraid to taint the miracle of her love by its fulfillment in this sordid world. Like André Walter, she is unable to conceive the ultimate and perfect communion with the beloved being, except in a purer, transcendental sphere. Like Luc, in *La Tentative amoureuse,* she suspects that desire corrodes and burns whatever it may touch. But she is also the sister of Ménalque and Nathanaël. Akin to those vagrant lovers, she prefers the sensation of thirst to the satisfaction of drinking, the unending quest to the transient illusion of happiness.

Her prayers and contemplations echo Gide's innermost thoughts. Her drama springs from the same striving unrest which is his basic impulse. Neither Gide nor Alissa is sure of God and His unfathomable intentions. Both agree that "to know God, is to seek Him." "You will not seek me," says Christ, according to Pascal, "unless you have found me already."

God—the God of Alissa, the God of Gide, our God—is not a fact but a problem; not a possession but a goal. The Pharisees, who deem themselves close to Him, are in reality farthest from His Truth. Not the knowledge of God is the truly religious experience, but the search for Him. He who dares to locate the Strait Gate, will go astray; he will find the broad one that leadeth to destruction. But everyone who asketh receiveth, and he that seeketh findeth.

The pious heroine of *La Porte étroite* speaks unmistakably in Gide's own voice, she vocalizes the heart and crux of his philosophy when she confides to her diary these bold and beautiful words: "I imagine the celestial bliss, not as a fusion with God, but as a continuous, infinite approach ... In fact, if I were not afraid of playing with words, I might dare to say that I would sneer at a bliss which is not *progressive*."

This is the wanderer's voice—the challenge and impetration of the eternal seeker. He does not believe in dwelling anywhere, not even in Paradise. To him Paradise is nothing stable or secure, but an elusive prospect—infinitely attractive and fascinating in its perpetual flux. Gide's whole work confirms what he divined in his youth, playfully disguised as Narcissus: that the Kingdom of Heaven (Paradise) will not be given to us by grace but will have to be sought and conquered. *"Le Paradis est toujours à refaire."* This axiom connotes a complex moral creed, from which a social and political credo may emerge in the future.

Only he who has overcome the inertia of selfishness will be prepared for the hazardous march toward God. The metaphysical quest presupposes the physical sacrifice. Thus the concept of progress fuses with the ethos of renunciation. Whoever wants to reach the Strait Gate must first pass through the bitterness of self-abandonment. Says the Lord:

For whosoever shall save his life shall lose it; but whosoever shall lose it, the same shall find it.

It is this word—at once so comforting and so frightful— which we will find quoted and hinted at, throughout Gide's entire work. He has interpreted it in many ways and in many different contexts; again and again he praised it as "the mysterious center of Christian ethics, the divine formula of happiness: the individual triumphs by renouncing the individual."

This sacred paradox is the gist and essence of that fragile and yet powerful composition, *La Porte étroite.*

From an artistic point of view, the novel marks a signal progress, compared, not only with *Les Cahiers d'André Walter*, but also with *L'Immoraliste*. As Alissa renounces her fleshly passion for the sake of a purer beatitude, the Gide of *La Porte étroite* seems to have forsworn all his literary mannerisms. There no longer are shrill or redundant outbursts; no glaring colorings, no hectic exaggerations. Everything in this novel is perfectly simple and, therefore, perfectly beautiful.

If the atmosphere in *L'Immoraliste* seems to phosphoresce with uncanny flares and flashes, the landscapes and interiors in *La Porte étroite* are bathed in an equable light, limpid and silvery. A pure, nacreous hue is cast over all things and faces; we can perceive that reflection in its sedate and yet passionate dialogues and, above all, in the fervent and delicate intonations of Alissa's voice. There is a strange overtone of serenity, even in her sorrowful meditations. She performs the gesture of sacrifice with an elegance that is truly heroic. Her affliction never becomes ugly or hysterical. She dies as she has lived and loved, placid and composed, a religious clairvoyant with superb manners.

The whole work has this tinge of classical conventionality: its shape and tempo seem calculated according to the august formulas of Corneille and Racine. The drama develops without any superfluous ballast—skillfully timed and measured, with a minimum of apparatus and personnel. All characters introduced are strictly necessary for the proceeding plot: besides Jerome and Alissa, there is just the traditional second couple—Alissa's sister, Juliette, and the boy who is in love with her, and, finally, the mother of the two girls, Madame Bucolin, whose objectionable conduct incites in Alissa the longing for sanctity. A few minor figures remain completely faceless and impersonal.

They are employed and abandoned with that lofty negligence shown by classical tragedians towards lackeys, confidants, and the like.

The opening scene is a masterpiece in itself. The setting is the garden of the Bucolin home, near Le Havre, a garden which is "not very large, not very beautiful, and which distinguishes itself by no particular feature from many another garden in Normandy." Yet it becomes the garden par excellence to everyone who reads and can appreciate the meticulous and plastic description. Small wonder that such a fastidious expert in French letters as André Gide was fully satisfied by this initial passage. "Certainly, the description of the garden is good," he notes in his diary. "But as for the rest . . . ?"

Of course, there are hours of doubt. Every creative mind is familiar with the downhearted moods Gide registers in his journal. "Yesterday I read to Jacques Copeau what I have written of *La Porte étroite*. It displeased me enormously. I was not far from throwing the whole thing into the fire . . ."

Copeau—one of the founders of the *Nouvelle Revue Française* and, subsequently, the director of an experimental theater, *Le Vieux Colombier*—saved the situation by his constructive advice. Gide changed his mind and spared his manuscript. But it took four more years before the novel could go to press. And in May, 1910, a few months after publication date, the author felt that, "if I died today, my whole work would disappear behind *La Porte étroite*. It is my only product that does actually count."

The notices in the press were about as clumsy and insidious as usual, but Gide seemed unusually sensitive this

time. The same critics who had first been shocked by
L'Immoraliste now disapproved of *La Porte étroite* as it
differed too glaringly from the former. What was he up
to, that vexatious imp of a Gide? They had just labeled
him as demoniac and a bit salacious. How could he dare
surprise the gentlemen of the press with all this sanctity
stuff?

"It perplexes my reviewers that these contradictory veins
have coexisted, and still coexist, in my spirit," Gide observed. "Whatever the book may be that occupies me, at
one point, I never give myself to it entirely. The subject
which is going to claim me next develops simultaneously,
at the other extreme of my being. If somebody believes he
might identify me with my most recent product, he is
utterly wrong. It is always from my last-born child that
I am most different."

Small wonder, then, that the hopes of his religious-
minded friends were presently disappointed. Did they expect this Proteus to abide by his pietist disposition? Before
long, the mystic vein manifest in *La Porte étroite* was to
be superseded by rather irreverent, even blasphemous
trends. Gide's literary output from 1910 to 1914 must have
been revolting to the devout Catholics among his readers.
But even when his religious strain became predominant
again, during the Great War, his philosophic and emotional
approach to God remained incompatible with the rigid
tenets of a Paul Claudel.

The friendship between Claudel and Gide is one of the
paradoxical features in the biographies of both men and,
incidentally, testifies to the spiritual rank and independence
of both. Their congeniality proved sound and stable

enough to outlast many an occasional quarrel and the principal divergencies of their views. Claudel, the Catholic, could forgive André Gide for his heresies as he was aware of his friend's deep and candid religiousness. As for Gide, he could overlook Claudel's almost brutal fanaticism, as it was free of any petty, hypocritical features, and always radiant with the flame of genius.

Moreover, Claudel's concept of Christianity harmonizes with Gide's in more than one respect. The notion of *joy*, this living germ of Gide's faith, is central also in Claudel's credo, for all its unyielding gravity and apparent somberness. Claudel's metaphysical fervor scarcely affects his attitude towards love and life. Ascetic morality is to him the poor and even somewhat disturbing daughter of the Christian religion. It is for the sake of the magnificent Mother that one has to tolerate the child and treat her with all exigible courtesy. Claudel must have sounded familiar and sympathetic to Gide when he exclaimed: "And surely we love Jesus Christ; but nothing on earth could make us love morality."

The situation became more precarious with regard to intellectual evaluations. No doubt, Gide was irritated, if not outright disgusted, when Claudel ranted against "that ass Goethe," or denounced, in his poem *Magnificat*, "*les Voltaire, et les Renan, et les Michelet, et les Hugo, et tous les autres infames!*" His rabid maledictions are indeed outrageously un-Christian. Or is it in keeping with the ethics of Jesus Christ to assert that the souls of those fallible but respectable men (including Goethe and Kant) are now with "the dead dogs," while their works rot with the gar-

bage? "They are dead," chides the Christian poet, "and
their names after their death still exhale poison and putre-
faction."

In other cases Claudel and Gide could admire together;
Rimbaud and Baudelaire, for instance, were their mutual
heroes. And still there were disagreements, even when their
judgments agreed. Claudel's interpretation of Rimbaud's
greatness irked Gide even more, perhaps, than his inordinate disparagement of Goethe or Voltaire. The seditious
poet of *Le Bateau ivre* and *Une Saison en enfer* became, in
Claudel's presentation, a herald of metaphysical ecstasies.
Gide had to witness how Rimbaud, the rebel and ruffian,
was claimed, usurped by the Holy Church. "Arthur Rimbaud is *my* friend," he insisted, "and if I love him otherwise than you do, I love him in the way he prefers to be
loved." But Claudel was equally persistent. Rimbaud meant
too much to him; he could not give him up.

Claudel's tenacity in this struggle for Rimbaud's soul is
comprehensible in view of the pivotal rôle the vagrant
genius played in his conversion. Paradoxical as it may
sound, it was under the impression of Rimbaud's glorious
blasphemies that Paul Claudel—eighteen years old, at the
time—discovered the sources of faith in the depth of his
dried-out and darkened heart. Rimbaud was the tool employed by Providence to illuminate this muddled and
blinded youth. Claudel describes the miraculous experience
in a moving account, "My Conversion" (published in
1913, twenty-seven years after the event). The spectacle
of the vespers at Notre Dame confirmed and completed the
revelation first started by Rimbaud's appeal. "All of a

sudden my heart was touched. I BELIEVED. It is true! God
exists—there He is! He is somebody, is a being as personal
and real as I am. He loves me, he calls for me!"

All converts are possessed by the fixed idea of converting
others. Claudel is a persuasive recruiting officer for the
holy ranks. His appeal is effective, almost irresistible, by
virtue of his dynamic personality and of his iron faith. Gide
has often described how puny and weak he feels in front
of Claudel's mighty stature. "He dominates me, he overwhelms me; he has more foundation and more surface,
more health, more money, more genius, more power, more
children, more faith—he has more of everything than I
have."

Yet Gide had more tenacity in resisting than Claudel
had in wooing him. Claudel made scores of Catholic prose-
lytes; but Gide was not among them.

"Drop your hideous Nietzscheanism!" he was urged by
Francis Jammes, who had seen the light, as far back as
1905. "Don't hesitate any more! The Church, France,
your friends—all of us want you to join us."

But his response was, *No*.

"Hurry up!" wrote another friend, Charles-Louis Philippe, the author of *Bubu de Montparnasse*. "Make up your
mind! Be a man! I know in advance what you are going
to choose. We will choose it all."

But Philippe's request was rash and emotional. He had
not yet made his choice himself, and he never did; or
rather, he made it against Catholicism. The example of
Claudel's vigorous harmony had almost induced him to
take the decisive step. "I am positive," Gide said in his
fine obituary speech about Philippe, in 1910, "that, at a

certain point, he was quite ready to submit himself to Catholicism." But then he points out that his late friend overcame at last the spell Claudel cast on him, and liberated himself of an influence which was "something more powerful, more important, and more dangerous than the authority of an individual writer. For what hid, or rather, did not hide, behind Claudel was the Church. I believe," Gide concluded this passage, "that I remain objective when I state that Philippe, after a long time of hesitation, deemed it a victory *not* to yield to this influence in the end."

One may say as much for Gide. More and more of his friends embraced the Catholic creed—Jacques Maritain, a former Protestant, and Charles Péguy, who had been anticlerical. During the bitter war years the number of conversions multiplied. Jacques Rivière—the highly gifted young critic and essayist whom both Claudel and Gide had wooed and influenced—finally made his decision in favor of the former: that is to say, he had recourse to the Church. So did Jacques Copeau and, most emphatically, Gide's old companion, Henri Ghéon. But Gide remained reluctant.

No doubt, he, too, was sensible to the vast attraction of Rome. There must have been hours when the holy harbor tempted his roving mind. The calamity of 1914 could not but afflict and disturb him to the very depth of his being. Everything he believed in and loved appeared imperiled, doomed. The world he knew—a hospitable world, boundless and bountiful—writhed and crumbled, shaken, as it were, by the grip of a wrathful god. Obviously, so sweeping a tribulation could not be without moral sense. It was imposed on man as a dire warning, if not as punishment. Something must be wrong, essentially, with our acts and thoughts, to provoke, to justify, such a devastating lesson. Nobody could exclude himself from the collective guilt as nobody is exempted from the general castigation.

What is my trespass, Lord? asked this solitary sinner, André Gide. *Surely, I too have failed. How? Why? What do You want me to do?*

It might be that he had missed the Strait Gate as he insisted on seeking it by himself? His solitude was his transgression, perhaps? If so, he had to give up his arrogant isolation, to join in the prayers of the community, of his people. What temptation!—to accept the shelter magnanimously offered by the Papacy. "You just anticipate what I may do in the nearest future," Gide wrote to a friend who became Catholic.

But he waited and wavered, torn by his contradictory qualms and inspirations. At one point he seemed inclined to side with the Royalist-Catholic-Nationalist movement of the *Action Française.* A message to Charles Maurras, in 1916, divulges this transitory mood. But he withdrew again —always evasive, oscillating between extremes.

It was easier and better to keep silence, rather than to adapt his words to any pattern or program. A brief essay on Baudelaire—a masterpiece, by the way—is the only thing Gide published from 1914 to 1919.

Not that he ceased to produce, on the contrary. The output of those years is voluminous, with *Si le Grain ne meurt* and *Corydon* as the two major items. But both works were published only several years after the end of the War, as was *Numquid et Tu . . . ?*, a slim booklet of religious meditations composed about 1916.

This aphoristic commentary on the Gospel is, in my opinion, by far the most significant piece of writing Gide accomplished during the War—definitely superior to both the somewhat disappointing autobiography and the painstaking treatise on homosexuality. A stirring document, profoundly marked by the anxiety of those trying days, it can well stand comparison with Claudel's *Conversion*. And yet the differences between the two accounts are even more revealing than the parallels. How humble and human is Gide's zealous uncertainty in contrast to Claudel's grand and triumphant faith! Gide's prayer seems to consist of passionate questions, whereas Claudel's credo is positive, stern, aggressive. Claudel's belief rests stolidly on the doctrines and the ritual; Gide has to conquer every truth himself—constantly beset by new doubts, enthralled and bewildered by new discoveries. The message of the Lord remains always surprising to him. "*La Promesse du Christ est toujours nouvelle d'une promesse infinie.*"

Claudel's vision is primarily transcendental; his religious pathos depends entirely on his faith in the existence of another world. Our transient affairs are real and relevant only because, and as far as, they are connected with the ultimate realities of Heaven and Hell.

But Gide says: No. It is here and now that we experience the real thing, the eternal life. For Jesus says, *I* AM *the way; I* AM *the truth; I* AM *the resurrection.* Eternal life is not only in the future. It is here, from now on, present in all of us. We shall possess it as soon as we consent to abandon ourselves, to attain the renunciation that gives us the resurrection in eternity.

"Neither behest nor ruling: simply the secret of the supreme felicity revealed by Jesus Christ in the Gospels. *'If ye know these things, happy are ye if ye do them.'* (John 13:17). Not *'happy shall ye be'* but *'happy are ye.'* Here and now we can share in that perfect bliss."

This paragraph is quoted, not from *Numquid et Tu . . . ?*, but from Gide's extraordinary essay on Dostoevski. It was only in 1923 that he concluded and released his studies on the Russian novelist-visionary. But the religious war diary proves eloquently, if implicitly, that Gide's passionate concern in Dostoevski's work dates from long before. "I am struck," says Gide, "every time I read the Gospels, by the insistence with which the words, *'Et nunc,'*—*'And now'*— are repeated over and over again. And certainly Dostoevski too was struck by it."

What Gide says about Dostoevski often sounds as if it had been said by somebody else about Gide. He writes: "But, you may well contend, if feeling is to overcome thought, and the soul know no state but this vague expectancy susceptible to every outside influence, what can result except complete anarchy? It has been said, and of late more frequently, that anarchy is the consummation of Dostoevski's doctrine. A discussion of his beliefs would lead us into a far country, for I can anticipate the storm of protest I should provoke if I dared to affirm that Dostoevski does not plunge us into anarchy, but simply and naturally leads us to the Gospels. On this point we must be clear. Christian doctrine as contained in the New Testament is usually seen by people of our nation through the medium of the Roman Catholic Church, as she has modified it, moreover, in harmony with her own needs. Now, Dostoevski abhors all churches, the Church of Rome in particular. He claims it is his right to accept Christ's teaching directly from the Scriptures, and from them alone, which is precisely what the Catholic cannot possibly concede."

But it was Gide, not Dostoevski, who said to Paul Claudel: "It is by no means free thought that prevents me, but the Gospel itself."

"Prevents you—from what?"

"Why, from entering the Church, of course. You Catholics don't know the Gospel. And not only do you not know it, you don't even know that you don't know it. You believe in all earnest you know it. That is why you continue to ignore it."

No, he could not come to terms with the Church. Like Dostoevski, like Kierkegaard, he preferred the direct dialogue with his Lord, without any go-between or interpreter. There are Lutheran undertones in his grim defiance of the Catholic tutelage. But even the system of strict Protestantism seems oppressive to him. His credo is: "I am neither a Catholic nor a Protestant; I am a Christian, quite simply."

Was it not Christ himself who destroyed obsolete formulas? Christianity will serve man as a prop and a spur for many years and centuries to come. But it must get rid of its outdated, cumbersome apparatus. The churches, whether Catholic or Protestant, have long become instruments of hindrance and restriction curbing man's approach to the Supreme Being.

The unfortunate development began with Paulus, whom Gide persecutes with the same obstinate antipathy Nietzsche had for that apostle. "It is never Christ, it is Paul who hurts me. In his sermons—never in the Gospel—I find again what once estranged me from the Lord." It is easier for him to believe in Christ's miracles than to accept the sophisms of Saint Paul. There occur things in the Letters to the Corinthians, and elsewhere in Paul's writings, that offend Gide's taste and logic. For there is one value he cherishes even more than his faith—namely, truth.

This uncompromising truthfulness is, perhaps, a part of his Puritan heritage. Honesty ranks above all other virtues in the hierarchy of Gide's evaluations. "*Honnêteté*," he notes in his diary. "*Tout ce qu'il y a dans ce mot.*" We may remember that it is this French term, *honnêteté*, which appears again and again in the German prose of Nietzsche. Gide rejects sternly what we may call the Jesuitic morality —the doctrine, that is, which holds that the aim justifies the means and that you can promote the truth by lying. Gide has dealt with this double-faced morality in one of his dramatic compositions, *Philoctète*, written soon after *Les Nourritures terrestres*. Here it is Ulysses who represents the conditional ethics according to which even felony is allowed, as long as it serves a noble cause—in this case, the interests of the Hellenic army. Philoctetus, abandoned by the Greeks on a desert island, and the young son of Achilles, supposed to rob him of his last belonging, the bow of Heracles, refute this purposeful morality. The forsaken hero is touched by the grace of the Olympians. He talks beautifully. "You are very eloquent," says Ulysses, "for somebody who suffers."

Philoctète: "Wherever I go, I am a son of Hellas."

Ulysses: "But you have nobody to talk to, any more."

Philoctète: "I have learned how to talk since I no longer address myself to men. I realize now that words are more beautiful when they don't serve any purpose."

Thus Gide adds his eulogy of the *disinterested word* to his philosophy of the *disinterested action*—a highly topical concept, in the days of the Dreyfus Affair. For it was under the impression of this rousing scandal that he conceived *Philoctète* and reaffirmed his unyielding notion of truthfulness above all. The adherents to army and church betrayed the truth for the sake of lofty abstractions which, in their turn, served as shoddy disguises of practical interests. Gide took the side of the Jewish Captain—that is to say, of truth.

We read in his journal, "*A propos de Maurice Barrès:* What he calls 'the Protestant spirit' is in fact that 'dangerous' spirit of probity which induced the Jansenists to write: 'To whatever country or whatever sect you may belong, you must not believe save what is true and what you would believe even if you belonged to another country, another sect, or another profession.' "

It seemed to him that those of his friends who became Catholics also became untruthful. Not only Henri Massis, the cunning Neo-Thomist, twisted the truth, and also his quotations from Gide's writings, according to his respective purposes. Even the candid Francis Jammes indulged in fabrications. Gide had to rectify publicly certain misrepresentations spread by his old friend—some of them innocuous, others fairly disagreeable. After having enumerated and corrected several "mistakes" and having closed his note, "*bien affectueusement, ton* . . . ," Gide had to add this amusing postscriptum: "I just happen to read, in the *Revue Universelle,* your poetic description of La Roque: drawbridges, decaying walls, an owl in your slipper, and so forth; all this is delightful. I cannot help believing, however, that a little bit of truth might have been even more interesting. But you feel, undoubtedly, that it wouldn't have fitted your style."

"*J'ai horreur du mensonge,*" André Gide said to Jacques Maritain. "I loathe the lie. It is, perhaps, through this aversion that my Protestantism manifests itself. The Catholics are not in a position to understand this. I have known many of them; in fact, all my friends are Catholics, with the one exception of Jean Schlumberger. The Catholics do not like the truth."

Whereupon Maritain answered, "Catholicism teaches the love for truth."

"No. Don't protest, Maritain! I have seen too often, and in too many cases, what kinds of compromises are possible. I know what you could answer me: that the Protestants often confound the truth and God; that they idolize the truth; that they fail to see that the truth is, after all, just one of the divine attributes . . ."

"But don't you think that the particular truth which your book intends to express might be dangerous?" asked Maritain.

The book in question was *Corydon.* Maritain tried very hard to talk Gide into withdrawing the scandalous opus, but in vain. Gide was adamant. He insisted: "However dangerous this particular truth may be, I believe that the lie which now covers it is even more pernicious."

The shocking book came out, in spite of all pious warnings. Most of Gide's Catholic friends turned presently
against him. Henri Ghéon, the playmate of happier days,
now vied with men like Massis and Béraud in slandering
the author of *L'Immoraliste*—a novel which carries this
dedication, "*A Henri Ghéon, son franc camarade, A. G.*"

Numquid et Tu . . . ? is dedicated to another neo-
Catholic, Charles du Bos, the eminent critic and philosopher. Even he—close to Gide for decades—expressed in
public his disapproval of *Corydon* and, from that time on,
concentrated his sagacious admiration completely on Paul
Claudel.

But, curiously, there was no break between Claudel and
Gide. The great Catholic poet was enough of an artist,
enough of a Christian, and enough of a friend, to understand and respect Gide's dogged and heroic nonconform-
ity. Maybe it was not without apprehension, but certainly
not without sympathy, that the bard of the *Magnificat*
watched the solitary pilgrim continue his hazardous march
on the narrow path. Would he stumble? Would he go
astray?

It occurred at times that Claudel worried about Gide's
endangered soul. Then he would urge his friend to confess, to make his peace with the Church. But Gide asserted,
half to tease Claudel, half to comfort him, "I have really
lost all interest in my soul and in its salvation."

"But God," replied Paul Claudel, "He has not lost
interest in you."

Which Gide may have known, at bottom, even before
Claudel told him so.

V. PROTEUS AND PROTESTANT

L'estre veritable est le commencement d'une grande vertu.

MONTAIGNE

Je ne suis peut'être qu'un aventurier.

ANDRÉ GIDE

*F*O R *whosoever shall save his life shall lose it;*
but whosoever shall lose his life, the same shall
find it.

Gide has quoted this Gospel word in many different
contexts and with many different connotations. The self-
sacrifice it implies is not necessarily the same in all cases.
There are many ways of abandoning one's own ego,
many forms of unification with more general, superior
entities. In Gide's vision the concepts of transformation
and sacrifice overlap and at times interfuse. To undergo a
change, to accept a disguise, means to transcend the limitations of introvert selfishness. Every metamorphosis is an
act of self-renunciation and, therefore, an act of love. "He
transforms himself into every being he loves," Gide says
about one of his characters. "And you must love him to
understand his being."

It is curious and illuminating to perceive the link
connecting Gide's philosophy of influences with his ethos
of renunciation. Characteristically, the first reference to

the above-quoted word of Christ in Gide's work occurs in
the treatise on *Influence in Literature* (1900). "A great
man," Gide says, "has but one concern: to become as
human as possible—to the point of seeming *commonplace.*
. . . And thus—how admirable!—he becomes most personal, too. Whereas he who withdraws from humanity to
the narrowness of his ego, succeeds only in becoming
whimsical, cranky, deficient . . . May I quote the Gospel?
Yes, for I do not think that I distort its meaning: *Whosoever shall save his life.* . . ."

The personal influences, it goes without saying, are at
least as crucial as are the literary ones: that is true of any
life, but particularly so in a case like Gide's, whose extreme receptivity is a vital and indispensable part of his
talent. "A great man commands not only his own intelligence but also the intelligences of all his friends." Gide
is wont to cite this sentence of Friedrich Nietzsche and,
furthermore, has paraphrased and amplified it in his
memoirs, *Si le Grain ne meurt.* What he tells us there with
an odd mixture of modesty and pride, is that he tried to
adopt and assimilate all those capacities and insights which
any of his friends may have had to offer as his personal
gift or "speciality." And while Gide always recognized
and respected the superiority of one of his companions in
this or that particular domain, he could not help feeling
superior to all of them as he focused and digested the
total sum of their various competences.

But not only is he sensible to the stimulus and the advice
of his friends, he responds also to the arguments of his
adversaries. It may occur in a dispute that Gide will drop

his own opinion and shift, if only temporarily, to the side of his opponent. He may go even further and make up additional evidence on behalf of his antagonist—abandoning, nay, betraying his own point of view, as it were, and playing wantonly the game of his enemy.

Is it a masochistic perversion that compels him to do so? Is it irresponsible cynicism? Or just a desultory whim? All these proclivities may have to do with Gide's treacherous penchant, which he acknowledges and condemns himself as a *"défaut d'esprit."* But this deficiency—which almost ceases to be one, once recognized and controlled—involves other aspects as well. For this weakness is but the negative and dangerous manifestation of artistic genius itself. All artists have, in a lesser or higher degree, this perplexing tendency: they are all inclined to change sides, to sneak from one identity to another, to betray their cause out of their indomitable love for disguises, masquerades, experiments. Every poet, indeed, every creative mind is a bit of an illusionist, an adventurer, and a Proteus.

Goethe's famous lament about the two souls dwelling, alas, together in his breast, is, of course, a glaring understatement. There were not only two souls fused in him, but a great many of them. The Faust-Mephisto formula is a simplification, just as it would be inadequate to reduce the vast complexity of Gide's being to the primitive antagonism between the Immoralist and the Saint. This contrast marks and dramatizes just the extreme potentialities of an individual disconcertingly rich in transitions and contradictions. *"Le sentiment de la complexité peut devenir une stupéfaction passionnée."* This is Gide at his best: the real Gide.

He is a virtuoso, among other things. His stunning versatility as an artist, the swift and gaudy sequence of his stylistic and philosophic "periods" might remind us of Picasso's kaleidoscopic manner, if it were not for the inexorable probity, inherent in the most casual gesture of André Gide but lacking even in Picasso's masterpieces. For Picasso, like Jean Cocteau, is essentially a performer juggling color and shapes (although the frantic intensity of his performance can at times assume truly tragic grandeur); whereas Gide, although his metamorphic skill sometimes suggests an irresponsible playfulness, never distorts or denies his incorruptible identity.

No doubt, his lifework includes a few things mostly, or at least partly, produced for the purpose of displaying the author's sovereign craftsmanship. Some of Gide's more recent books may belong to this category—*L'Ecole des femmes* and *Geneviève*, and certainly *Isabelle* (1911).

What he had really meant to bring out, after *La Porte étroite*, was *Corydon*, the treatise about the Hellenic Eros. But when he read the opening dialogue to his friends, their reaction was indeed discouraging. They appeared grieved, bewildered, altogether aghast. Their unanimous warnings could not but impress on Gide the utter risks involved in his enterprise. He wondered, wavered, and dropped the idea, for the time being. (Later, in his preface to the definitive edition of *Corydon*, in 1924, he quotes a word of Henrik Ibsen to the effect that "our friends are dangerous, not because of what they induce us to do, but rather because of what they prevent us from doing.")

Just as Oscar Wilde jotted down *Dorian Gray* to make good his boast that he could write a novel, Gide improvised *Isabelle* to convince his friends that he was able to produce something entirely inoffensive, idyllic and humorous, free of any diabolic touch. The result is a strangely impersonal but engaging tale full of minute observations and wistful jocularities.

As for the plot, Gide has not been very particular: a young man who becomes involved, half against his will, in the affairs of a quaint ménage of old people—among them a frustrated girl, whose yellowed love letters fall into the young man's hands and disclose to him a dusty and foiled romance that took place—or rather, did not take place—many years before. The setting of this melancholy humoresque is a country house called Quartfouche—a meticulous portrait, incidentally, of a delapidated villa not far from Gide's own estate of La Roque. One day he paid a visit to the decaying building, accompanied by his friend Francis Jammes. Both writers were considerably impressed by the drowsy and bewitched scenery. Jammes composed presently an extensive poem describing the very place which Gide, in his turn, re-created in *Isabelle*.

The young man, Gerard Lacase, who witnesses and reports the story, bears scarcely any autobiographical features. He sounds a bit like André Walter, especially as he admits, right in the beginning, that "at the age of twenty-five I knew life exclusively out of books." But this theme, and a few other reminiscences of Gide's previous writings, are just casually hinted at; they are not integrated into the texture of the ironic idyll.

Undeniably, *Isabelle* falls short of all other major works by André Gide. Yet I would not like to miss this quaint interlude. Its pensive serenity adds an amiable, somehow reassuring touch to the disquieting variety of Gide's artistic palette. Between the two great efforts of *La Porte étroite* and *Les Caves du Vatican*, it has the effect and the function of a relaxing exercise, like one of those minor feats the acrobats are wont to perform, left-handed, so to speak, before they fling themselves into the breath-taking adventure of the *grand écart*.

Gide's *grand écart*, his big number and uncanny stunt, has become famous under the name of *Les Caves du Vatican* (1914). The impish spirit, which begins to manifest itself in *Isabelle*, suddenly effervesces, grows indomitable, assumes rampant dimensions. The sedate chuckle becomes tempestuous laughter, elementary, sweeping, explosive. The whole book is one staggering hoax, utterly irreverent and altogether delightful. A veritable classic in humorous literature, *The Vaults of the Vatican*—or *The Vatican Swindle*, or *Lafcadio's Adventures*—refutes, once and for all, Gide's reputation of being ponderous and obscure, all heavy weather, no fun.

It is surprising that even an eminent connoisseur like the American scholar, Albert Guérard, should foster the prejudice that Gide is lacking in a sense of humor. Of course, the professor is right in principle when he stresses, in his remarkable book, *Preface to World Literature*, the element of "earnestness" prevailing in modern realistic fiction. Guérard writes: "Hitherto, born of parody and satire, the novel had retained a strong tinge of the comic. Chaucer, Boccaccio, Rabelais, Cervantes, Lesage, Defoe, are among those writers whose first aim is to amuse; and this was to remain true of Smollett and even of Fielding. When they have a serious purpose, it comes in almost surreptitiously. *Manon Lescaut*, on the contrary, is frankly a tragedy. It opens a long line of psychological narrative without a trace of frivolousness: the fictionist is a medical observer or a confessor rather than a jester. This is the kind that was illustrated by Benjamin Constant in his *Adolphe*, by Stendhal in *The Red and the Black*, by Tolstoi in *The Kreutzer Sonata*. It was to lead to Paul Bourget, André Gide, and Marcel Proust. . . ."

Excellent definitions, these. But why label André Gide as a follower of the Abbé Prévost, whose *Manon Lescaut* he admired with reservations, when his literary ancestry comprises exactly those illustrious jesters whom Mr. Guérard enumerates as his antagonists? As for *Les Caves du Vatican*, it has obviously more to do with Rabelais and Boccaccio, Cervantes and Defoe, Smollett and even Fielding, than with Paul Bourget or *The Kreutzer Sonata*. *Les Caves du Vatican* is the work of a man whose first aim is to amuse—that is to say, to amuse himself and, therefore, his reader. Gide pokes fun at a demure and tiresome novelist who appears in the book and proclaims gravely, "I don't write to amuse myself." That's why he is such a bore. Gide, on his part—the Gide of *Les Caves*—rather follows the example of Voltaire—the Voltaire of *Candide*—in reference to whom Gide observes, "*En s'amusant, il amuse.*"

It is by no means a psychological novel the author of *The Vatican Swindle* meant to bring about, "*en s'amusant.*" In fact, Gide does not present his book as a novel but as a *sotie*, which is not quite adequately translated by "farce." Yet the difference between a "farce" and a "sotie" is of faint, rather elusive nature. Both are derived from the ancient "morality," "an allegorical drama, in which the characters are abstractions: principles, virtues, vices, classes, and conditions of men. This simple definition covers a wide range of varieties, from the theological to the journalistic."

It is again from Guérard's meritorious work, *Preface to World Literature*, that I quote these elucidations. He informs us, moreover, that at a certain point "the morality had almost merged with the *sotie*, a satirical play acted by the clerks of the Paris Law Courts, and with the farce." In respect to the particular genre of the "sotie," Mr. Guérard adds the following footnote: "*Sotie:* so called because the association of merrymakers called themselves *sots* (fools); cf. popularity of the Ship of Fools theme at that time, and the election of a Pope of Fools. For some recondite reason, André Gide has elected to call some of his works *soties*."

Frankly, I do not know what is "recondite" about his calling *Les Caves du Vatican* a "sotie"; if we need any special explanation for this meaningful caprice, we may obtain it from Mr. Guérard's own text. For he refers expressly to a certain hilarious ritual performed by the association of merrymakers—namely, the election of a Pope of Fools. And this happens to be the central plot in Gide's Vatican farce: an association of audacious merrymakers elects and enthrones a Pope of Fools, thus fooling and bedeviling Christianity. What, then, is a *sotie*, if not this impudent, sparkling fancy? To me, it is the *sotie* of *soties*, the *sotie* par excellence, the hyper-*sotie*, if there is such a thing. It is a farce and a morality, and a farce about phony

moralities, and a moral, merrymaking challenge to all fools
and to all popes of fools and to all popish follies and foolish
poperies. In short, it is a gorgeous extravaganza and the
most ravishing harlequinade.

Its aggressive wit is by no means one-sided but comprehensive. It mocks not only the high clergy in Rome but
also the obtuse materialism of certain "free-thinkers" such
as Professor Armand-Dubois, the freemason, who dissects
rats, believes in Progress, and, in jocose vein, would refer
to God as *Monsieur le Principal.*" But in the end a pretty
tenuous "miracle" illuminates this smug gentleman; he fore-
swears freemasonry—thus ruining his worldly career—and
becomes a religious fanatic.

Professor Armand-Dubois makes an ass of himself. So
does Julius de Baraglioul, his brother-in-law, a successful
novelist of the mundane-Catholic type. He aspires to the
French Academy and allows the association of merrymakers to mystify him with a vengeance. His sister, Comtesse Guy de Saint-Prix, is no smarter. The chief of the
merrymakers, a philosophic crook called Protos, pays a
visit to her and—oh, shame! oh, fun!—she falls for his pre-
posterous rodomontades. The crook, disguised as a priest,
convinces the grand lady that His Holiness the Pope has
been kidnaped by the freemasons and is imprisoned somewhere in the vaults of the Vatican, while a counterfeit
Pope receives the homages of Christianity. It is a complicated intrigue, shrewdly woven and circulated. The kidnap
affair is somehow linked with the mystery of Meyerling,
where the Austrian Crown Prince was found dead with
his mistress—a joint suicide, according to the official version,

but a dire crime, according to the merrymakers. The murderer of Prince Rudolph shares the prison of His Holiness. Several kings and wicked cardinals are involved in the lurid plot. Everything is extremely secret and dangerous. Comtesse Guy de Saint-Prix is expected to contribute a considerable sum to the funds for the Crusade to rescue the Holy Father.

Madame la Comtesse writes a check and confides the secret to her best friend. The best friend's husband, a certain Amédée Fleurissoire, ventures on a pilgrimage to Rome, determined to unmask the Pope of Fools and to liberate His Real Holiness. He is a queer old chap, Amédée Fleurissoire, awkward and pathetic but not without engaging qualities. First, he has a terrible time with the bedbugs in Italian inns. In Rome, a member of the merry gang lures him into a brothel. There Amédée loses his innocence. An experienced girl, Carola, seduces, or rather, rapes him. Amédée bursts into tears when the sinful act is over. It is a moving scene, quite apart from its being screamingly funny.

In Naples, Amédée meets a bogus cardinal—a cardinal of fools. Protos shows up again as a priest. His intelligence, remarkably developed by nature, is somewhat obfuscated and confused by Nietzschean slogans. He wants to be a superman, beyond good and evil. He, too, makes an ass of himself.

As for poor Amédée, somebody pushes him out of a running express train, between Rome and Naples. He is gone for good, assassinated by the reckless merrymakers, we suppose?

Wrong, again. Protos had no interest in killing Amédée

Fleurissoire. In fact, nobody could benefit by the crime. Yet it was committed. Who, then, committed it—wantonly, senselessly, just for the murderous fun? Who is that cynical, that monstrously cruel?

It's Lafcadio—who else could it be? Lafcadio, the old pal of Protos (but not mixed up in the pseudo-Nietzschean racket); Lafcadio, the half-brother of Julius de Baraglioul and of the Comtesse Guy de Saint-Prix whose father, the old Count de Baraglioul, once had an affair in Bucharest with a woman of signal beauty and hospitality. A son resulted from this frivolous liaison. And what a son! What an amazing fellow!

From his jolly *maman* Lafcadio inherited his looks, his sensual attraction, his irresistible smile, and the complete absence of any scruples or inhibitions. His brilliant manners must come to him from his father's side—this nonchalant elegance typical of his gait, speech, and outfit. A badly fitting suit is to him what a lie is to a Calvinist.

He is nineteen years old—Lafcadio without a country and without a conscience, the spirited good-for-nothing and rakish adventurer. He possesses nothing, except a fine vocabulary in six languages which he picked up in the boudoir of his mother; nothing, except his wit, his youth, his pride, his instinct, his vitality. He is very generous, Lafcadio, and alarmingly erratic. He defies all sacred laws of society but imposes upon himself the severest castigation when he has somehow transgressed his own self-styled, capricious code of honor. Reckless to the point of outright brutality, he still risks his life to rescue a child from a burning building. He has features of Balzac's Rastignac and of a young, well-bred horse. He resembles Stendhal's juvenile hero, Julien Sorel, and he has also elements of an ordinary impostor. He has something of a child and of a genius and of a monster. He has not much in common with Dostoevski's haunted amateur criminal, Raskolnikov, although his, Lafcadio's, character seems at times to be conceived as a parody of the somber Russian.

Both young men, Lafcadio and Raskolnikov, commit an unmotivated crime—the former, by pushing an innocuous old gentleman out of a running train; the latter, by slaughtering a pathetic old woman. But Raskolnikov's murderous impulse springs from an intellectual obsession: he wants to prove that he is a superman. (Lafcadio's crony, Protos, commits felonies out of similar considerations.) Lafcadio, however, acts under a sort of facetious compulsion: he simply feels like doing what he does. There is no principle or purpose behind his action; he does not care to prove anything but is impelled by sheer energy. His wanton misdeed is *l'acte gratuite*, the disinterested effort in its purest form, pushed to its utmost, paradoxical extreme. He is aware of all risks involved while he acts; but to him danger means an additional, or it may be the decisive, attraction. No doubt, he would accept his punishment, even death, if need be; he is perfectly prepared for it. But he does not seek it, as does his pensive cousin in St. Petersburg. Raskolnikov is torn by remorse; the whole novel is but the story of his repentance, climaxing in his final confession. Lafcadio, much more buoyant and more cynical, does not think of confessing, nor would he fall in love with a humble prostitute. Not that he has anything against prostitutes in principle; he has an affair with one, at the beginning of our story. Carola—the same Carola who subsequently seduces

Amédée—is sincerely in love with Lafcadio—the same Lafcadio who lives with her only "for hygienic reasons" and
who will assassinate poor Amédée out of similar motives.
Carola, the good-natured whore, is dropped, bluntly and
brutally, by her radiant friend, who is all nature, no goodness. In the end he is busy conquering a sweet and serious
young creature of finest stock (the stock couldn't be finer:
it is Lafcadio's own). The girl in whose arms we leave him
happens to be the daughter of Julius de Baraglioul, the tiresome novelist, whose enterprising father had also begotten
Lafcadio, nineteen years before, in Bucharest, Rumania.

No, he is not going to give himself up to the police. He is
going to live. He will abandon the girl who now covers his
face with her kisses. She loves him, and will continue to do
so, notwithstanding his crime and his instability. So does
Gide. So do we, the readers. How could we help loving
Lafcadio, the jester, the crook, the hero? Who could be
angry at him? Who would take him to task for his daring
follies, since the world surrounding him seems to be popu-
lated exclusively by swindlers and their stooges?

And then, what he has done may be grisly; but, after all,
it's only a merrymaker acting in a *sotie* . . .

All living creatures mirror and explain their creator, or
at least one aspect and potentiality of the creative mind
from which they emerge. Just as all men bear the mark of
their divine descent—however blurred or distorted—the
characters conceived by one novelist are all akin to each
other as they are all akin to their poet. Every work of art
is a self-portrait.

We recognize Gide's grave and spiritual physiognomy

behind Lafcadio's impishly charming grimace. Yes, this
dashing and dangerous youth is made from the same stuff
that is André Walter's and Alissa's and the Immoralist's.
His inordinate antics and paradoxes, his innocence and his
tricks, all his emotions and actions are imbued with the unmistakable flavor of Gide's style and personality.

"It is certainly easier for me to make one of my characters speak than to express myself as myself, undisguised."
This is Proteus' confession. He continues: "There is nothing in my work I have written with more easiness than
Alissa's diary or the monologues of Lafcadio, nor is there
anything better. When producing such things, I forget who
I am, if I have ever known it . . ."

Does he abandon himself to become Lafcadio? Or is the
fictitious individual an emanation of his own substance and
energy? But what is the difference? Is there any difference,
really?

The question becomes somewhat more perturbing in the
case of an unpleasant and untruthful character such as the
hero in Gide's following book, *La Symphonie pastorale*
(1919). The Calvinist minister, whose diary communicates
the whole story, is an unctuous hypocrite who not only
cheats his environment but also deludes himself. With complacent circumstantiality he dwells on every detail of his
little drama. We see the winter landscape of the remote
mountain valley in Switzerland where his parsonage is situ-
ated, and we sense the glacial peace of the night when the
minister was called to a moribund old woman, somewhere
in the snowy solitude. It was in her hut that he found the
wretched creature that was to play such a decisive rôle in
his life—Gertrude, the blind niece of the defunct old

woman; a pitiful half-wit, filthy, unable to speak, almost beastly.

No doubt, the pastor's spontaneous impulse to take the poor idiot along is in itself noble and laudable. He is a Christian, he feels sorry for the miserable orphan. But, again, is he not a little bit too pleased with his own charity and goodness? And, besides, there is his wife at home—a commonplace, sturdy person without understanding for his immoderate generosity. He knows, of course, that she will disapprove of his eccentric gesture. But he also knows that she will be, nevertheless, as practical and helpful as usual. It is she—the pastor's homespun wife, not the inspired pastor—who tackles the unappetizing job of transforming her unwished-for guest, Gertrude, from a fetid wreck into a clean human being. As for the pious man, he contents himself with awakening, little by little, the girl's darkened and frightened mind.

His diary informs us of her gradual progress. She learns how to speak and to laugh, how to believe in God and in His earthly representative, the pastor. She is innocent and lovable. He loves her.

Is his love still pure and fatherly? His notes divulge what he does not admit to himself: that his feeling for Gertrude has long transcended the sphere of paternal-pedagogical interest. This is not sympathy, any more: it is passion.

He refuses to grasp the obvious, palpable truth, even when his violent jealousy dramatically reveals his emotional entanglement. His son falls in love with the sightless belle. The pastor, blinder than his angelic protégée, raves but still fails to realize why. He keeps lying, doggedly, desperately; lying to his wife, who looks through his obvious devices;

lying to his son, who yields to the paternal authority and renounces Gertrude; lying to Gertrude herself, whose idea of the world and of his own character he falsifies and confuses with his mendacious, purposeful eloquence.

The swindle ends as Gertrude gains her eyesight, thanks to an operation. Now she sees, and she understands. It is the young one she loves—the pastor's son, not the pastor. She recognizes at last the true nature of the old man's devotion. She shudders. Everything palls on her. She has perceived the existence and might of Evil too suddenly and overwhelmingly to be able to bear it.

The end is tragedy, with the son joining a Catholic order (the most scathing gesture of protest against his Calvinist father he could possibly think of); with Gertrude committing suicide, and the pastor left all alone—alone with his homely, frustrated wife, with his guilt and his distress. He tries to cry, but his heart is "as arid as the desert." From his withered heart rises his desolate prayer: *Our Father which art in Heaven* . . .

Now, what has Gide in common with this miserable and hypocritical man? Where is the affinity between the created character and the creator? Or is *Pastoral Symphony* just another *tour de force* executed with detached mastership?

But there can be no doubt that Gide has furnished his dreary hero with certain features inherent—more or less latently—in his own personality. In fact, he lays many an idea of his own into the mouth of the deceitful minister, where they presently tarnish and lose all validity. The cunning lover employs big and beautiful words—Gide's words —to camouflage or to excuse his illegitimate passion. How cleverly he tosses about such grandiose notions as "pure love," "True Christianity versus Puritan prejudices," "educational fervor," "self-sacrifice," and so forth. When Gertrude—still without eyesight—asks him whether there is anything evil about her being so fond of him, he answers, slyly and evasively, "Love can never be evil." And when his poor wife reproaches him, rather early in the course of the story, with preferring the blind stranger to his own children, he invokes the Gospel sacrilegiously. Does not Jesus teach us that a sheep that was lost and has been found again is more valuable, indeed, more lovable than the rest of the flock that never went astray? And Gertrude, blind and dumb as she was, must she not be considered a lost sheep? So why should we not rejoice and be glad? For this thy sister was dead, and is alive again; and was lost, and is found.

But the pastor's wife does not rejoice and is not glad at all. Nor was Gide, I suppose, when twisting and polluting his own favorite tenets by lending them to his hideous double and self-caricature. He, who never admitted that a fine cause could ever justify evil means, now mirrored himself in a man who abuses the finest reasons for the sake of an evil cause.

If it is an act of paradoxical unselfishness to invent arguments for one's own enemy, as Gide does at times, it implies much more of a self-inflicted torture to make a hateful person employ and misuse one's own thoughts and principles.

Conceived as the utmost contrast to the cheerful escapade of *Les Caves du Vatican;* saturated with the gloom and the anxiety of the preceding war years, *La Symphonie pastorale* is the subtlest and most scathing self-indictment Gide has ever issued—more relentless, indeed, than *L'Immoraliste*, and much more bitter than the hilarious self-irony of *Paludes*, where the most acrid criticism is mitigated by a hearty laughter. But there is no trace of gaiety in *La Symphonie pastorale*. The setting is of bleak austerity; the coloring, dismal and murky. Proteus does not allow himself the faintest smile. This time his metamorphosis looks terribly like a self-flagellation.

Lafcadio is in the habit of tormenting himself with a red-hot knife when he has violated one of his own arbitrary taboos. For what secret transgression did André Gide want to atone when he punished himself with the glowing steel of his well-turned, revealing word?

"There is no monster or miracle on earth that concerns me more than my own character. . . . The more I explore and scrutinize myself, the more my deformation amazes me—the less can I understand myself."

It is with wholehearted approval that Gide quotes these words, in his brilliant *Essai sur Montaigne* (1929). The great French humanist of the sixteenth century is one of his most beloved and most trusted masters. It is by no means Montaigne's famous "skepticism" by which Gide feels mostly attracted. The noncommittal gesture *"Que sçais-je?"* would not in itself be helpful and constructive if it were not for the new humanistic pride and probity already inherent in such sturdy agnosticism. "To Pilate's cruel question, *What is truth?* which re-echoes down the ages," writes Gide, "Montaigne seems to have assumed, though in a quite human and profane manner, and in a very different sense, Christ's divine answer, *I am the Truth*. That is to say, he can know nothing *truly* but himself . . ."

This is the twofold lesson Gide obtained from his illustrious friend, Michel Eyquem de Montaigne: that self-scrutiny, self-analysis, complete sincerity towards oneself, is the beginning and, perhaps, the crown of all wisdom; and, that the most pertinent way of teaching anything to anybody is to communicate—frankly! without retouching! —what one may have found out about one's own inmost conflicts and condition.

Gide is delighted by what he calls Montaigne's *"heureuse audace dans l'indiscrétion personelle."* He relishes all details the lusty nobleman confides to him as to his most intimate experiences, psychological or somatic. To Gide, it is greatly interesting news that the author of the *Essays* is able to hold his water for ten hours or so. If the fact as such is not startling, Montaigne's indiscreet wish to disclose it is charming and significant in itself. This unusual frankness implies much more than sheer exhibitionism, according to André Gide. It connotes a valiant protest against canting conventions, against what is concealed in general. Everything devious and stealthy is precisely what fascinates him most and what he likes to display.

King Candaulus, we remember, was prompted by similar impulses when he revealed his wife—a flagrant slip for which he had to pay with his life. Gide, who dramatized this edifying story, cannot be unfamiliar with the antagonism between shame and sincerity. And yet his "indiscreet wish" to exhibit his secrets, his pedagogical proclivity to teach the world a lesson by unveiling his privacy—this innate disposition to expose himself got the better, more often

than not, of any conventional scruples. His extensive autobiography, *Si le Grain ne meurt* (published in 1926), is of
a meticulous straightforwardness compared with which
Montaigne's "fortunate audacities" look almost conventional.

I am afraid that I may have been unduly hard on this
particular work of Gide when I referred to it in a preceding chapter. Did I not call it "somewhat disappointing"?
What a rash and superficial judgment! I am tempted to
take it back, but I cannot. I want what I write to be as
sincere as is the author it deals with. How, then, could I
mince or modify my words? The truth is that I was disappointed when I first read *Si le Grain ne meurt*, and that I
cannot help feeling the same way whenever I read it again.

That is not to say that Gide's memoirs are lacking in
unforgettable scenes and images; there are many of them,
particularly in the childhood chapters, but also in the following parts. What he tells us about his first literary impressions and religious qualms comes off beautifully, as do
certain of the school memories—especially the first acquaintance with Pierre Louÿs, at the *Ecole Alsacienne*. The third
volume offers a good deal of lively information about the
literary milieus in Paris around 1890; there are striking
sketches of Mallarmé, Herédia, and the sophisticated crowd
that flocked to their receptions. The Algerian episode, finally, with its elaborate double portrait of Oscar Wilde
and Lord Douglas, is perhaps the climax of the whole account.

It is there, in the African chapter, near the end of the
story, that the "shocking" details occur—six pages or so,
in a work that comprises about six hundred. Evidently,

these risqué passages have attained a popularity entirely
out of proportion. I have heard people discuss *Si le Grain
ne meurt* as a salacious book—"the book, you know, in
which he tells all that dirty stuff about Wilde and Douglas
and the little Moors,"—while, in reality, Gide's memoirs
are mainly concerned with such earnest matters as Sym-
bolistic art, Puritan pastors, Beethoven, country life, bot-
anizing spinsters, and young André's innocent romance
with Mademoiselle Emmanuèle.

Why, then, do so many readers choose to remember
solely the interlude with the Arabian lads? There must be
more serious reasons for this undue emphasis than just the
ordinary predilection for the sexual sphere. It might be that
the Algerian adventure strikes the reader as particularly
thrilling and colorful since the rest of the book is somewhat
poor in color and suspense. Moreover, the "revelation of
the desert"—as one of Gide's biographers, Léon Pierre-
Quint, terms the African episode—seems to be the logical
climax, indeed, the solution our story was driving at all
along. The anguish and apprehension of André's childhood; his abrupt and irrational outburst, *"Je ne suis pas
pareil aux autres!"*; the moral struggle of his later years; the
strangely seraphic flavor of his relation to Emmanuèle: all
this becomes intelligible in the light of what has happened
under Wilde's devilish auspices. By disclosing his "deformation"—to quote Montaigne's formula—Gide provides us
with the clue to the labyrinth of his inner drama.

There can be no doubt, of course, that Gide's erotic
penchants and experiences are of signal relevance to his development in all respects. One does not need be an unconditional adherent to Freud's doctrines to recognize the vital

bearing of sex on the human life. It was not the founder of
the psychoanalytical school but Nietzsche who called sex
the root and basis of all artistic creation. According to him,
a man's sexual inclinations can be traced even in the most
lofty and disinterested manifestations of his genius. And
still we ought to beware of premature conclusions in general, and especially in so far as Gide is concerned. *"Ne me
comprenez pas si vite, je vous en prie!"* His request is as
applicable to his erotic problem as to any other aspect of
his character.

· Let us be frank and factual. Gide discloses, in his memoirs, that he has had sexual intercourse with young Ara-
bians in Algeria, fifty years ago. That is all, or rather,
would be all, if it were not for a brief but significant phrase
following the scene with Mohammed—a sentence to the
effect that this escapade helped him in finding his "normality." We are not told, however, whether this normality implies a lifelong fixation on Arabian boys. In fact, Gide is
much more discreet than his reputation suggests and than he
wants to appear. As far as reading can tell one, his whole
work, including his *Journal*, contains no direct reference to
his sexual experiences except the one passage in *Si le Grain
ne meurt*. We are not told whether the Algerian incident
was followed by others of a similar kind. There are scarcely
hints at any young men among Gide's acquaintances, save
Marc Allegret, the companion of the Congo journey, who
happens to be descended from a family very close to
Gide's. Nor do we learn much about the women who
might have played a rôle in his life. I have tried before to
stress Gide's extraordinary reserve with regard to his marriage. He is not more expansive in respect to other alliances.

How about the liaison which resulted in the birth of Gide's daughter? The young lady was presented as his niece, as long as Madame Gide was alive. But with Emmanuèle deceased, the widower recognized his illegitimate child officially. Yet the published version of his *Journal* offers no clue to this love affair of great consequences.

One of Gide's most intimate friends once said to me: "He is terribly difficult to understand, our great André. It amuses him to bamboozle all of us. Think of his relation to women, for instance! Most people take it for granted that he doesn't care much for them. Wrong! Women mean more to him, in a sense, than do men. And it's *not* only Emmanuèle I am thinking of. As for *her,* she has more power over him than any other being, male or female. I believe he would sacrifice his dearest friend if Emmanuèle insisted . . ."

Gide's work seems to confirm what his intimate divulged to me. The female element among his characters is at least as significant as the male. As for the topic of homosexuality, it plays but a secondary rôle. One voluminous treatise, *Corydon,* is devoted to this subject, and there occur allusions—not very obvious ones, though—in *L'Immoraliste* and *Les Faux-Monnayeurs.* And yet it seems out of the question that Gide would ever have recourse to such masquerades as were employed by Marcel Proust, for instance. On the contrary, Gide disapproved, repeatedly and sharply, of Proust's cunning policy which consisted of presenting the boys he was interested in disguised as girls. The Albertine, in *À la Recherche du temps perdu,* was actually an Albert—a fact well known in Parisian literary life.

Gide sounds indeed rather angry when he notes in his

diary (1921): "Perplexed and indignant after having read the last pages of *Sodome et Gomorrhe* (in the December issue of the *Nouvelle Revue Française*). Knowing Proust's nature and opinions the way I do, it is difficult for me to see there anything but a feint, prompted by the desire for self-protection. His camouflage is as clever as could be; for nobody could be interested in unmasking it. Yes, this offence to truth is likely to please everybody—the heterosexuals, as it justifies their prejudices and animosities; and the others, who will profit by the alibi and by the lack of resemblance between them and the characters Proust portrays. In short, *Sodome et Gomorrhe*, more than any other piece of writing I have ever read, is apt to foster the general cowardice and to encourage public opinion to abide by its fallacies."

What annoyed Gide, furthermore, is the way Proust seems to confound homosexuality and effeminacy. Baron Charlus, the macabre hero of *Sodome et Gomorrhe*, is indeed the embodiment of degeneracy. Not that the portrait of Charlus is unfairly or malignantly drawn in itself; there are plenty of gentlemen very much like the Baron. What may be considered unfair is that Proust presents this morbid snob as *the* invert par excellence, while transposing the more appealing experiences of another character, Swann, into the less controversial sphere of heterosexual love. According to Gide, however, a bumptious freak—namely, the Baron Charlus—is by no means typical of the homosexual as such. To speak of "*the* homosexual" is as erroneous as to speak of "*the* Jew" or "*the* artist."

It is the main thesis of *Corydon* that homosexuality, just like heterosexuality, "comprises all degrees, all shades—from

Platonism to salaciousness, from renunciation to sadism, from joyful soundness to pathological gloom, from the most primitive satisfaction to the most refined perversities. The 'inversion' (i.e. effeminacy) is just one annex of it. Moreover, there are innumerable transitions between exclusive homosexuality and exclusive heterosexuality. Yet, in general, people are wont to contrast what they call 'normal love' with what they deem a form of love 'opposed to nature'; and, for reasons of sheer convenience, they take it for granted that all noble passions, all beauty of spirit and of emotion, are reserved to the 'normal' side, whereas the others have to content themselves with I don't know what kind of scurvy substitutes . . ."

This distinction between the "invert" (or effeminate type) and the "normal homosexual" (namely, the male lover of male youth, in the Hellenic style) goes as a leitmotiv throughout the didactic dialogues of which the treatise consists. M. Corydon—quite an expert in his particular field—tries aptly and patiently to convince his somewhat naïve questioner that homosexuality is neither a crime nor a disease. A spirited and conscientious teacher, he tackles the matter from all conceivable angles—medical, literary, philosophic, sociologic, historic, and religious. He quotes Montaigne and Darwin, Pascal and Goethe, Plato and Walt Whitman. His argument includes the habits of dogs and geniuses, Christian and pagan ethics, the testimonies of statesmen, doctors, and priests. He is unusually bright and brave—that imaginary Mr. Corydon, undaunted apologist of an unpopular cause.

Frankly, it is difficult to see why Gide's friends and advisers should have been so worried and bewildered about this semi-scientific, impersonal essay. Nor does one quite understand why Gide was in such a state of excitement and happiness when he composed *Corydon*. According to his *Journal*, no other work elated and thrilled him in an equal degree, since the hectic days of *Les Cahiers d'André Walter*. Only then, as a callow, inspired youth, was he possessed by the same enthusiasm. *Les Cahiers d'André Walter* and *Corydon* are the only two books Gide believed to be of utmost significance, indeed, indispensable, while he was engaged in writing them.

As for the former, it may be deemed an indispensable document within the whole of Gide's lifework: whoever loves André Gide's production in its entirety, certainly would not want to miss *Les Cahiers*. In the case of *Corydon*, however, I do not feel quite the same way. If I had to sacrifice one of Gide's major works, I would choose *Corydon*, without hesitating. It is a useful book but not an inspiring one. Far from being unduly emotional and bold, it is rather lacking in these qualities. It presents and develops its thesis, sturdily and effectively, and with an impressive display of eloquence and erudition. But it does not include the antithesis; in other words, it is not dialectic, not musical, not artistic, not disinterested. It wants simply to prove its point. In order to be persuasive, Gide sacrifices what is indeed the source and secret of his persuasion—the iridescent complexity of his style and thought.

Proteus seems a little awkward and uncomfortable in the rôle of a propagandist. He is more himself—he is indeed at his best—when he plays and puzzles; when he changes his shape and shifts from one position to another; when he phosphoresces and oscillates and intrigues.

This explains, perhaps, the relative tenuity of *Si le Grain ne meurt* and *Corydon*. In both cases Gide tries to come out undisguised, as a man who tells his story and who puts forward his argument. But, curiously, the authentic story and the direct, unconditioned testimony fall short of his subtle, noncommittal devices. Paradoxical as it may sound, Gide sounds less cogent, indeed, less truthful when he conveys the plain truth. For the plain truth is never *his* truth. The plain truth is a simplification.

The more disguised, the more authentic is Proteus. We recognize his gesture and his message, whether it comes to us in the make-up of André Walter or Ménalque, of Narcissus or Candaulus; with the saintly smile of Alissa or with the feverish glow of the Immoralist; with Lafcadio's triumphant turbulence or with the deceitful dignity of the Calvinist pastor: they are all stigmatized and blessed with his mystery, his charm, his savor, his unmistakable hue.

And this is true not only of Gide's fictional self-presentations and self-transformations but also of his essayistic masquerades. Precisely as in his novels, he at once veils and reveals his own personality when scrutinizing and evaluating the works and characters of Stendhal or Dostoevski, Baudelaire or Nietzsche, Montaigne or Charles-Louis Philippe. His polemics against Barrès, his notes on Chopin, his studies on Goethe or Racine, are indeed as integral a part of his lifework as his stories or plays. Gide's fervor and intuition are no less creative and original in the field of literary criticism than they are in the narrative or dramatic spheres. The importance of his essayistic volumes equals that of his novels, tractates, and tragedies.

There is a profusion of delightful and illuminating things in the collections of Gide's literary-analytical prose—*Prétextes* (1903), *Nouveaux Prétextes* (1911), and *Incidences* (1924). But even more delightful and illuminating are the countless reflections and *aperçus* scattered throughout his central and cardinal work, his diary. The volume I cherish most among all things he has written, is the complete edition of his *Journal, 1889–1939*—more than thirteen hundred pages, handsomely presented by the *Bibliothèque de la Pleiade*. It is a treasure of a book, not inferior, in my opinion, to Montaigne's *Essays* or to Goethe's *Conversations with Eckermann*.

Of course, the art of the journal, like epos or tragedy, has its own inherent laws and logic, its specific style and its specific dangers. The journal, as a particular medium of expression, must not be confounded with the "confession," of which we have so many samples in world literature, from St. Thomas Aquinas to Jean-Jacques Rousseau, Thomas De Quincey, and others. But the confession, like the autobiography, is retrospective; its objective and function is to review the way that has led to a certain climax or terminus to which the confessor shows the road. The account is necessarily colored and purposeful. The same is true, for different but equally obvious reasons, of personal letters as a literary device. Only the diary is sincere, if it deserves to be called a diary.

Some of the most illustrious journals can hardly be considered genuine. The diary of Friedrich Hebbel, for instance—the best-known document of this type in German literature—is an impressive compilation of axioms and aphorisms rather than a day-to-day report of its author's factual and emotional life. As for the brothers Goncourt, their celebrated *Journal* is really a social and literary chronicle, entirely journalistic in its purport and policy.

In other cases, again, the journal is sincere but insignificant. The daily notes of Goethe or Tolstoi, Stendhal or Dostoevski, yield certainly a good deal of enjoyment and instruction to any reader truly interested in those masters; but nobody would ever count these casual and desultory entries among the main achievements of the great men who jotted them down to keep track of their daily doings.

There are much-vaunted journals by some authors who have nothing else, or almost nothing else, to their credit. The reputation of Marie Bashkirtseff, for instance, is due entirely to her *Journal*, as is that of Madame de Sévigné to her letters. But a diary that constitutes a lifework can never have as much fascination and significance as has a diary that accompanies, elucidates, and completes a great literary contribution.

If it is true that André Gide's *Journal* would be less attractive and less important if his other writings did not exist, it is also true that his work would be fragmentary without his diary. This is not so in most other cases. We are able to appreciate the grandeur of Dickens or Balzac, Poe or Byron, Milton or Descartes, without knowing their diaries. But to know Gide we must know his journal. Far from being an accessory, it is an essential—the heart and center of his creative effort.

Gide is a matchless master in this particular field. All his novels and tales, from *Les Cahiers d'André Walter* over *Les Caves du Vatican* and *Les Faux-Monnayeurs* to *L'Ecole des femmes* and *Geneviève*, are written, partly or completely, in the form of personal diaries. The *Journal* which he signs himself, sums up and reaffirms all those fictitious monologues and imaginary confessions. It also contains the essence and the résumé of his intellectual endeavor, the candid and continuous chronicle of his inner adventures and actual experiences. It is not only the most valid and conscientious self-analysis in modern literature, but also the liveliest survey of a great, eventful period in European history. By registering, day by day, the oscillations, transitions, and complications of his own quest and drama, he portrays—unwittingly, as it were—the currents and vicissitudes of spiritual life at large. His most intimate experiences mirror and at times anticipate the general trend of intellectual motions.

Gide's *Journal* is a self-portrait in motion: hence its extraordinary charm and efficacy. Not a statue but a moving picture, it presents a creative mind in the very state of roving, striving, erring, seeking, questioning, creating.

"*Je ne peints pas l'estre. Je peints le passage*" (I depict the process of *becoming*, not the status of *being*). Gide not only quotes this maxim of Montaigne but also follows its advice. He, too, describes movement and change, the wandering, the reluctancies, the unending transformations.

What is his purpose in doing so? But art has no purpose; it is disinterested, an aim in itself, a sublime waste of energy. The adventures of Proteus are as many gratuitous actions.

Or is there an objective, after all? Proteus does need, perhaps, a medium to express his visions and apprehensions? Proteus is a Protestant, as we should not forget. What the Catholic confides to his confessor, the Protestant submits to God directly. As it happens in the case of professional writers, the directest approach to God goes at times over the reading public.

The Protean Protestant is free: he belongs to no hierarchy. Responsible to no authority save his own conscience, he might easily lose his sense of direction and go astray, if it were not for his constant self-observation which is tantamount to constant self-control. That is why Proteus cannot content himself with assuming ever new and ever suggestive forms, but has to render account of the metamorphosis itself. In other words, he has to keep a diary, the daily chronicle of his fleet adventures, the lasting monument of his restlessness.

VI. THE FUGUE

Without Contraries is no progression.
Attraction and Repulsion, Reason and
Energy, Love and Hate are necessary
to human existence.

WILLIAM BLAKE

Les extrêmes me touchent.

ANDRÉ GIDE

AT THE age of fifty-seven, André Gide published his first novel.

That is to say, he had published five other novels before, or, to be more precise, three full-length novels and two novelettes. Yet he deemed it appropriate, for one reason or another, to present *Les Faux-Monnayeurs* (1926) as his first novel. The dedication reads:

A Roger Martin du Gard
je dédie mon premier roman
en témoignage d'amitié profonde.
                                        A. G.

What, then, is Gide's idea of a novel? Obviously, he must harbor a very exacting conception of what a novel should be if he feels that neither *Les Caves du Vatican* nor *L'Immoraliste* nor *La Porte étroite* deserves this particular designation.

Who are the great novelists he admires most and whose style serves him as model and stimulus?

Two facts are noteworthy and somewhat surprising. First, Gide does not believe that French writers have excelled particularly in the field of the novel. In his opinion, the English and Russian novelists definitely surpass their French competitors. Secondly, he is but faintly interested in the contemporary novel. Daringly progressive, even revolutionary, in his social and psychological views, Gide is rather conservative in his literary preferences. About all of his reading time and of his critical wit are devoted to the classics.

As for the former point, it is profusely documented in Gide's journals, letters, essays, conferences, and so forth. One of the most revealing statements in this context is an article, "Les Dix Romans français que . . ." featured in the *Nouvelle Revue Française,* in 1913.

A prominent daily paper had approached Gide with an inquiry concerning the ten most important French novels. Why so chauvinistic? Gide seems irritated by this undue limitation. After having announced his two favorites— Stendhal's *La Chartreuse de Parme* and *Les Liaisons dangereuses* of Choderlos de Laclos (1782)—he becomes reluctant.

France, according to this great Frenchman, is a country "of moralists, incomparable artists, composers, orators, and architects. What have other countries to offer that could be matched against Montaigne and Pascal, Molière, Bossuet, and Racine? But, on the other hand, who is a Lesage compared with a Fielding or with a Cervantes? Who, an Abbé Prévost compared with Defoe? And even a Balzac—who is he, in view of a Dostoevski? Or, if one prefers this angle, what is a *Princesse de Clèves* in comparison with a *Britannicus?*"

Yet the master novel of Madame de Lafayette (1634–1695), *La Princesse de Clèves*, ranks among Gide's chosen ten, notwithstanding its inferiority to both its contemporary British novel and its contemporary French tragedy. Then our fastidious judge falters and wonders again:

"For want of *Moll Flanders*, should I indicate, at this point, our *Manon Lescaut?* Perhaps. Hot, human blood circulates in her veins. And still I cannot help feeling slightly embarrassed by this book. It has too many readers, and the worst ones, too. I would much rather *not* be fond of Manon . . ."

Three other classics included in the list can hardly be reproached for immoderate popularity: Furetière's *Roman bourgeoi*, Fromentin's *Dominique*, and even *La Marianne* by Marivaux, are as unknown—outside of France, at least—as Gide could possibly wish for.

When it comes to the nineteenth century, however, he cannot avoid altogether the more popular sphere. One title out of Balzac's epic treasure is obligatory in such an enumeration. Gide makes his choice in favor of *La Cousine Bette*. Flaubert and Zola? No chance to get around them. Let us select *Madame Bovary* and *Germinal*.

Evidently, Gide feels rather apologetic for admitting that great barbarian, Emile Zola. True, he says, ruefully, none of the praises due to Stendhal would make sense if one tried to apply them to Zola. Whereupon he expresses his astonishment that such a book—namely, *Germinal*—should have been written "in our language"—namely, in French. But then, is it not equally difficult to imagine that work couched in any other idiom? It's an annex of literature, Gide concludes. It ought to be written in Esperanto. Yet, there it is; self-evident, irrefutable, vital. We cannot change it, nor can we wish, at bottom, that it were written differently.

So much for Zola. Is Gide's reaction more enthusiastic in the case of Honoré de Balzac? Naturally; but . . . but why, then, does he open his paragraph about *La Cousine Bette* with a sentence to the effect that "it is advisable to read Balzac before one's twenty-fifth year; afterwards it becomes rather tedious . . ." That does not sound very flattering, particularly in view of what was said before about *Les Liaisons dangereuses*. With regard to that eighteenth-century jewel, Gide congratulated himself on *not* having discovered it before his thirtieth year, when he was really able to gauge and relish its merits.

No doubt, Gide's admiration for Balzac is infinitely more cordial and unconditional than what he feels toward Zola. "It is vital to have read Balzac, the *whole* Balzac," he says. "Some literati believed they could do without him. They were compelled in the end to recognize their mistake, or else the readers recognized it for them."

And again, there are ironic reservations in which Gide never indulges when discussing Goethe or Dostoevski. Is it the national relationship that makes him carp at Balzac? We are all inclined to be unduly hard on those we know too long and too intimately. Perhaps it is out of such an overcritical affection that Gide conceives his charmingly malicious notes in reference to Balzac. For instance: "*Car il n'est jamais naivement sublime; jamais moins sublime que quand, naivement, il croit d'être.*"

With respect to Flaubert, Gide's response is even more ambivalent. The author of *L'Education sentimentale* is probably the French novelist he used to love most profoundly, after, or along with, Stendhal. But while his devotion to Stendhal remains intact and increases rather than declines, his love for Flaubert is less stable and becomes more and more problematic. Gide was still young, and still under the spell of Flaubert's genius, when he noted in his diary that among his sacrilegious thoughts which he hardly dared admit to himself, was the faint, secret suspicion that the beginning of *Madame Bovary* is perhaps, after all— don't tell anybody!—a pretty poor piece of writing.

Twenty-five years later, he is more outspoken, more relentless to Flaubert as well as to himself. "*J'ai tant aimé Flaubert!*" Gide will exclaim, in 1922, and continue, after three sad and suggestive points: "Every word written against him grieved and wounded me. For more than five years his *Correspondence* replaced the Bible on my bookshelf. He was a source of energy to me. What he offered to my striving heart was a new form of sanctity. I suppose that the disciples of Gustave Moreau may have had a similar veneration for their master. But, nevertheless, Gustave Moreau is not a great painter, just as Gustave Flaubert, alas, is not a great writer. His style is not quite good enough considering his dogged efforts to write beautifully. The true masters—Montaigne, Saint-Simon, Bossuet—did not work under this frantic strain. When I reread Flaubert today, no longer blinded by reverence, it is never without embarrassment and chagrin. I sense everywhere the tenseness, the gaucherie . . ."

What Gide misses in the French novel at large—not only

in Flaubert's ambitious craftsmanship—is, among other things, the virile élan of adventure and exploration, the salty breeze from the sea, the wide horizons and open spaces. "Where is in our literature that tonic ozone I breathe with gratitude and delight in so many English-written books?" Gide asks himself, wistfully. And he adds that he chose deliberately the expression "English-written," not "English," in order not to exclude "the most glorious one of them all, *Moby Dick*."

Melville's name is among those frequently invoked and praised in Gide's diary. Also, he remains faithful to E. A. Poe—one of his early loves—and refers respectfully to Hawthorne. Concerning modern American writers, however, he appears less receptive and less informed. In fact, Gide's voluminous critical work contains but a few scarce allusions to contemporary Americans. Some remarks about Henry James (with whom he was on cordial terms during the First World War); a few cordial words about Thornton Wilder, whose *Bridge of San Luis Rey* seems to him "*de la littérature, mais de la meilleure, et même quelque chose de plus*,"—greatly in contrast to Upton Sinclair, one of whose early novels he happened to read in 1907 and found "*quelque chose de fort mauvais, tout à fait hors de littérature.*" What he has to say concerning John Dos Passos does not sound much more amiable. And that is about all. Not a word about Dreiser or Anderson, O'Neill or Lewis, Wolfe or Hemingway.

Not that there are any national prejudices involved— definitely not. Gide's preference for the dead is equally obvious in his notes on English novelists. His *Journal* teems with remarks about Richardson and Fielding, Dickens and

Meredith. But as for the contemporaries, Joseph Conrad seems the only one who really arouses his curiosity. The occasional remarks about Kipling and Thomas Hardy sound rather casual and perfunctory. The name of H. G. Wells is consistently omitted, as are those of Joyce and Virginia Woolf. Aldous Huxley, whom one might think rather to Gide's taste, is dismissed succinctly and cruelly: *Point Counterpoint* is referred to as "unreadable."

This utmost reserve regarding modern writers, including his French colleagues, is indeed a strange feature of Gide's critical approach and policy. According to Gide, all our appraisals of contemporary literature are inevitably lacking in detachment and validity. "I am under a vow to restrict myself to discussing only the dead." With this sentence Gide opens an essay on Marcel Proust, who was still alive at the time.

In fact, Proust seems the only novelist of this century— except Conrad, perhaps—in whose work Gide took a lasting and intensive interest and by whose example he could really profit. It is true that certain elements of Proust's style and character repelled Gide at first and always remained unpleasant to him. He openly disapproved of Proust's crafty, not to say dishonest, mode of dealing with sexual matters. Moreover, Proust's social snobbism, his fawning upon the Faubourg St. Germain, could not but strike Gide as somewhat fatuous. But such extraneous objections faded away completely as soon as Proust's work, at once fragile and powerful, became perceptible in its mellow splendor and complexity. No doubt, there was a vision, was an epic scheme akin in many ways to Gide's idea of what a novel should be like in this century. Marcel Proust realized, as did André Gide, that it would be futile and tiresome to re-employ the realistic or romantic patterns of the nineteenth or eighteenth centuries in communicating problems and emotions from the twentieth. The novel of the twentieth century should differ from *Nana* or *Pamela* as a motor car differs from a carriage. "Among all forms of literary expression," Gide says, "the novel offers by far the richest and most variable possibilities."

That is to say that the novel, under certain circumstances, may almost cease to be a novel in a traditional sense. Do Franz Kafka's hallucinatory fragments belong to the category of the novel? And if not, to what other category do they belong? And what about the epic experiments of James Joyce? And Thomas Mann's Joseph saga? To all these authors André Gide might have written what he wrote to Marcel Proust: "Your work is not a novel. There is no plot whatsoever, and yet I have never read any story with more ardent interest."

A la Recherche du temps perdu may seem amorphous, without structure and without suspense, compared with the master novels of past epochs. But then, is not life—our life—also disorderly, lacking in logic and in composition? With ancient hierarchies cracking and old illusions fading away, how could the novelist cling to ready-made formulas and obsolete clichés?

There is a crisis of the novel as there is a crisis in economics or in psychology. New patterns, new approaches must be defined and tested, in the realm of the novel as in the fields of aviation or of medicine. This is a period of transition and experiment.

Marcel Proust had his way of dealing with the crisis of

the novel, and James Joyce had another way, and others have other methods again. None of these methods is André Gide's—naturally not. For there is no second writer whose obsessions and insights are precisely the obsessions and insights of André Gide.

Neither Proust nor Joyce was vitally concerned with moral or social issues. Their sole preoccupation was how to present, to mirror, to express life; not how to meet its actual conflicts and requirements. In other words, they were fundamentally, almost exclusively, artists, whereas André Gide was and is a moralist with artistic genius. To him, ideas are more exciting, indeed, more real than emotions; or rather, it is with an emotional fervency that he approaches ideas. He is a lover of ideas—an intellectual lover, a cerebral visionary.

The organisms of *Ulysses* and *A la Recherche du temps perdu* are dominated by all kinds of sensual images and sensations: rhythms, smells, colors, melodies, a profusion of flitting reminiscences. The structure of *Les Faux-Monnayeurs*, however, is organized around a center of moral, intellectual energies. The drama developed in this ample and diffuse composition is primarily ideological. Gide's novel is a novel of ideas.

That is why it appears comprehensive and yet exclusive —almost anarchic in its bountiful variety, and at the same time lucid, architectonic, pure. An amplitude of elements is fused in the microcosm of this extraordinary book; but all elements it contains are essential, *pure*—no accessories and arabesques are admitted.

"To purge the novel of all elements which do not belong specifically to its character!" demands the author of *Les*

Faux-Monnayeurs, and continues: "One does not bring about anything worthwhile by mixing incoherent patterns. I have always abominated what they call 'the synthesis of arts,' and which, according to Richard Wagner, should be effected in the theater. Hence my horror of the theater—and of Wagner . . .

"Tragedy and comedy have attained, in the seventeenth century, a high degree of purity; the same is true, by the way, for all other genres, whatever their scope and their significance—fables, character sketches, maxims, sermons, memoirs, letters, and so forth. Lyric poetry can be purely lyric—and the novel could not be purely a novel? (Purity, in art, as everywhere, is the only thing that matters.)

"Nobody has succeeded, neither then nor later, in creating the *pure novel*—not even the admirable Stendhal, who came closer to this ideal than any other novelist. As for Balzac, however, he may be our most potent narrator, but he certainly is the one who surpassed all others in fusing and amalgamating the most heterogeneous elements. His novels are crammed with ingredients essentially strange and inadmissible to the novelistic form. That is why each of his massive books overwhelms us with its power and its imperfection, its flaws and its dynamics. It is remarkable that the English, whose drama has never become perfectly *pure* (in the sense in which the tragedies of Racine are perfect and are pure) have attained so early a much higher degree of purity in the novels of Defoe, Fielding, and even Richardson."

This statement, paraphrased from Gide's *Journal des faux-monnayeurs*, may be apt to clarify the innermost intentions and aspirations that induced him to write his "first novel." The composition he dreamt of, would have to be informed with the whole confusion and disquietude of this critical moment in human history—not just echoing the anxieties, but elucidating, dramatizing, purifying their impact. To render the chaos transparent, to organize the disorder, to rationalize the crisis—what a bold, wonderful task! The result might turn out to be something at once intricate and lucid, a labyrinth constructed with mathematical precision, akin—to what? To the fugues of Johann Sebastian Bach, perhaps.

"What I would like to produce," Gide admitted, "is something in the line of the *Kunst der Fuge*. I don't see why it should be impossible to accomplish in literature what has been possible in the sphere of music."

Gide acknowledges that a novel can be "impure" and yet great. (The case of Honoré Balzac.) The reader might be inclined to ask whether a "pure" novel is necessarily a great novel; or, more bluntly, whether *The Counterfeiters* may be called a great book.

An outstanding connoisseur of novels, and an outstanding novelist, E. M. Forster, answers this question in the negative. Gide's book is, according to Mr. Forster, "among the more interesting of recent works: not among the vital: and greatly as we shall have to admire it as a fabric, we cannot praise it unrestrictedly now." Whereupon he chooses to "glance again at *War and Peace:* here the result is vital."

The book from which I just quoted, *Aspects of the Novel*, is one of the acutest, most delightful achievements in the field of literary criticism. Forster has an admirable manner of discussing Proust and Meredith, Tolstoi and Joyce, Anatole France and Dickens. It is from Dickens that he jumps directly to André Gide. He senses an affinity between *Bleak House* and *The Counterfeiters*—"a novel which for all its modernity has one aspect in common with *Bleak House:* it is all to pieces logically. Sometimes the author is omniscient: he explains everything, he stands back, *il juge ses personnages;* at other times his omniscience is partial; yet again he is dramatic, and causes the story to be told through the diary of one of his characters. There is the same absence of viewpoint, but whereas in Dickens it was instinctive, in Gide it is sophisticated; he expatiates too much about the jolts. The novelist who betrays too much interest in his own method can never be more than interesting."

The last sentence is strikingly, scathingly true. Besides, Gide is fully aware of the dangers inherent in his constant self-observation and auto-analysis. His double and mouthpiece in *Les Faux-Monnayeurs*—the novelist Edouard, who is occupied with writing a novel about counterfeiters himself—muses over his diary: "A good novel should be conceived and composed much more naïvely and instinctively . . ."

But what is a "good" novel? Or an "interesting" or a "vital" novel? Both Edouard and E. M. Forster employ their evaluating epithets in a somewhat arbitrary fashion. Why should an interesting novel not be good, or vital, or even great? That is to say, great and vital in its historic function, and according to the demands and standards of its period.

Why compare a novel of ideas with an epic saga of

Homeric dimensions? It's like comparing a tennis champion with a heavy-weight pugilist. They are of different statures; they respond to different requirements; in short, they do not compete with each other. The same is true of the two novels, *War and Peace* and *The Counterfeiters*.

Of course, Gide may look slim in comparison with the Russian giant. But then, who wouldn't? Who does live up, nowadays, to the impressive dimensions of the nineteenth-century masters?

The stature of an individual is something relative—not an absolute. Each epoch has its specific pattern of greatness—an inherent maximal norm which an individual may attain, if he can. In the Renaissance this "maximal norm" was of tremendous caliber: Ibsen or Degas would appear ridiculously puny with Michelangelo or Shakespeare around, as would our contemporaries contrasted with the creative plethora of the preceding period. True, André Gide is not quite Tolstoi or Dostoevski, just as Stravinski falls short of Bach; Claudel, of Dante; Picasso, of Rembrandt and Leonardo.

But the only relevant question is whether Gide can compete with the maximal stature of this century, and also whether *The Counterfeiters* represents the highest and finest attainable to this artist. Both questions must be answered in the affirmative. No doubt, Gide's rank matches the most exacting standards set by our epoch; and, undoubtedly again, he gives in *Les Faux-Monnayeurs* the best he has to offer, the crown and climax of his genius.

And now let us have a look at the novel proper.

We must keep in mind, first of all, that the opus we are

dealing with is a fugue, not a symphony. That is to say, the novel is not built in several major episodes, each with an individual theme of its own; but the whole polyphonic score develops one central theme, varying and transforming it most ingeniously, according to strict contrapuntal rules. As for this central theme . . . But perhaps we ought first to outline the scheme of the variations.

The texture of the novel consists of a multitude of dramas, all of which are interwoven with the utmost skill and a great deal of musical tact. The reader is allowed, or required, to visualize every character as belonging to several groups simultaneously and as playing a rôle in several actions at one time. That is the way life works. A schoolboy, say, is not exclusively a schoolboy: he is also a son and a brother, and perhaps he is a lover or a criminal or a genius or what not. So every actor in the ample cast of *The Counterfeiters* has his function on several stages and in various capacities. The central character, if there is such a thing in this book, is involved in all dramas at once.

This central character, if anybody, is Edouard, the novelist who is engaged in writing a novel called *Les Faux-Monnayeurs*. Edouard is André Gide, almost undisguised. Through Edouard's diary Gide expresses his own views and reflections with regard to *The Counterfeiters* and the world in general. While Gide attempts to bring about a novel of ideas, a pure novel, his character, Edouard, dwells theoretically on all problems involved in such a delicate task.

But Edouard is by no means just a commentator; he actively takes part in the various plots. There are links between him and all other groups. His position is mainly, but not solely, that of a go-between, mediator, confessor, and confidant. Somehow ageless of type, he belongs half to the camp of the youngsters, half to the side of the grown-ups. Both parties trust him and tell him about their troubles. And they have plenty of troubles, all of them.

It may be more correct to speak of three main camps, not just two. For the youth sector is split in itself: the children and the young people live on different planes. The young men, between seventeen and twenty-five, are as remote from their little brothers of ten to fifteen as they are from their aging parents and professors.

The most prominent characters of the intermediate group—in fact, the two leading figures, after Edouard, of the whole composition—are Bernard and Olivier, intimate friends but very different from each other. Bernard is the secretary and collaborator of Edouard, whose half-sister, Pauline, happens to be Olivier's mother. Her oldest son, Vincent, belongs half to the adult, half to the juvenile world, while Pauline's youngest boy, Georges, plays a crucial and rather terrible rôle in the children's drama. He is a pupil of Pastor Vedel, who runs a boarding school with his wife. One of Georges' schoolmates is Boris, the grandson of old La Pérouse, who is Edouard's former teacher.

The Vedels have four children—a boy and three daughters, one of whom, Laura, is the mistress of Vincent (son of Madame Pauline, brother of Olivier and Georges, nephew of Edouard). He abandons Laura for an exotic and glamorous woman, Lady Griffith, the mythic incarnation, as it were, of luxuriance and sex appeal. Lady

Lilian comes from a gaudy and gorgeous world wondrously different from anything ever known by Madame Pauline and her boys. That is why Vincent is so sensible to Lady Griffith's attraction, while his brother, Olivier, responds with equal eagerness to the cunning appeal of Robert de Passavant, a devilishly brilliant gentleman, Lilian's male pendant, so to speak, and a great friend of hers, for that matter. Passavant amuses himself by corrupting Olivier, which irritates Edouard. For he, Edouard, too has a definite weakness for Olivier.

Now the following dramas develop, skillfully coördinated:

First, the boarding school drama, in which two youngsters have the leading parts: Georges (brother of Olivier and Vincent) in the rôle of the villain, with Boris (grandson of old La Pérouse) as his partner and victim. Georges, and some other lads, are mixed up with a gang of counterfeiters; they pass false coin and behave like veritable criminals. When this becomes too dangerous (the police are after them), they establish a rather weird kind of club, "The Association of Strong Men," the main objective of which is to drive Boris into suicide. The tragedy of Boris is the climax of the boarding school drama, which involves also Pastor Vedel (a hypocritical Puritan akin to the minister in *La Symphonie pastorale*); Madame Vedel, who forces herself to appear more irresponsible than she is, as she prefers to ignore the lurid goings-on around her; Grandfather Vedel; the four Vedel children, including the abandoned Laura, Sarah—somewhat seditious and comparatively loose, Rachel—more on the demure side, and Armand, whose high-minded and imaginative nature is

distorted and stained by resentment against the stifling
milieu in which he has been brought up. Finally there is
old La Pérouse, grandfather of young Boris. Old La
Pérouse performs his own minor drama, proud and isolated and inconsolably sad. His abysmal pessimism accompanies the action and predicts the undoing of everybody—
a bleak, discouraging oracle.

As for Edouard, he is connected with the counterfeiter
affair in various respects. The false money circulated in
Paris gave him the idea of his novel, to begin with. Moreover, he is keenly interested in all developments in Vedel's
pension, not only out of his general curiosity, but also
because of Georges (his nephew, Olivier's brother), because of old La Pérouse (his former teacher), and, finally,
on account of Laura, with whom he happens to be on
good terms.

The drama of Laura and Vincent and Lady Griffith
would in itself yield sufficient material for a full-length
novel. Lady Griffith occupies a strange position among the
other characters of the book. Radiant with sin and seduction, she appears utterly devoid of moral consciousness.
While Robert de Passavant, the sophisticated tempter, is
essentially and consciously evil, Lilian is soulless, an element rather than a human being. She cannot be solved
like a problem, but has to be stamped out like a snake.
And that is what Vincent does: he kills her, throwing her
out of her sumptuous yacht, somewhere on the Nile, and
then abandons himself to a mild form of insanity.

The central triangle, however, is that of Edouard,
Olivier, and Passavant. Olivier, delicate and attractive,
oscillates between the two men who wish to influence him.

Edouard wins. He rescues Olivier from Passavant. The final union with Edouard is more excitement and bliss than the sensitive youth can endure. He attempts suicide but fails—in contrast to the little Boris who—alas!—succeeds. This twofold climax—Boris' end and Olivier's awakening—coincides, furthermore, with Bernard's ultimate trial. He meets his angel, literally. The young man and his demon rove together through the streets of Paris. A fight takes place between them. But in the end the two wanderers, boy and angel, understand each other.

Bernard is more virile, more adventurous, more resilient than his friend Olivier. Olivier needs a mentor and wavers between two; Bernard is in search of himself, of his star and his demon. He runs away from home when he finds out that he is not really the son of the dignified old gentleman whom he has thought to be his father. He is a bastard, like Lafcadio, with whom he has also other features in common. The *Journal des faux-monnayeurs*—Gide's commentary on his book when it was in process of construction—tells us that Lafcadio was supposed to be the leading character, according to the original plan. Is Bernard, then, Lafcadio in disguise?

No, he resembles too much the Prodigal Son to be Lafcadio's double. He is less irresponsible, less impish and primitive than the radiant vagabond of *Les Caves du Vatican*. Bernard is reflective, not without a certain youthful gravity, for all his dashing élan.

"For what cause should I use the forces that I sense in me?" Lafcadio is not likely to ask this question which occupies Bernard.

"How to make the best out of myself?" Bernard muses.

"By concentrating on one particular goal? But as for this goal, how could I select it? How can I know what it is like, as long as I have not yet attained it?"

And as Edouard says something to the effect that "to live without a goal means to live without direction," Bernard replies, "I'm afraid you don't quite understand what I am trying to say. When Columbus discovered America, did he realize what he was up to? His sole goal was to move, just to go ahead. His goal—he carried it in himself . . ."

Is this, then, the clue, the leading thought in virtue of which the incongruous elements of this book cohere and can become a living entity? Is Bernard's angel the secret center of the composition, rather than Edouard's diary with all its incisive reflections?

Yes, the heart and hero of the book is the demon—not just Bernard's, but the demon in general and as such.

The demon is not sheer, rampant energy such as impels Lafcadio to commit his inspired larks. Nor is this demon of a purely spiritual nature like the one haunting Alissa and the Immoralist. The demon of *Les Faux-Monnayeurs*— Bernard's demon: André Gide's demon—is double-faced, complex, dialectic, as is the demon of the Prodigal Son.

Reason and Energy, Love and Hate, destructive and constructive impulses are combined in the truly demoniac disposition. We can trace the authority of the demon in all characters of the novel, with the one exception of Lady Griffith. She belongs completely to the realm of nature. Her cynicism is natural. Nature is not demoniac; spirit is.

The demon manifests itself, diabolically, in the cynical elegance of Robert de Passavant, in Vedel's hypocrisy, in

La Pérouse's rigid and arrogant gloom. No doubt, Georges and his fellow-pupils, or fellow-felons, are possessed by the demon; their grisly and dangerous plays are obviously inspired by his genius. Who stands behind Laura when she abandons her husband? As for Vincent, the *Journal des faux-monnayeurs* makes it very plain what force it is that guides and confuses him: "Vincent complies with the diabolic spirit, who penetrates him little by little. He feels himself becoming diabolic; just when everything he touches prospers and succeeds, he realizes his doom more than ever. He would like to warn his brother Olivier, but everything he tries in order to save him turns out damaging to the other, profitable to himself. . . . He senses the grip of Satan, but at the same time continues to wonder if the Evil One exists in reality. His mind is haunted by the Devil's terrible whisper: 'Why are you afraid of me? You know perfectly well that I do not exist . . .' In the end Vincent comes to the point of believing in the reality of Satan *as he believes in his own reality;* that is to say, he identifies himself with the Devil."

The demon harasses and mystifies the smug, canting citizens: the pastors and housewives, teachers and officials, who lie to each other and commit by stealth their dreary little crimes, unaware of the demoniac lights and voices alluring and leading them. Bernard is stronger and more lovable than his demure father (who is neither really his father nor really so demure), as he, Bernard, attempts at least—and how passionately! how bravely!—to scrutinize his own being and to disentangle the staggering pellmell of devastating and constructive impulses.

For the demon has always a twofold tendency and a

double appeal; the important thing is to recognize the ambivalent impact of his spell and persuasion. That is what
Socrates was driving at when he advised the youth of
Athens to listen to the demoniac whisper of their inner
voices. If the unconscious is the Devil's retreat, we have to
lift the darkness from this hiding place. Sigmund Freud
agrees with Socrates: what matters is to shed light upon
the shadowy realm of the unconscious.

Gide agrees with both. Those characters in his novel who
openly admit the presence and the power of the demon are
in a better position, and are better characters, than the others who deny or conceal their own devilish tendencies.
Even the murderous youngsters in Vedel's boarding school
are preferable to the mendacious pastor. They follow their
demon into mortal adventures, blindly and naïvely; whereas
the old liar protects himself and breeds pestilence as do
those who desire but act not.

Edouard recognizes his demon and follows him, unafraid.
"Every being acts according to his inherent law," says
Gide, "and that of Edouard compels him to experiment incessantly. He has a good heart, to be sure; but at times I
would prefer to see him act out of interest, rather than out
of a generosity which is often only the companion of his
indomitable curiosity. And this curiosity might become
very cruel."

And yet Edouard's greatest adventure does not spring
from his demoniac curiosity; or, if it does, it changes its
character, almost miraculously. There is nothing playful
or cruel about Edouard's "experiment" with Olivier. Ennobled and transfigured by love, the demon reveals, for
once, the sacred flame of his divine descent.

But only for transient moments, never in the long run, is the demon altogether good or altogether evil. "There are in every man, in every moment, two simultaneous tendencies," Baudelaire remarks in his *Journal intime*, "one toward God; the other toward Satan." Gide, who quotes this sentence in his admirable preface to *Les Fleurs du mal*, underlines, in parentheses, the cardinal importance of the word "simultaneous" in this particular context, and then dwells on the double proclivity of human nature. The will of every individual to maintain his own identity coherent and consistent, is constantly counterbalanced and at times counteracted by the reverse instinct which is centrifugal and disintegrating, tending towards division, dissociation, and dissolution. Prodded by this uncanny, this truly demoniac impulse, the individual is always inclined to jeopardize his own logic, to run risks, to gamble, to split, to go to pieces, to lose his poise or to transcend his limitations. And André Gide—although fully aware, of course, of all dangers inherent in this "centrifugal," schizophrenic trend—suggests nevertheless: "Are here not the first signs of a new radioactive energy of incalculable value, the power of which may be such that the ancient theories, laws, conventions, and pretensions, all of them, may fade away before long?"

Do we recognize him, this revolutionary, dynamic demon, whose contradictory magic can compel us to fall into dire depths or to soar to glorious heights? William Blake, for one, was on appallingly intimate terms with that divinely devilish Being. "This Angel," we read in the *Marriage of Heaven and Hell*, "who is now become a Devil, is my particular friend; we often read the Bible together in its infernal or diabolical sense, which the world shall have if they behave well."

Gide invokes the "Proverbs of Hell" in his fascinating essay on Dostoevski, to which I referred before, in another chapter and in a different context. The work in question, a cycle of lectures delivered in 1922, at the *Théâtre du Vieux-Colombier*, is what remains of one of Gide's favorite projects: a "Life of Dostoevski" for which he compiled material as far back as 1910. This biographical study, meant for publication in Charles Péguy's magazine, *Cahiers*, was conceived somehow along the lines of Romain Rolland's *Beethoven* and *Michelangelo*. But Gide's "Dostoevski" was not destined to come into being; history interfered. A bitter loss, to be sure.

And yet, it may be questionable whether the full-length biography, if written before the pivotal year of 1914, would have turned out to be as illuminating in respect to both Dostoevski and Gide as are the conferences held in the very year when Gide ventured on the composition of *The Counterfeiters*. The rousing shock of the First World War was necessary, perhaps, to reveal to Gide the whole impact of Dostoevski's mysticism—"so much closer to Asia than to Rome"—and of his psychological profundity. It may be that this perspicacious critic, André Gide, had to pass through many a calamity and many a transformation himself, to grasp fully the inherent logic of what appears as morbid inconsistency in Dostoevski's figures. Far from concealing this uncanny desultoriness of his heroes, the great Russian displays and emphasizes it deliberately. That is to say, what fascinates him most in a human character is the profusion of incoherent, contradictory trends and energies coexisting in his shadowy, unfathomable depth. That co-existence appears often all the more paradoxical and disconcerting as Dostoevski pushes the emotions of his characters to the extreme or even exaggerates them to the point of absurdity.

And what of André Gide? Are not the emotional reactions of his figures often pitched to almost unbearable heights? Olivier's attempted suicide is as illogical, as "inconsistent" as any mystic vagary of any Dostoevski character. The demon who corrupts Georges and destroys Boris is hardly more rational than Raskolnikov's murderous whim or the reveries of Prince Myshkin in *The Idiot*. If Dostoevski's martyrs and visionaries are split personalities, divided within themselves, what should be said of the Prodigal Son or the Immoralist?—or of Lafcadio? *"Je suis une être d'inconséquence!"* he rants in his childlike fashion. The double optics of *Les Faux-Monnayeurs*, with Edouard's fictitious novel reflecting and criticizing the methods of André Gide's fiction, suggest a mild case of schizophrenia. Or is it just that genius has a penchant for complicated devices and by instinct prefers the indirect approach? William Blake is right, then, when he says: "Improvement makes strait roads; but the crooked roads without Improvement are roads of Genius."

To Blake's "Proverbs of Hell," quoted by Gide with so much amused approval, he adds these two tenets of his own credo: "It is with fine feelings that one produces poor literature"; and: "There is no work of art without the collaboration of the demon." Then he tells us that every work of art is a token of the marriage of Heaven and Hell, which serves him as a pretext to cite Blake once more: "The reason Milton wrote in fetters when he wrote of Angels and God, and at liberty when of Devils and Hell, is because he was a true poet and of the Devil's party without knowing it."

But after having dwelt on the demoniac aspects of Blake's and Dostoevski's genius, Gide reminds his listeners of the essential fact that both are so utterly overwhelmed by the truths of the Gospel that their "ferocity" cannot but be of transitory nature, the momentary consequence of a kind of holy blindness. Gide would like to quote some of Blake's "Songs of Innocence" to counterbalance and rectify the impression he conveyed by citing the "Proverbs of Hell." As for Dostoevski, his Christian ethos has by no means always a somber or savage tinge. He is also a great lover; he adores this life and this world—this "vast world of delights," to use another of Blake's phrases. To illustrate this streak of exuberant optimism in Dostoevski, Gide reads to his listeners this suggestive fragment of a dialogue from *The Possessed:*

" 'Are you fond of children?'
" 'I am,' said Kirilov, in a rather indifferent way.
" 'Are you fond of life too, then?'
" 'Yes, I do like life too. Does that astonish you?' "

André Gide is interested in children because he is interested in life—in its growth and development, in its unending potentialities, in the unending promise it enfolds. That which *is* fascinates him more than what *has been.* But even more exciting than the present is the future—that which could be and, therefore, *will* come into being. "What is now proved was once only imagin'd," William Blake says.

And his spirited disciple, André Gide, adds, "What we imagine now will be proved in the future."

One might object, at this point, that Gide's imagination is dismaying as far as the coming generation is concerned. Are his callow counterfeiters and suicides, his little runaways and neurotics, the future we have to look forward to?

Yes and no. They bear the germs of the future, those erratic youngsters who perform their drama in *Les Faux-Monnayeurs*. True, their drama is lurid and disorderly. But is it their fault? Or rather is it not the fault of a society which abides by untruthfulness, oppresses the instincts, postpones and pollutes the evolution of man? The disorderly demon of youth, iridescent, uncertain, dynamic, might become the demiurgos of a truly new order.

Boris and Georges go astray—poisoned by the blight of hypocrisy that palls M. Vedel's institute. But perhaps Olivier will find his way, guided by Edouard? And Bernard—did he not come out victorious from his fight with the angel? And what do we know about Bernard's younger brother, Caloub? Edouard is curious to find out what this little stranger may be like. The voluminous, involved composition of *Les Faux-Monnayeurs* ends with a casual but suggestive reference to this imminent meeting. The last entry in Edouard's diary, the last sentence of the novel reads: "*Je suis bien curieux de connaître Caloub.*"

Thus the fugue resumes and reaffirms its intrinsic theme, which connotes and guarantees new themes and new fugues to come. The infinite melody of which romantic musicians dreamt—there it is, full of prospects and promises, severe and serene, playful and faithful and proud.

Gide shows us, with relentless realism, a generation be-

wildered and confused in the midst of the rampant turmoil
that is our present life and our present society. He shows
the struggle, the efforts, the vices secret or open, the triumphs, the aberrations. He wants future generations to receive this dialectic confession, the fugue of our contradictory drama, *le roman pure*, the undisguised account of our
crisis. He supposes that it may be profitable for the generations to come to be familiar with our adventures and our
sufferings. He is an optimist, the author of *Les Faux-
Monnayeurs*. To write for future generations indicates
optimism.

Gide never cared much for the immediate success of his
writings. In the beginning, however, when he composed
Les Cahiers d'André Walter, this detachment had a rather
melancholy flavor. In that time, he was not interested
enough in the present to aspire to present success. But thirty-
five years later, at the time of *Les Faux-Monnayeurs*, he
was too keenly interested in the future to be primarily concerned with his prestige among contemporary critics. The
indifference as such remained the same. But the feelings
from which it springs had altered.

André Walter said, somewhat drearily, "I don't care
whether or not I am understood and liked by my generation."

André Gide—the André Gide of *The Counterfeiters*—
says, "My fervent hope is that I may be understood and
liked by generations to come."

"Why," he says, "why should we not be able to attain
a sympathetic perspicacity, in virtue of which we could
anticipate what is in the offing and in the making? What
problems will perturb the coming generation? It is for

these coming ones that I write. To answer yet unspoken questions! To respond to yet indistinct longings! Those who are children now will be surprised, one day, to find me on their path."

VII. FREEDOM AND DISCIPLINE

Wherever a man comes, there comes revolution.
RALPH WALDO EMERSON

Je vous assure que le sentiment de la liberté peut plonger l'âme dans une sorte de détresse; (expliquer et developer).
ANDRÉ GIDE

I N *Les Faux-Monnayeurs* André Gide reached the climax of his artistic experiment. It is to this book that his
international prestige is mainly due—particularly his
fame in the United States. In France the critics were at
first somewhat hesitant to acknowledge the unique significance of this astounding "first novel." Little by little, however, the reading public grasped its revolutionary impact.
What Gide had accomplished, this time, was much more
than a successful novel. It was a new pattern, encouraging
and foreshadowing other works in the same line to be put
forth by the same author or by his followers—other intellectual fugues, other pure and passionate surveys of our
emergency and of our future. Gide's first novel is pregnant
with infinite suggestions and promises.

"What is a book?" he asked, decades before he wrote
The Counterfeiters. "A lot of dead letters? No, a sack full
of grain."

Would he be able to sing them out himself—these new

tunes already introduced in the ample scheme of this extraordinary composition? Apparently the composer felt somewhat depleted when he had brought this score to a provisional end. "Could be continued." Gide was tempted to conclude his book with these words which deny that there is a conclusion. Is Edouard to produce a second volume of his *Counterfeiters*? Or will Bernard prove spirited enough to describe his fight with the angel in the form of a novel or a comedy?

As for Gide, he realized at bottom that he had communicated the valid formula of his message. From that point on, the center of his interest shifted from fiction to the moral and philosophical sphere. The demon who hitherto obsessed all Gidean characters, including his own, gradually withdrew, to be superseded by a more rational inspiration. The romantic period of Gide's quest seemed to have reached its end.

There is nothing abrupt or paradoxical about this antiromantic development. The tendency away from the romantic spell is inherent in Gide's writings, from *Les Cahiers d'André Walter* to *Les Faux-Monnayeurs*. André Gide, as an artist, seems preoccupied with one primary concern: to clarify and simplify his style; to purge it of all exaggerations and redundancies; to come as close as possible to the ideal of classical perfection. From book to book his idiom becomes more transparent, more concise. What a difference between the dithyrambic grandeur of *Les Nourritures terrestres* and the crisp sobriety that prevails in *Les Faux-Monnayeurs!* In Gide's early books everything floats and phosphoresces; now, each word is to the point, there are no shrill, hysterical tones any more. André Walter reveled in fancy images to describe a flower or a bit of music; the author of *Les Faux-Monnayeurs* remains composed, almost dry, when he has to introduce an angel. All we are told is that Bernard had never seen any angels before, but was hardly surprised when he saw one. The angel said, "Come!" and Bernard, swift and obedient, got up to follow him. Gide renounces, with self-imposed austerity, all rhetoric effects to which the situation might have invited a less-disciplined writer.

Of course, the reader is free to object that the appearance of an angel in a modern novel means in itself a dubious adjustment to romantic tastes. The moderation of Gide's vocabulary may seem surprising rather than reassuring, in view of the baroque fantasies in which he indulges simultaneously.

But what would be the artistic and moral value of this stylistic sedateness, if it were *not* the result of a conscious ethical effort? Classical simplicity is a bore, when it springs from sheer lack of temperament and imagination. It is Gide who tells us that "the classical work of art cannot be vital and fascinating, except in virtue of its *dominated romanticism.*"

"*Qu'est-ce qu'il y a de plus mystérieux que la clarté?*" The clarity to which Paul Valéry refers in this sentence (which occurs, incidentally, in an essay devoted to Gide's and Valéry's common master, Stéphane Mallarmé)—this mysterious clarity has nothing to do with naïveté and cloudless innocence; it is the prize and result of a long, painful struggle, a triumph over chaos.

The idea of heroism plays an integral rôle in Gide's concept of classical art. "The human soul requires heroism," he proclaimed as a young man, in 1904, in an address attacking the triteness of naturalistic literature. Modern society no longer admits heroism, except in its passive form, as acceptance and resignation. Art, therefore, has to be the inspiring example contradicting and surpassing a dreary reality. Art must become antirealistic, classical once again. It is by no means the function of art to repeat the reality; quite the contrary, it behooves the artist to intensify and to ennoble his opaque material. Art is selection, contraction, purification. What a mistake to believe that art could ever be "free"! It will remain obedient to its self-styled, inherent law, or else will mar and finally forfeit its own dignity.

Gide admires Racine more than any other poet, even more than Shakespeare. For it is Racine's work, more than any other achievement in literature, that conveys and fulfills the idea of artistic perfection. There are critics (Gide quotes one of them) who prefer the British genius to the genius of France, because the heroes and heroines in Racine's tragedies cease to live once the curtain goes down, while the Shakespearean characters appear for some unforgettable hours in front of the audience, then withdraw to continue their dramas somewhere else, on other planes, with unabated passion and grandeur.

But this is exactly what Gide loves and admires in Racine's lofty figures—their sublime conventionalism, the graceful and strict preciseness of their contours, the serene elegance and royal discipline with which they accept the limitation and stylization of their solemn existence.

Shakespeare is nature: his cosmic work resounds with natural cries and laughters, sweeping emotions, rampant and violent life. But Racine is the crown and essence of art: at once economic and generous, well-balanced, noble, urbane, and profoundly intelligent. "Each work of art," Gide says, "is primarily a product of *reason*."

Astonishing words, these, coming from a man who recognized and hailed the demon as the source and kernel of artistic creation. But so did Goethe, and yet he attained harmony, by virtue of reason and of discipline. Gide often quoted his German master, who said that no work of art is valid and effective unless it inheres and communicates what Goethe calls *"das Schaudern,"* that is, the fearful and lustful shudder caused by the demon's touch. The author of *Faust* and *Tasso* was certainly familiar with that weird and sublime sensation. He knew and controlled the demon.

This is true also of the Greek tragedians and of Racine; of Johann Sebastian Bach and Poussin, of Gluck and Pascal, Stendhal and Molière—of all those, in short, André Gide loves most faithfully. He loves them for their aristocratic discipline, their tact, their measure, their heroic urbanity, and for what he calls *"leur qualité la plus exquise: la réserve."*

Is this André Gide praising measure and limitation?— the same Gide who told us, not once but dozens of times, that the idea of option and fixation is intolerable to him? He, the vagrant and erratic spirit, does he glorify the exacting rituals of the classical tragedy?

No doubt, there is a strange contrast between the floating uncertainty of Gide's emotional and philosophic attitude, on the one hand, and his will for architectonic clarity, on the other. This dualism, perplexing as it may appear at first, is one of the intrinsic qualities of Gide's nature and one of the sources from which his genius springs. The rampant disquietude of his thought and feeling is counterbalanced and tamed by the august tranquillity of his artistic style. The more daring and seditious are the questions he asks, the more sedate and graceful the formulation. His most indiscreet confessions are couched in the most discreet manner. The elegant discipline of his literary idiom smoothes and clarifies the paradoxical or rebellious ideas he wishes to put forward.

To him, artistic expression is tantamount to purification. He wants art to be detached, disinterested, unaffected by the passions it echoes and transmits. Amidst a general flux and flurry, art represents the principle of stability. Immutable and perfect in itself, it mirrors and transfigures the glorious imperfection and unending motions of life. Gide might apply to his own work what he said in reference to Proust's: "Detached from life, he remains closely connected with it. Bent to its depth, he contemplates it, or rather, he contemplates his own reflection in it. And the more unquiet the image, the more placid the mirror, the more contemplative the gaze."

Do we recognize the enchanted dreamer all absorbed in his own immaculate image? After so many adventures and tribulations through which he has passed, he still is the one we surprised and admired in the solitude, near the pool— still lovable, still inaccessible, still Narcissus.

No, he is not the same—not altogether, not essentially. He has changed since 1890, since the days of youth and Symbolism. His classical attitude, the solemn grace of his gestures, have assumed a different meaning and serve other purposes. Now he has recourse to the immutable harmony of perfect forms, not to escape from harsh realities, but in order to dominate their chaotic turmoil. He does not want to dodge the insoluble contradictions of which human life consists; nor does he wish to be overwhelmed by their savage disorder. That is why he needs art as a balm and a clue, as a weapon.

But can a purely æsthetic discipline suffice to meet and master the tremendous conflicts of life? Can one solve the basic paradoxes inherent in the human condition, simply by defining them in crystal prose or verse? Is the perfection of forms an adequate remedy for the glaring imperfection that prevails in nature and society? What is the sense and the value of a perfectly organized style amidst a disorganized, disintegrating world?

The Gide of *Les Nourritures terrestres* seemed yet unaware of these questions. His hedonistic credo, addressed exclusively to the individual, disregarded all social issues and responsibilities. An individual—Nathanaël—was encouraged and urged to enjoy life, to relish its sweetness and its mystery—regardless of any collective restrictions or requirements; against society, if need be.

"A social question?" asked Gide, in 1895. "Certainly. But the moral question is primary. One man is more interesting than mankind; it is the individual, not the race, whom God has shaped according to His image. *Each* man is more valuable than *all* men."

Throughout his youth, up to the time of *The Counterfeiters*, we will find Gide on the side of the individual whenever there is a conflict between collective interests

and individual ethics. His violent reaction against Puritanism brings him to the verge of anarchy. His iconoclastic
fervor repudiates the whole code of restrictions and pro-
hibitions through which the appointed guardians of society
—the priests, the teachers, the judges, the officials—try to
shackle and domesticate the individual. Gide feels, with
Ralph Waldo Emerson, that "society is everywhere in conspiracy against the manhood of every one of its members."
That is why there comes revolution, wherever a man
comes.

There comes a man, André Gide—a rousing, challenging
voice. He protests against all hierarchies, all taboos, all
oppressions; against the tutelage of the family and against
the lies of nationalism; he debunks hollow slogans and
obsolete prejudices; he defends the outcasts and the sinners
—the Son of Man against the Pharisees.

But the same rebel and protestant recognizes and recom-
mends the strictest laws, the most exacting discipline in the
artistic sphere. While questioning and transgressing all
social and moral conventions, he preaches and practises a
sublime conventionalism as an artist, in his artistic effort.
He who rejects the authority of any rules imposed on him
from without, accepts and follows a discipline the legiti-
mation of which is derived from within. For this obedience
is voluntary, self-styled, and gratuitous—as voluntary and
gratuitous as is Alissa's sacrifice, Lafcadio's arbitrary taboos, or Bernard's submission to his angelic antagonist and
mentor.

There is, indeed, a vital affinity between Gide's voluntary adherence to artistic discipline and his concept of the

gratuitous action. A gratuitous action is a *free* action, conceived and performed without any pressure from the outside world. It is disinterested, creative, a *human* action. "I have always believed," we read in one of Gide's early writings, *Le Prométhée mal enchaîné* (1899), "that this is the quality in virtue of which man distinguishes himself from the animals: the capacity of acting gratuitously. To me, man is the animal capable of acting without recompense, even against his material interest."

The individual confirms and amplifies his independence by overcoming his innate selfishness; the disinterested act, the voluntary sacrifice, is the postulate and the consequence implied in Gide's individual ethics. His exaltation of the gratuitous action and his obedience to the classical rules of art spring from one central idea and motive.

It is fascinating to perceive how the contradictory components of Gide's vision are all interrelated like the threads in a finely woven tissue. The most divergent elements of his philosophy seem to merge, to penetrate each other, when visualized from one particular angle. Gide's classicism becomes recognizable as an aspect and a manifestation of his individual ethics when he tells us that "the triumph of individualism and the triumph of classicism are identical. For the triumph of individualism springs from the self-renunciation of the individual."

And it is in this context—speaking of classical style—that he quotes once again the Gospel word he finds relevant to so many different issues and situations: *Whosoever shall save his life shall lose it; but whosoever shall lose his life, the same shall find it.*

The ethos of self-discipline and self-renunciation becomes increasingly predominant in Gide's thought and work, after *Les Nourritures terrestres*. And yet we must not forget that this moral doctrine remains the expression and self-correction of an absolutely individualistic, not to say anti-social, attitude. If Alissa's futile generosity proves the transcendental sources of this disinterested energy, the example of Lafcadio discloses drastically its anarchic potentialities. In the light of individual ethics, an unmotivated crime is as natural and as laudable as an unmotivated sacrifice.

Gide has always been exceedingly interested in crimes and criminals. The phenomenon of the illegitimate action, its psychological roots and implications, puzzled and preoccupied his mind from the beginning of his conscious life. Always fascinated by the exceptional, he has portrayed and analyzed all kinds of aberrations and anomalies, from childish pranks to the most sinister felonies. An Arabian lad—Moktir, in *L'Immoraliste*—who pilfers a pair of scissors, opens a long parade of adventurers and counterfeiters, murderers and impostors, who constitute an important sector of the personnel in Gide's dramas and *soties*.

But this passionate concern in criminology manifested itself not only through the medium of creative writing. If *Les Caves du Vatican*, *Les Faux-Monnayeurs*, and other mystery stories, show their author as an expert in the affairs of the underworld, another document, *Les Souvenirs de la Cour d'Assises*, reveals the source from which these insights are in part derived.

In this entertaining and instructive little book—written in 1912, published in 1914—Gide appears not only as an

observer and commentator but also as a judge, or rather
as a juror. It had long been his secret dream to serve on
a jury, but somehow he had never had the opportunity.
Whenever he arrived in a new city, he would rove around
the law-court, attracted by the fortresses of civic justice
as Raskolnikov was by the uncanny charm of the com-
missioner who will eventually unmask his crime and pre-
pare his atonement.

At last he had the chance to act as a juror at the assizes
in Rouen. But as soon as the first trial began, his courage
and determination dwindled and were superseded by the
most painful doubts. The callous complacency of his
fellow-jurors struck him as monstrous. How could they—
how could *he*—have the nerve to judge this little thief, or
that man who had raped a girl, or even this innocuous-
looking youth who had killed his mistress? Who knew the
real motives behind their deeds? Who was familiar with
the specific conditions from which these motives originated? And how could anyone dare to judge unless he
understood the causes of the offense?

This sensitive juror was disconcerted, appalled by the
perfunctory fashion in which the court handled and decided upon the most complex and most delicate cases. Did
those smug citizens and officials not realize the scope and
weight of their responsibility? One member of the assizes
at least could not sleep at night, perturbed and puzzled by
the intricacies of a drama in which he was supposed to play
his part as a judge. And yet he felt rather like a defendant.

The stillness of his room seemed to echo the commandment of Christ: *Judge not!* How alarming and menacing
sounded this benign advice to a rueful Christian, who

understood too much to condemn anything, and did not dare to condemn unless he understood.

Ne jugez pas!—Judge not!—that is the leitmotiv of the curious memoirs of a Rouen juror. "Not that I believe society could do without tribunals and without judges," Gide adds, reasonably and dutifully. "But . . ."

But, he says, the judges should be milder and better men; better informed, less biased and less bored, more humane, more conscientious. The question is whether Gide would have acknowledged their authority, even if they had been paragons of friendliness and wisdom. Was he not biased himself?—in favor of the so-called criminals, to be sure. Was he not a partisan, in his turn?—a faithful champion, that is, of all outlaws and all pariahs, of all nonconformists, all exceptions, of all dangerous and endangered minorities.

It is only seemingly a paradox that his interest in exceptional individuals turns out to be the root and the nucleus of Gide's social consciousness altogether. First he emphasized and defended the independence of the personality against the encroachments of the social order. Those, however, who have to be protected from such encroachments, constitute a collective group in themselves, an underprivileged sector of the social organism. To come out for the underprivileged, against the rulers and judges, foreshadows, or already implies, a truly revolutionary spirit. Books like *Corydon* and *Les Souvenirs de la Cour d'Assises* contradict and arraign certain principles and practices of the bourgeois order. These indictments transcend the scope of individual ethics. The issues of legislature and public morality are, no doubt, primarily of a social nature. The fight for certain minorities results almost inevitably in social criticism. Do I need say that social criticism presupposes and proves social consciousness and the acceptance of social responsibilities?

André Gide, the individualist, became a supporter of outcasts, prompted by his unyielding truthfulness, his chivalrous generosity, and also by his passionate concern in everything unusual, dangerous, and devious. He came out for Captain Dreyfus because he thought him innocent and unfairly treated. He went out of his way for the petty crooks in Rouen because he believed that their transgressions clamored for understanding rather than for punishment. He did homage to Oscar Wilde when the hypocrites and the snobs ribaldly betrayed their former favorite. He risked his own reputation (and jeopardized forever the Nobel Prize, a seat in the French Academy, and other advantages) when he ventured on the delicate topic of homosexuality in *Si le Grain ne meurt* and *Corydon*. And he offended not only the moral prejudices but the material interests of the French bourgeoisie when he exposed the outrages of French imperialism in his brave and realistic account, *Voyage au Congo* (1927).

It has often been asserted that Gide's Congo expedition, in 1925, marks the turning point of his moral development, the awakening of his social and political conscience. Even an intimate friend and competent critic like Jean Schlumberger perceived and presented the situation in this simplified manner. "It was during his African journey," Schlumberger suggests, in the *Nouvelle Revue Française*, "that Gide found himself for the first time confronted with the phenomenon of social injustice and also with the alternative of whether or not he ought to come out against it."

That is not quite so, as Gide points out to Schlumberger, in a most interesting reply. According to Gide's own version, it was by no means as recently as in 1925 that he first discovered the glaring inadequacies of our social system. He had been aware of these shortcomings, long before he exposed them in his Congo book. Of course, he noticed the ugly and ominous aspects of capitalist colonization and exploitation when he roved through North Africa as a young man in easy circumstances but with an anxious mind. True, he did not allow, at the time, these hideous things to invade and mar the pure realm of his artistic vision. Under the influence of Mallarmé and out of his animosity to the naturalistic school, the young traveler deemed only "the absolute" fit subject for his art. Deliberately and strictly, he omitted in his *feuilles de route* any reference to political or social issues. "I would have considered myself dishonored as an artist," Gide explains in his answer to Schlumberger, "if I had had any dealings with such sordidly vulgar affairs. . . . Besides, I still adhered, at the time, to the absurd cult of specialists and experts—economists, administrators, generals. I had confidence in them; I took it for granted that the things that caused my indignation would irk and disturb them as well, and that they were much better qualified than I to expose and to correct the outrages, the extortions, the injustices, the mistakes."

But when he went to the Congo, he had to realize that the terrible things he witnessed would remain concealed from the conscience of France, of the world, unless he,

Gide, spoke them out. The colonial officials, missionaries, and business men—the only representatives of France in those regions—were compelled to keep quiet, either by interest or duty. "This time," Gide says, "I had to speak, as I was the only one who could. I was by no means anti-imperialist when I left France for Africa, and it was not for the sake of anti-imperialist principles that I disclosed the ugly things I witnessed down there, alas. Yes, it was only a long time afterwards that I was induced by un-escapable logic to grasp the causal connection between those particular outrages and a system which tolerates, indeed praises, such crimes because it profits by them. This system, I realized at last, is obviously and completely foul."

This he wrote in 1935, ten years after the journey. As for the travel account itself, it is far from being a *J'accuse*. Just as the public unduly emphasized certain details in *Si le Grain ne meurt*, so has the revolutionary character of *Voyage au Congo* been greatly exaggerated. True, there are grim and factual reports on terror and exploitation. The wretched plight of the Negroes is revealed in scores of appalling examples. But Gide describes solely what he observed himself—individual acts of brutality, the blunders and offenses committed by certain inhuman officials. At no point does he indulge in generalities and abstractions. The general cadence of his prose is by no means that of a political manifesto but rather that of a half-scientific, half-narrative account. The style of *Voyage au Congo* resembles the solemn pedantry of the aging Goethe, rather than the flailing accusation of Zola or of Victor Hugo.

Characteristically, Gide was reading Goethe's novel, *Die*

Wahlverwandtschaften, while he traveled in the Congo valley. The sedate tempo and conscientious neatness of his own idiom seem to echo the well-turned phrases of the German master. With a truly Goethe-like accuracy, Gide dwells on the particularities of landscapes, weather conditions, and native rituals. Insects and flowers, the formations of trees, mountains, and butterflies, are described with the utmost minuteness. Especially when it comes to botanical observations, the French explorer appears almost as competent as the illustrious botanist of Weimar. The question is whether Goethe, less affable and much more august, would have been equally interested in the personal worries of such humble men as the Negroes who accompanied the caravan of André Gide and Marc Allegret. While the ambitious young man took pictures for the travel film he was preparing, Gide would have a chat with one of their guides or carriers. How much did the fellow make? Under what conditions did his family live? How much did he know about Europe? What were his feelings toward his white masters? Gide, in his book, repeats the things he heard—the monotonous stories, the timid complaints, the hopeless sighs, and the ominous curses.

The African report is completely lacking in fantastic or humorous elements. It deals with serious and simple matters. There is nothing funny or fantastic about a starving Negro, or about a big river, or a palm tree, or the malaria fever, or a cobra. Nature has no sense of humor, especially in the Congo zone.

Packed with factual material, unemotional and undramatic, Gide's chronicle exhales the savage vastness of the solitudes it describes. It carries the aroma of wilderness

and jungle, as the novels of Joseph Conrad are imbued
with the ozone of the open sea. In both cases, however—
in the epic diary of the roving Frenchman and in the
maritime sagas of the English-writing Pole—the soulless
grandeur of nature is ennobled by undertones of protest
and compassion.

Voyage au Congo is dedicated "To the memory of Joseph
Conrad."

Home in Paris again, Gide toyed for a while with the
idea of writing a satirical novel about slavery. He meant
to contrast an owner of Negro slaves with an employer
of white, freeborn men. The plan was to have the slave-
owner turn out to be much more careful and humanitarian
in his treatment of his slaves than was his "liberal" com-
petitor in his dealings with his "free" employees. The
slave-owner has had to pay good money for every working
man: each slave is as valuable to him as four chickens or
half of a horse. His more modern neighbor, on the contrary, realizes that "free citizens" do not cost much; for
every free man who dies, because of unduly hard work
and unduly poor food, there are plenty of others to take
over his job.

"What a subject for Swift!" exclaimed Julian Green,
to whom Gide disclosed this project. The two writers
had a chat about racial questions, stimulated by the visit
of a certain Mr. Cook, a Negro professor at Atlanta University. The professor was charming and talked French
beautifully—with a vivacity that struck Green as Jewish
rather than Negroid, according to his *Journal*. It may
have been this resemblance which caused the two friends

to delve into the complex issue of racial discrimination in general, and particularly in so far as the United States was concerned. Gide, old champion of minorities, racial or otherwise, conveyed his hope—half-facetiously, though—that the Jews and the Negroes might absorb before long those other sectors of the population that now look down on them.

No, the Gide who returned from the Congo was no "changed man" in any obvious or spectacular way—no individualistic Saulus who came back as a socialist Paulus. Gide was not changed but changing, which means that he was unchanged. He was in search of himself, as before —as always.

His literary output of that particular period hardly indicates an abrupt transformation. The next major work, after *Voyage au Congo* and *Le Retour du Tchad*, is a novel, or rather, two short novelettes conceived and published simultaneously, *L'Ecole des femmes, suivie de Robert* (1930). After several years this double-composition was followed by a third part, *Geneviève* (1936), adding the story of a half-grown daughter to the confessions of Eveline and Robert.

The psychological themes treated in this slim trilogy are familiar enough—typically Gidean topics. Eveline, once passionately devoted to her husband, gradually ceases to love him: that is to say, she begins to see him as he actually is. He turns out to be not quite as wonderful as she at first thought him, not quite as noble and excellent as he still believes himself to be. It is a tale of disillusionment, the bitter end of a matrimonial romance.

Eveline would like to leave Robert, for she no longer

loves him and sees through his unctuous feints. But, being a decent woman and also a Catholic Christian, she proves only too sensible to the admonitions of her confessor and her family. They all tell her that it would indeed be very wicked to abandon Robert. Doesn't she think of her innocent little daughter?—of her own womanly honor?—of the family reputation? And, last but not least, doesn't she think of God? He, according to the priest and the family council, is strictly against divorces.

Eveline—thinking of her child, her honor, the business interests of her earthly father and those of her own soul—renounces the foolhardy idea of leaving the man whom she has ceased to love. She is a good woman, an unhappy, cowardly woman. The life she will lead from now on is a dreary farce.

As for her daughter, Mademoiselle Geneviève, she is no longer so very innocent when she submits her memoirs to the very man who exposed the tragedy of her mother—namely, to André Gide. The personal letter enclosed with her manuscript sounds rather ill-tempered and complacent. "There I am," says Mademoiselle Geneviève. "I don't care whether you like me or not. I am a modern woman—by no means a romantic heroine. I have my serious problems and my reasonable hopes, as you will find out when you read my paper. What worries me are not vague and general questions, but the realistic and specific issue of my own plight and future. What can an intelligent, independent girl expect from life, nowadays? What are her chances and rights? What obstacles is she likely to meet? How can she overcome them?"

Moreover, she informs Gide—and Gide's readers—that

her story is not going to be a lot of fun and excitement
but just a plain, homespun report. Unhappily, her warnings turn out to be justified.

Geneviève is like a female character from an Ibsen
drama, with their most amusing qualities missing. She commands neither Nora's quivering naïveté nor the impressive
hysteria of Hedda Gabler. Her intelligence is rather commonplace—deliberately so, to be sure; her emotional life
is unoriginal, even a little embarrassing at times. Her ideas
in respect to equal rights for women are well enough,
one supposes. But she cuts a rather clumsy figure when
she calls on a gentleman whom she thinks attractive—a
certain Doctor Marchant—and scares him with the dis-
closure that she would like a baby from him. Just like that,
without any beating about the bush. Doctor Marchant is
nonplussed, and so are we, the readers. The situation becomes all the more awkward in view of the fact that
Geneviève's mother, Eveline, happens to share the taste
of her forward daughter. She, too, had at one time been
susceptible to the doctor's charm, but she would not have
made an ass of herself by asking the gentleman for a baby,
as if it were a cigarette or a new hat.

Geneviève feels ashamed when she finds out about her
mother's faraway, frustrated romance. Her heart contracts
as she sees her mother's lips pale and tremble. "How much
more respectable!" clumsy Geneviève muses, "how much
more authentic are mother's subtle and secret feelings compared with my selfish rashness!"

Eveline wasted her life because she was unable to overcome the conventions imposed on her by her caste. Will
Geneviève ruin herself, out of her inability to control what

she cherishes above all—her beloved, dangerous freedom?

This question, not new in itself, is new as a central theme in Gide's work. Hitherto, he had conceived only its religious implications, not its social impact. His primary subject was freedom, not discipline. If the individual ethics required self-control, it was a matter of personal pride (the case of Lafcadio) or a mystic caprice (Alissa's sacrifice). In neither instance are any social issues involved at all.

As for *Les Faux-Monnayeurs*, it is undoubtedly a social panorama, not the confession of a solitary soul. But the society it portrays and arraigns is a society in disintegration, at once rigid and disorderly. The personnel of the novel consists in part of frustrated, narrow-minded bourgeois (the Vedels, La Pérouse, Bernard's ostensible father, and so forth); in part, of cynical bohemians (Lady Griffith and Robert de Passavant); and, finally, of striving, uncertain youth. Olivier and Bernard, Vincent and Armand, even the poor little Boris and the devilish little Georges— all these keen and muddled young men, are they not clamoring and longing for a new valid order, an acceptable discipline? Are they not tired, the whole lot of them, of their aimless existence amidst a social and moral vacuum? The way things stand, they feel drifting and derelict. It may be all right, for a while, to debunk the slogans of Nationalistic demagogues, or the pretentious chatter of snobbish literati, or Pastor Vedel's pious swindle. But does it suffice, in the end? Bernard—among all the young men Gide has ever presented, the most spirited and most intelligent one—articulates the question which perturbs all his comrades and which will be resumed by Mademoiselle

Geneviève: How can we use our freedom? For what purposes? To what ends?

Bernard, wandering through the Luxembourg Gardens, feels perplexed and elated as he contemplates his life, its veiled perils and promises, its bewildering uncertainty. He does not see the garden; he actually sees his life—right there, in front of him, ocean-like, an immeasurable mystery. They say that there are routes leading across the seas; but they are scarcely marked, those routes, and Bernard does not know how to find the one he is supposed to take.

But at this point his angel appears. He will guide him.

Geneviève has no angel. She believes in science and progress as firmly and doggedly as her poor mother used to believe in virtue and in God. Moreover, Geneviève's author, André Gide, does not seem in a frame of mind, just now, to play with cherubim. He has become very sober, almost alarmingly so.

Evidently, something curious and a bit depressing had happened to Gide's style, simultaneously with his new emphasis on social issues. For years he had tried to suppress the lovely mannerisms of his playful youth. At this point he attained at last—if only temporarily, in a queer, paradoxical fashion—what he had so long been striving for: a perfectly simple, classical diction, impersonal, austere, lusterless.

What was the design and objective of this new form of asceticism? Did it result from artistic impotence? Was it a caprice? Or a failure?

No, this deliberate and obvious absence of élan and color manifests a moral attitude, a new renunciation, another sacrifice.

Gide was a very young man, still given to extreme in-

dividualism and other vagaries, when he asserted that to
become human means to become commonplace. The artist,
aristocratic by nature and conviction, renounces his splendid isolation by identifying himself with the preoccupa-
tions and the vocabulary of the common people. He
discusses plain things; he becomes plain himself. He gives
up the ornate words and big gestures; in short, he ceases
to be a great man, to become *a man*, quite simply.

The so-called great men—the heroes, rulers, exploiters—
always delude themselves and their victims. Their glory
is based on a lurid mire of lies and feints, whether they
know it or not. King Œdipus, for instance, remains long
unaware of the grisly entanglements to which he owes
his seemingly brilliant career. He is to find out, however.

Gide's drama *Œdipe* (1931) is a more significant contribution, I think, than the strangely perfunctory novelettes about Madame Eveline and her daughter. Not that
Gide's rationalistic interpretation of the antique myth
could compete, as a work of art, with the immortal original; in fact, it falls short of certain modern adaptations
of Greek legends. Jean Cocteau's version of the Œdipus
legend, *La Machine infernale*, is undoubtedly more colorful than Gide's sober experiment. And yet the grim simplicity of Gide's dramatic essay possesses and conveys a
certain tonic seriousness and authenticity in which Cocteau's entrancing fireworks are definitely lacking.

Just as Mademoiselle Geneviève lives up to her initial
warning that she is going to tell a plain, homespun story,
King Œdipus makes good the promise he formulates in his
prologue: that he wants to put forward succinctly and
directly whatever he has to say, and will not indulge in

fancy words, sublime poses, and beautiful lies. The drama
in which he acts as the leading figure—not to say, as the
hero—is free of swollen rhetoric and by no means unduly
rich in artistic beauties. Its significance and suspense spring
exclusively from its moral and intellectual purport.

The tragedy of King Œdipus is the tragedy of extreme
individualism. The master of Thebes and husband of
Queen Jocasta cheats himself, his family, and his people.
He pretends to be happy and to govern happily, although
his happiness and his government rest entirely on his "individual ethics," in other words, on a pack of lies. He has
long mismanaged his life, and Jocasta's, and the collective
life of his people, but he still keeps ranting and jubilating,
"How remarkably happy I am! How fortunate all of us
are!" At this point, the plague has already devastated the
City of Thebes, and before long the martyred people will
have to find out why their wayward gods are so direly
angry with them: King Œdipus is, of course, the son and
murderer of the legitimate monarch, King Laius, which
means that his wife, Queen Jocasta, is his mother, and he,
the boastful king, a pitiful and fearful criminal. Blinded
by his selfish optimism, he must atone for it by losing his
physical eyesight. This is the punishment he deserves and
accepts for his having wantonly disregarded the obvious
intimations from his unfortunate wife and mother, his
vulgar but upright brother-in-law, Creon, and his pedantic
high priest, Theresias, a disagreeable but shrewd old gentleman.

The most telling warnings, however, did not come from
any individual but were pronounced by a collective voice
—the voice of the people, the anxious men and women of

Thebes. Their sturdy chorus—the chorus of common sense —accompanies the drama of the King, which parallels and causes the drama of the community. The voice of the people demurs to Œdipus' foolish assertion that everybody is happy. "Not so," grumbles the chorus. "We, the little fellows, the forgotten men, we aren't happy at all." The left-wing group of the chorus goes even so far as to suggest that there might be a causal connection between the King's much-vaunted prosperity and their own wretchedness. "We cannot help feeling," they say, ominously, "that your fortune and our misfortune have somehow to do with each other."

These are new accents and new accusations—new as far as André Gide is concerned. Their novelty is all the more discernible and all the more exciting as they are interwoven into a composition rich in self-quotations and in allusions to familiar themes. Œdipus behaves in a typically Gidean fashion when he quarrels with the tiresomely reasonable clergyman, Theresias, and defends his "individual ethics" against the high priest's rigid orthodoxy. But the confusing thing is that in some of these disputes the author seems to sympathize with the inflexible traditionalism of Theresias rather than with the buoyant blindness of Œdipus' heedless libertinage. It chances, more often than not, that the unpleasant priest says the right thing, while the pleasant King indulges in illusions.

And this is true also of the dialogues between Œdipus and his brother-in-law. Does not the former make an ass of himself when he seems so pleased to be an illegitimate child? True, Gide has always had a weakness for bastards: his two most engaging characters, Lafcadio and Bernard,

both are the fruits of "free love." In the particular case of
Œdipus, however, the situation is unusually involved and
delicate. Even this easygoing adventurer would pale and
shudder if he knew what we know—the horrid degree of
his illegitimacy.

But he is too deeply entangled in his self-delusion—
blinded and doomed as is the Calvinist minister in *La Symphonie pastorale*. His pious daughter, Antigone, trembles
with sinister forebodings—as did the minister's homely
wife—when she hears her tragic father rant about his "in-
fallible instinct" and about the private deity on whose
advice he depends. Antigone—a meek and heroic creature
akin to Alissa in *La Porte étroite*—agrees with Theresias
(and so does the author, we may presume) when he chides
the King for his sacrilegious self-assurance. "This ostensible
deity you pretend to carry about," grumbles the bilious
priest, "is your own ego, deified."

But when it comes to the last argument between the
priest and the King, Antigone as well as Gide is in favor
of Œdipus, for the first time without reservations. The
incestuous murderer accepts his fall and his castigation,
not only stoically, but with humble joy. He leaves the
City of Thebes, determined to communicate his inner light
to all people—whoever they are, wherever he may meet
them. His voice has the force and the persuasion of truth
when he announces his beautiful decision. The voice of
Theresias, on the contrary, sounds hard and loveless when
he snaps back, "It is not joy we should seek and transmit;
it is the salvation of our souls."

This time the man of the church is wrong; the martyr-
monarch is right. For he is no longer a monarch, only a

martyr; not a great man, just a man; just an eyeless wanderer among others, a stumbling pilgrim among many
equally blind, equally fallible. He has joined the chorus.
An anonymous beggar, he may find the Strait Gate that
leads to the real Kingdom.

The spiral line of Gide's development appears at times
erratic and confused. In *Œdipe*, and at this stage of his
biography in general, he resumes certain moods and trends
of the *Strait Is the Gate* epoch and fuses them with the
rationalistic and rebellious accents of *Les Caves du Vatican*
and *Les Faux-Monnayeurs*. That is to say, he varies and
revaluates one of his basic ideas, the ethic of sacrifice and
self-renunciation, and gives it a new meaning, a different
tendency. The polarity between two possible ways of individual behavior—namely, asceticism and hedonism—is
now replaced by the antagonism between unrestricted individualism and an individualism controlled and limited by
social responsibilities. The new theme, already sketched
in *The Counterfeiters*, further developed in *Geneviève* and
Œdipe, is not transcendental but human and practical.
For both notions at stake, freedom and discipline, belong
to a category which does not involve God directly. The
new conflict takes place on an earthly plane: among men,
so to speak; it hardly affects man's attitude towards the
Supreme Being. Irrelevant, perhaps, in the sphere of the
absolute, this dualism—personal liberty versus collective
interest—is greatly relevant to our worldly affairs, however
relative and transient they may be. Hence the sturdy,
realistic tenor of Gide's style at that time.

Not only the demon seems now to be banished from

Gide's heart and work; an estrangement from God, indeed, from Christ Himself, has evidently taken place as well. His new effort tends exclusively to the solution of human problems; no help from the divine authority is required. Humanistic pride and manly self-reliance prevent Gide's having, at this point, recourse to metaphysical props.

This new anti-mystic, anti-romantic, almost anti-religious orientation is noticeable, not only in his writings of that period but also in the selection of his reading material. It is now that his intimacy with Montaigne reaches its highest point—Montaigne, who repudiated so bravely and obstinately all supranatural comfort and advice. Gide's fine essay on the *Essays* dates from that epoch, 1929. Along with Montaigne's chivalrous and reasonable figure, his favorite companions are Goethe, La Fontaine, and Racine, Swift, Dryden, and Pope. The taste for Pope's didactic poetry is particularly characteristic. The Gide of that rationalistic interlude, between *Les Faux-Monnayeurs* and the communist adventure, comes palpably close when one reads and relishes a diary entry like the following one of 1930.

"I resume the delightful habit of reading a book while I walk—somewhat less attracted, just now, by the spectacle of the street. Pope walked with me, these days. I found these lines, in his *Essay on Criticism:*

> Those rules of old discovered, not devised,
> Are Nature still, but Nature methodised:
> Nature, like liberty, is but restrain'd
> By the same law which first herself ordained.

"Perfect; it couldn't be better. (What reasonable truth!

And how reasonably formulated! Completely anti-poetic. What's the difference?)"

Gide's enthusiasm about Pope's rhymed aphorism is noteworthy, not only, or not mainly, because of the literary taste it indicates. What he liked in this neatly couched commonplace is the dry realism with which the limitation of liberty is taken for granted.

This reasonable and inevitable restriction of freedom, necessitated by the interests of the community—could it not turn out to be compatible with the finest form of individualism? It was in speaking of Goethe that Gide coined the formula of *serviceable individualism:* "I do not mean slavish, but serviceable, ready to serve. He was a man of duty: yes, of duty towards himself. His apparent and obvious egotism leads him to it and submits to it. Those who have accused him of this egotism seem to me to have misunderstood the austere demands that a healthy individualism often implies."

"He was a man of duty." Thirty, or fifteen, years before, Gide would hardly have used these words to eulogize a great poet. Nor would he have said, in presenting the first novel of a young French writer: "I am particularly grateful to him for having elucidated this paradoxical truth, which seems to me of extraordinary psychological importance: that the happiness of man does not spring from freedom but lies in the acceptance of duty."

This remarkable statement occurs in Gide's preface to *Vol de nuit* by Saint-Exupéry (1931). In introducing a new literary name, Gide announces and defines a new phase of his own quest and effort—a new flight, a new adventure, the adventure of duty.

VIII. THE CRISIS

The time is out of joint: O cursed spite,
That ever I was born to set it right!
SHAKESPEARE

Il faut être sans loi pour écouter la loi nouvelle.
ANDRÉ GIDE

T H E authority of a writer is a capital that accumulates slowly, almost unnoticeably: it does not result from one sensational triumph but is due to a sum of imponderables. More is needed than just genius to make a real master; tenacity and faith, pedagogical intuition and patience are equally indispensable—especially patience, a great deal of it.

The true rank of a work of art does not depend on its immediate success but on its durability. Gide is wont to say that he hardly cares whether his new books are read; what matters is that they be reread when they are not new any more. He treasures the balance sheet of his publisher which indicates that five hundred copies of *Les Nourritures terrestres* were sold from 1897 to 1917—just five hundred in the course of twenty years! "The book was completely boycotted by the literary critics," Gide stated, forty years after the original publication. "As far as I remember there appeared only two articles about *Les Nourritures*—both by personal friends of mine. This would not be noteworthy,

if it were not for the extraordinary resonance my book was
to have subsequently. Today it exercises a considerable
influence on the young generation."

Neither boastful nor bashful, but in a casual, matter-of-
fact fashion, the aging master acknowledges the actual and
evident state of affairs. Everybody knows that he has never
run after fame: yet there it is; he has become one of the
great figures of world literature. All his gestures and experiments carry the weight of glory. Whatever he says
and does is eagerly discussed in the vanguard magazines,
book sections, and literary cafés of five continents. All his
major works are translated into all major languages. There
are critics, not only in France but also in distant countries,
who specialize in the exegesis of Gide's writings as if they
were *Das Kapital* by Marx or the Gospel. During a certain
period—say, from 1928 to 1938—the author of *Les Faux-
Monnayeurs* was more talked and written about than any
other modern writer, except, perhaps, Proust and Joyce.
For a while, the literature on Gide was considerably more
voluminous than his own output.

That is not to say that he idled. If he dodged all social
temptations and obligations that result from fame, he was
all the more conscientious about his literary responsibilities.
His correspondence assumed vast dimensions. He participated in public symposiums and polemics, wrote prefaces,
epitaphs, and book reviews. Many a striving talent has
been encouraged and criticized by this unflagging reader
and sensitive connoisseur. At the same time he took to
translating again: the first act of *Hamlet*, for instance,
could be featured in the bilingual magazine *Echange* as a
literary novelty, "French by André Gide."

In 1932, the *Nouvelle Revue Française* began to publish the monumental edition of his *Œuvres complètes*, presenting not only all his novels, novelettes, plays, and essays in their chronological sequence but also a profusion of miscellanies and the complete journal. The job of compiling and editing this bountiful material was handled with painstaking accuracy by a competent *famulus*, L. Martin-Chauffier. He was assisted, however, by the author himself, who supervised the layout of the fifteen portly volumes available up to now. (The luxurious enterprise, financially guaranteed by a small number of international subscribers, had to be discontinued, temporarily at least, on account of the political developments. Tome xv—the last one to come out—includes the *Journal*, from 1928 to 1932, the essay on Montaigne (1929), the "Notes about Chopin" (1931), and a selection of minor critical writings. The *L'Ecole des femmes* trilogy and *Œdipe* are scheduled for an additional volume promised for the near future.)

Martin-Chauffier had a hand also in the setup of a series of booklets, *Ne jugez pas!*, initiated and sponsored by André Gide. The idea was to present a collection of criminological cases to reaffirm and illustrate the tenets first put forward in the *Souvenirs de la Cour d'Assises*. "Surrender, Judge!" is the quintessence of Gide's message. "Give place to the doctor!" And to reveal the shortsightedness and inhumanity of modern jurisdiction, he submits meticulous reports on two cases—neither particularly exciting but both of symptomatic significance. *L'Affaire Redureau* and *La Sequestrée de Poitiers*—Gide's own contributions to the *Judge Not!* library—are convincing accounts; unassuming, candid, factual. It may be that they are somewhat lacking in artistic color and verve, which has to do, perhaps, with the fact that Gide dictated them. This new technique of production—new, as far as Gide is concerned—does not seem quite in keeping with the cadence and countenance of his style.

But then, this was not a climactical moment in Gide's literary career. He produced slowly, under difficulties. The diary entries concerning his current work sound indeed rather dreary. As soon as he left his desk, the thought of his forthcoming novel, *L'Ecole des femmes,* palled on him, became vapid and irrelevant. He might have postponed, or even renounced altogether, the conclusion of this novelette, if it had not been for the editors of an American magazine, *Forum.* Prodded by their trans-Atlantic persistence, Gide, half-grudgingly, half-amused, made a last minute effort and actually met the deadline.

His frame of mind and general state of health resembled the nervous depression he passed through during the years between *L'Immoraliste* and *La Porte étroite.* At once languid and erratic, he kept moving from the South of France to North Germany, from Paris to Munich, Zurich, or Tunisia. When Madame Gide expected him at Cuverville he would surprise friends in Biarritz or Toulon with improvised week-end visits. More cometary than ever, he showed up in Cambridge or Heidelberg, or disappeared completely, roving incognito through one of the territories between the North Sea and the Mediterranean.

Sometimes the foreign lands seemed even more difficult to bear than France with all her familiar pettiness and fatuity. In Germany, of course, there were always plenty of things to irk and puzzle an observant traveler. Italy was more than irritating with the hollow grandeur of its sham Empire. It was in Naples that Gide coined the striking formula, "architectural journalism," to characterize the showy palazzos from which the Fascist bureaucracy tyrannized over an easygoing, vain, and ignorant people.

Time and again the fatigued wanderer would seek recreation in one of the famed watering places. But the noisy ugliness of the bourgeois crowds in Karlsbad or Vittel got so painfully on his nerves that no salubrious well could make good such an annoyance. The situation became quite unbearable when the smarter ones of the hideous crowd tried to prove their sophistication by addressing Gide as "*cher maître*" and complimenting him on his books. The "dear master" writhed with embarrassment when a garrulous lady buttonholed him at the promenade or in the hotel lobby, cruelly determined to cry out her admiration for "your cute little novel, *Unfinished Symphony*," (meaning *La Symphonie pastorale*, probably), or to rave about "that masterpiece of yours, *A la Recherche du temps perdu*."

Were these the readers he was writing for? Did his audience consist of such fatuous snobs and smug Philistines? Was it to them he owed his fame? Was it for their sake he suffered and endeavored? Was it worth-while to work for the desultory pleasure of these decadent parasites? Was there no other form of society in which writers would be less disconnected and less derelict? As things stood now, the writer's social position was half that of a clown, half that of a pariah. Those well-to-do morons on the promenade or in the hotel lobby insulted the spirit, whether they ignored or cheered its creations.

The author's place and function within the framework of modern society—it was not the first time that Gide found himself haunted and preoccupied by this vital issue. It was in his most individualistic, anti-social period—in *1897*, the year of *Les Nourritures terrestres*—that he jotted down these revealing lines: "Gloom and lassitude. I want to serve the community, the State; I recognize its authority but I do not see what sort of service I could render to it. It seems that the State does not need us. It ought to need us, though. But how convince the State that it needs people such as I?"

It is the same apprehension we sense in the violent disquiet of Bernard, in *The Counterfeiters*. Like his juvenile hero, the aging Gide keeps looking for a route across the ocean, a formula to give life a new purpose and a new direction. Terrified by the disintegration and emptiness of modern society, the Gidean characters, and the sovereign intelligence that created them, long for a new ethical code, an inspiring and yet feasible creed, a bold and practicable scheme for which they could work and fight, a humanistic Utopia—daring and distant enough to incite their adventurous instincts, and yet near and actual enough to be loved, to be believed in, to be suffered for.

Neither *Les Faux-Monnayeurs* nor Gide's other writings, up to *1931*, contain any hints as to the coloring and shape this desired scheme would assume, if and when it was discovered or invented at last. The new order might have been religious and traditionalistic: there are elements in Gide's books that seem to intimate such possibilities. Or the Utopian program might have turned out to be a poetic phantasmagoria, playful, sensual, aristocratic. It would have been hazardous to predict, in view of *L'Immoraliste*, *La*

Porte étroite and *Les Caves du Vatican*, that the new order
to emerge from this long uncertainty was to be of a glaringly red hue—a socialist credo, a revolutionary design.

The first hint of this new development occurs in Gide's
diary, under the date of May 13, 1931. "Above all," he
notes, "I would like to live to see the Russian plan triumph
and the European peoples compelled to recognize what
has been so long and viciously slandered. How could such
a vast reorganization have been carried out without a
transient period of disorganization? Never before has my
mind been bent to the future with so passionate a curiosity.
I applaud wholeheartedly such a gigantic and yet entirely
human effort."

It is not yet a definite declaration of faith; a new mood
rather than a new determination. A few months later Gide
is struck by the beauty and purity of certain war letters
written by German soldiers, in 1914, and published subsequently. "I have often said," Gide adds, after having
praised some especially fine samples of the German collection, "that there are much more decent men than we
think usually—men capable of heroism, sacrifice, and so
forth. . . . And that is what prevents me from being revolutionary, or rather, which renders it so difficult for me to
abandon myself completely to my revolutionary impulses.
I can wish for the coming victory of communism; but,
while doing so, I can still disapprove of the horrible methods proposed by the Communists for the attainment of
their objectives. I could hardly embrace a philosophy
according to which noble ends justify ugly and cruel
means. It's all right to tell me that one cannot attain certain
things without acquiescing in certain others. But how, if

this preparatory stage is too dreadful to pass through? . . .
It is good to know that in Russia at least these hideous
'requirements' have already been carried out. May the
lofty ends be secured, solidly and for good, so that it will
not be necessary henceforth to have recourse to the hateful
means!"

If this statement still sounds somewhat conditional and
reserved, the tenor of Gide's pro-Soviet proclamations will
soon become more decided and more provocative. In
1932, he interrupts himself in telling a psychological anec-
dote which he had meant to report in a detailed way: "For
I do not want my journal to deal exclusively with the
Soviet Union. And yet there seems to be nothing else I am
really interested in." And in the fall of 1933, stirred and
alarmed by the ominous developments in Germany and
elsewhere, he speaks already like an experienced fellow-
traveler. His message to the "Committee for the World
Congress of Youth against War and Fascism" might as well
have been formulated by an editor of *L'Humanité, New
Masses, Pravda,* or *Die Rote Fahne.* The fastidious author
of *La Porte étroite* speaks like any propagandist when he
asserts that the only "Soviet propaganda" there is does not
consist of words but obtains its efficacy from facts—the
glorious, self-evident, irrefutable facts of the Soviet reality: "The example of the October Revolution has made
the peoples aware of the state of suppression and wretchedness in which they are kept by the capitalist system."

No wonder that the public was astounded to hear so
fierce and primitive a jargon from André Gide, the matchless master of suggestive overtones and iridescent subtleties.
He who had been evasive and noncommittal, drifting from

one complicated uncertainty to the next, appeared now all resolution and aggressiveness. His statements, far from being airy and enigmatic, became almost shockingly blunt. Asked how he managed to reconcile the philosophy of Montaigne and the doctrines of Lenin, he replied succinctly that it was by no means his ambition to marry these two humanistic visions: they follow one another.

So now it was Lenin's turn, according to André Gide? The rumors, then, were correct? He had made up his mind? He had made his choice? Taken a stand at last? He adhered to the political and philosophical orthodoxy of the Comintern—or didn't he? It was a conversion—or wasn't it? Gide insisted it wasn't.

"Don't speak of conversion!" he admonished the excited commentators. "I have not changed my direction. I have always marched straight ahead, and continue to do so. But for a long time I could not see anything ahead of me, save the reflection of my own fervor. Now, I have a goal again. I feel that my vague longings take on a definite shape and that my dream is on the point of becoming reality."

It sounded convincing enough. The term "conversion" was, perhaps, an inadequate simplification. Was the word "evolution" more appropriate to define Gide's newest adventure? Yes and no, he said, and explained in a detailed way why he did not think the image of "evolution" really pertinent to describe the experience he passed through. This experience, he said—his new faith in communism—was not only derived from his primary and basic creed—Christianity—but was its direct continuation and consequence, not to say its fulfillment. "What you call my 'conversion' or my 'evolution' springs logically and organically from this initial Christian formation (or deformation?) of my mind."

He who had repudiated, solemnly and obstinately, the Catholic creed *on account of the Gospel,* now yielded to the anti-religious doctrine of Karl Marx, *on account of the Gospel.* Or rather, it was not the Marxian philosophy that attracted and captivated him in the socialist ethos; his attitude towards that founding father of "scientific-revolutionary materialism" remains chilly or becomes downright inimical. "The climate in the writings of Karl Marx is suffocating to me," he admits, in the middle of his "Marxist" period. "There is something lacking, I don't know what kind of ozone indispensable to my mental respiration."

And he draws the candid, paradoxical conclusion: "I found my way to communism thanks to the Gospel—not thanks to Karl Marx."

"I still am the simple Christian I have always been," Gide emphasized, while the reactionary press shuddered over his ostensible "conversion to atheism." In reality, he remained faithful to both his devotion to Christ and his animosity to the Christian churches. Communism, as he conceived and stylized it, appears more akin to the original Christian message than is the rigid dogmatism of the Catholic Church. Do you not see, André Gide wondered, that communism, too, is a form of religion—a religion, that is, without mythology: a reasonable religion. Gide's vision confirms the prophecy of the anticlerical mystic, Sören Kierkegaard, who predicted that "that which had a political countenance and imagined itself to be political, will one day be unmasked as a religious movement."

But, presuming that Gide's pietist past was compatible with his revolutionary present, does not even this religious version of the socialist creed betray and contradict his former individualistic tenets?

Gide's diary—his highly important *Nouvelles Pages de journal, 1932-1935*—anticipates and refutes this objection. "The individual, even today, is infinitely more interesting to me than the masses," Gide asserts, in 1932, at the peak of his communist enthusiasm. "What matters above all, however, is to organize the living conditions of the masses in such a way that the sound development of the individual would be guaranteed."

There is a change, no doubt, in the vistas and requirements of this great individualist—a change which he admits expressly and the vital character of which he stresses again and again. The pivotal, profound change is this, according to the *Nouvelles Pages de journal:* "Up to very recently I believed that the primary necessity was to transform man; that the revolutionary process ought to start in the sphere of individual life. That is why I wrote that the moral question was of greater significance than the social question. Today I am positive that the individual cannot change, unless the social conditions invite and enable him to do so: which means that we ought to occupy ourselves with them— that is, the social conditions—above all and before anything else."

To define and to propagate a religious form of communism and a socialist form of individualism—this, then, was Gide's task, at this juncture of his ambitious quest. Moreover, he insisted on the supremacy of truth, on the absolute integrity of the spirit, even while admitting and emphasizing the revolutionary-propagandistic function and mission of literature. An unrealistic, servile intelligence is hardly apt to serve the cause of progress. The efficacy and persuasion of art, science, and philosophy depend entirely on their detachment, their incorruptibility. "There is a certain intellectual honesty," (*une certaine honnêteté de l'esprit*) Gide insists, "which the young Communists must not betray for opportunistic reasons. Honesty, probity, truthfulness are laical virtues, the exercise of which demonstrates the righteousness of our cause."

No wonder that Gide's monologues, during the period of his affiliation with the Comintern, have at times apprehensive overtones. There are despondent moments, hypochondriacal veins, when the author of the *Nouvelles Pages de journal* conceives his new preoccupation with social issues as a direct result of his artistic sterility. "Why should I fool myself?" he broods, in such downhearted hours. "Those issues simply replace the creative demon, who has long withdrawn from my mind." At once proud and discouraged, he compares his own development with Tolstoi's, who would not have dallied with dubious political programs, if his genius had still been pregnant, at the time, with such colossal visions as *War and Peace* and *Anna Karenina*.

Like the aging Tolstoi, the Tolstoi in decline, Gide comes to questioning the validity and timeliness of art as such. The vagaries and visions of the artistic genius seem appallingly void and flighty, in view of the weight and vastness of our actual conflicts and the actual sufferings of our fellowmen, everywhere. Art has to be "disinterested" and aloof, or else it ceases to be art. "But whoever

remains contemplative and detached, these days," says
Gide, "discloses an inhuman philosophy or a monstrous
blindness."

I recall having heard many utterances of a similar kind
from Gide directly. His personal conversation confirmed
what his diary suggests in such grave, sorrowful accents:
his searchings and doubts as regards the significance, or
insignificance, of literary efforts at this critical moment of
history. The following account from Julian Green's journal (under the date of March 15, 1932) is as typical as any
dialogue I might recollect. "Saw Gide this afternoon. He
told me that he cannot concentrate his thoughts on anything, except Russia and Communism. What is the use of
producing books? It seems meaningless, considering the
tremendous events to take place in the world. I asked him
whether this state of affairs is disturbing to him. 'No,' he
said, 'I find it exalting.' "

There are, indeed, accents of true and powerful exaltation in the slim but dynamic book which Gide concluded
in that time, notwithstanding his profound skepticism as
to the relevance of his poetic message.

Les Nouvelles Nourritures (1936) is conceived and presented as a direct continuation of Les Nourritures terrestres,
from which it resumes and develops many images and
ideas. Just because of its intimate and deliberate affinity
with Gide's early work, Les Nouvelles Nourritures testifies,
most eloquently and most movingly, to both the organic
unity and rich versatility of his genius. Every detail in this
extraordinary manifesto—one of the most arresting things,
no doubt, Gide has ever written—is at once daringly new

and familiar. We recognize, with tender gratitude, the unmistakable tenets and intonations of Gide's youthful credo, widened, deepened, intensified, all imbued with a new revolutionary purport and pathos.

There they are again, the glowing raptures of the vernal days, the sweeping gestures of cosmic tenderness and immeasurable delight. Once more, life is glorified as the mystery of mysteries, the joy of joys, the incomparable, inscrutable adventure. *"Tu ne t'étonnes peut'être pas assez de vivre,"* André Gide said to Nathanaël. Now he addresses the same lyrical admonition to somebody whom he calls "comrade," as the name Nathanaël sounds too unreal and too plaintive.

"Omit everything that is only plaintive or only playful!" the revolutionary Gide urges his imaginary comrade. "Try to organize your life in a way that renders all complaints superfluous. Do not beg from others what you can conquer and accomplish yourself.

"I have had my life," says the aging poet. "Now, it's your turn, my comrade. All my faith, all my hopes are with you."

It sounds like a farewell, and yet *Les Nouvelles Nourritures* exhales the spirit of youth. The author who commands such a style and such a confidence has remained youthful, for all his experienced wisdom.

Only a youthful heart is capable of the effusive gratitude which Gide cries out to this creation and to the Creator. His fervent, bewildered love for this "astonishing earth"— what is it if not a form of religious ecstasy? His prayer has the whole passion and purity of his early impetrations as he invokes Him whom he never ceased to seek and to adore: *"Je reviens à vous, Seigneur Christ, comme à Dieu dont vous êtes la forme vivante. Je suis las de mentir à mon coeur. C'est vous que je retrouve partout, alors que je croyais vous fuir, ami divin de mon enfance."*

The entrancing authenticity of these words is not affected by the vagueness of Gide's emotional pantheism as we find it formulated in certain passages of his book. He sounds like a disciple of Spinoza, or like Goethe's Faust, when he identifies God and Nature. It is remarkable, however, that his idolatry of the material and mortal world somehow implies the faith in the immaterial, immortal Creator. "It is more difficult than one would believe not to believe in God," says Gide, after having passed through a period of relative indifference toward the Supreme Being.

Yes, he has remained young; he is young again. He believes in the mysteries of Creation, Joy, and Motion. But his cult of joy no longer is the selfish hedonism in which he used to indulge. Now the postulate of joy has become something like a social program. The relishing of irresponsible sensations is not recognized as joy any more. "My happiness consists in increasing the happiness of others," says Gide, who once contented himself with vagrant, noncommittal delights. "I need the general happiness to be happy myself."

This explains what he means when speaking of an "imperative obligation to be happy"—an essentially moral obligation which he strongly feels and joyfully accepts. And, again: "I have long understood that joy is something infinitely rarer, more difficult, and more beautiful than sadness. . . . And I decided to be happy."

Nature indicates that man is destined to attain happiness:

what is life if not the pursuit of joy? And the term, "joy," is to be conceived in its sublimest and coarsest sense, as mystic enthusiasm and also as primitive amativeness. We recognize the rampant sensuality of *Les Nourritures terrestres* when Gide proclaims, in the *Nouvelles Nourritures*, that he has obtained more instruction from lust than from books. "It is in the ecstasy of the flesh that we become most intensely conscious of our own being."

And yet his concept of love has undergone a crucial modification, while maintaining its unabated impact of carnal lust. But the cosmic lover is not satisfied any more with embracing and praising the universe; he has become eager, at this point, to participate in its organization and in its improvement. He is enough of a Marxist to agree that it behooves the philosopher to change the reality of this life, not just to define its causalities.

For he who sings "the Body Electric" cannot but be interested in the physical well-being, whether present or future, of the living masses, the masses to be born, "the armies of those I love," to quote Walt Whitman—particularly pertinent in this context. The voice of the American poet, which resounded through the dithyrambs of *Les Nourritures terrestres*, is recognizable in many a formulation of the inspired sequel.

Gide, who formerly joined Whitman in his sensual exaltations and echoed the ebullient tunes of *Calamus*, now sings with him, "Victory, union, faith, identity, time, the indissoluble compacts, riches, mystery, Eternal progress, the cosmos, and the modern reports."

There it is, the word Gide avoided, almost as anxiously and consistently as the word "Democracy": *Progress:* the tritest word and the greatest. It had become stale and hollow, the magic word that inspired our ancestors. "Why, I could jeer at progress as well as the next fellow, even as well as Flaubert." Gide's assertion sounds convincing enough, especially when he continues: "The bourgeois idolatry of progress got on our nerves—naturally it did. Progress of business and industry! Progress of art—what stupidity! Progress of knowledge, all right. But what really matters is the progress of man himself."

The notion of progress, if conceived and interpreted by a profound and passionate spirit, is ample and flexible enough to focus and integrate the whole complexity of modern thought. Gide could recognize the essential features and motive powers of his philosophy in this simple formula, *Progress:* his ardent love for changes and experiments, his cult of motion, his dynamic restlessness, the vagrant and virile energy of his approach to life. Alissa, the gentle and spirited heroine of *La Porte étroite*, already understood what her author now reaffirms with such captivating eloquence: that happiness is not a state but a movement; that we cannot, and must not, imagine a form of bliss that is not *progressive*. Alissa's pilgrimage, too, was progress; but a progress towards metaphysical goals, a transcendental quest, aimless and endless according to the logic and the interests of this life. The generous frenzy of her sacrifice assumes a new purport and significance, it becomes reasonable and meaningful in the light and under the influence of this new social credo. The wasteful and floating motion is finally disciplined, oriented towards attainable ends, like a cataract the dynamics of which have been dominated and rendered serviceable. "The individual never affirms himself more definitely than when forgetting and abandoning himself." Gide resumes his old tenet, the living gist of his creed, with a new urgency and a new ethos.

Man has to overcome the limitations of his selfishness to live up to his intrinsic potentialities. Progress means the striving for self-identification and self-fulfillment, the ultimate humanization of the human race. The belief in progress implies the belief in man and the belief in Utopia.

Gide takes certain "realistic" young people to task for their sterile, superstitious fear of that inspiring term, Utopia. Petty and faithless minds are afraid of losing their dignity when adhering to "utopian" ideals and programs. "As if not every great progress of man were due to realized Utopia!" Gide exclaims. "As if the reality of tomorrow could be anything but the result of today's Utopia! A future that would merely repeat the present conditions of life—that is indeed the one prospect I consider unbearable."

Love and reason, common sense and faith are necessary to promote and finally fulfill Utopia. Only a movement in which those energies—emotional ardor and constructive will—are organically combined—only such a movement has a chance to serve Progress and Utopia. And there was only one movement that lived up to these requirements, according to the Gide of the early thirties—the Communist International. "The voices of my heart and of my intelligence compel me to choose this path—the path of communism," he proclaims in *Les Nouvelles Nourritures*. "Enthusiasm and reason make me abide by this program. It may be that the voice of reason is even stronger in me, at this point, than any emotional motive. And if it has depressed me, at times, to see certain Communists indulge in cold abstractions, another fallacy seems now equally grave to me—that is, to perceive and emphasize exclusively the sentimental impact of the communist doctrines."

He speaks of fallacies but fails to grasp his own. How admirably young he is!—this extraordinary old boy of almost seventy. With generous naïveté and disarming innocence, he confounds his solitary vision with a political orthodoxy; he tries to coördinate his daring dreams and the unscrupulous tactics of the Comintern. Did he not foresee the inevitable fiasco of his high-minded, ill-starred experiment? Blind and bold, a lovable and slightly ridiculous Don Quixote, he plunged into this dangerous, absurd adventure.

André Gide, addressing a Communist mass meeting—one must have watched this curious spectacle to realize the foolhardiness of his political escapade. How bashful and yet haughty, how movingly isolated and out of place he appeared among all those glib or violent agents of a powerful party machine! The speakers preceding and following him recited their perfunctory variations of current party-line slogans. Gide spoke out what he thought to be true and important. He said simple and serious things, in a simple and serious manner. Renouncing all rhetorical devices and intellectual fireworks, he insisted on a few vital points— that Fascism is evil; that another imperialistic war would be a major disaster; that the fighting republics of Spain and China deserve the moral and material support of all decent people; that the means of production should be socialized; that Hitler, Franco, and Mussolini are wicked and dangerous men; and that social conditions have to be reorganized, or else human culture is doomed.

None of these disclosures can have been very startling to a proletarian audience. What startled and moved them was rather the sacerdotal gravity with which these truisms were conveyed and formulated. If Gide's political speeches were lacking in news-value, the fact that he delivered them was big news in itself. The author of *Les Cahiers d'André Walter* and of *L'Immoraliste* haranguing the workmen from the "red suburbs"! The illustrious æsthete and intellectual aristocrat, joining in the oratory of Henri Barbusse, Marcel Cachin, Vaillant-Couturier, and other notorious comrades! It was indeed something to get excited about.

The hullabaloo assumed sweeping proportions. Everybody, all parties and coteries, had to contribute their bit of approval or disapproval in respect to Gide's stunning performance. The Stalinists, needless to say, triumphed and jubilated. Their propaganda machinery, geared up to a staggering pitch, blared and raved about this sensational, miraculous, incredible, logical, symbolic, meaningful, amazing conversion. The very embodiment of bourgeois culture embraces the doctrine of the glorious proletariat! Celebrated artist abandons ivory tower! Grand old man of French letters finds his way to the camp of the future and the revolution! Greatest living writer recognizes greatest statesman of all times, Joseph Stalin! The fact that Gide paid homage to the Little Father in Moscow was sufficient proof, in the opinion of the Communists, of his, Gide's, literary genius. Party scribblers who had never read a book by the newly discovered comrade went suddenly into raptures about *Les Caves du Vatican* and, even more vehemently, about *Voyage au Congo*, which was vaunted as a revolutionary classic. Paul Nizan wrote in *L'Humanité* (the official organ of the Communist Party in France) that Gide had really been a communist for a number of years, unwittingly and by stealth. Ilya Ehrenburg, the most gifted literary agent of the Kremlin in Western Europe, praised Gide with enthusiastic sagacity. The left-wing vanguard, splendidly represented by André Malraux and Louis Aragon, congratulated themselves on this powerful asset to the intellectual People's Front.

Outside of the Party, however, the reaction to Gide's red extravaganza was less favorable. Not only the reactionary jingoists jeered and scolded; the anti-Stalin revolutionaries and adherents to Leon Trotski were equally shocked and angered. One of them, Claude Naville, devoted a whole pamphlet to the issue of *André Gide et le Communisme* (1935). To him, Gide's affiliation with the "Stalinist reaction" was a *"malentendu dramatique,"* a glaring blunder due to a basic misconception. What a dilettante Gide was to imagine his "socialist individualism" would be tolerated, in the long run, by the rigid Party bureaucracy! Did he really believe the Kremlin wanted strong and independent personalities? It was not without a grim laughter that Claude Naville asked this question.

And not only Gide would be disappointed, according to Naville's prediction. The Comintern, too, should beware of their new herald and favorite. Did they expect him to renounce for good his metaphysical caprices? How could they hope to make a reliable partisan out of an obstinate old nonconformist? Did they forget the spiritual sources from which Gide's character and philosophy were derived? He was a disciple of Nietzsche and Dostoevski, Wilde and Mallarmé—wasn't he? What could be more remote from Marxism than the heritage of these masters! What could be less Marxian than Gide's message and faith!

The radical young polemicist proved with incisive wit the infeasibility of the alliance between André Gide and the Third International. His exposé, the last work of a spirited fighter who died before his manifesto was published, is rich in striking definitions and testifies to both the revolutionary fervency of the author and his sympathetic familiarity with Gide's thought and work. This anti-Gidean and anti-Stalinist pamphlet reveals indeed a more profound socialist ethos and a more intimate knowledge of Gide's character than do most of the Party-inspired eulogies that appeared about the same time. The booklet by Maurice Sachs, *André Gide* (1936), is one of these trite and one-sided documents. Mr. Sachs attempts to be popular and concise, but succeeds only in being shallow and primitive. A handful of Marxist clichés do not suffice to analyze and to evaluate so rich and intricate a phenomenon as are the writings of André Gide. To adorn the title page of a book on Gide with a Stalin sentence is in itself an embarrassing *faux pas*, especially when this motto reads as follows: "For the proletariat, there is but one way to attain the Revolution—the way of the Communist Party; but every intellectual can join the revolutionary forces in his own fashion."

The most thorough and most revealing examination of Gide's communism took place under the auspices of a Catholic group, the *Union pour la Vérité*. Some of the most prominent Catholic writers—François Mauriac, Jacques Maritain, Gabriel Marcel, Henri Massis, and others —participated in the extensive debate, which was attended also by several liberal authors, such as Jean Guéhenno and Ramon Fernandez, who has a brilliant book about Gide to his credit. The date of the meeting was January 23, 1935. Gallimard (the publisher of the *Nouvelle Revue Française*) presented subsequently the complete record of the discussion in the form of a booklet, *André Gide et notre temps*, one of the most substantial contributions to the voluminous André Gide literature.

The debate develops on a remarkably elevated level. I cannot but admire the civilized moderation displayed by the Catholic speakers, considering the provocative tenor of certain anti-Catholic statements made by Gide, shortly before the meeting. "Religion and family are the two worst enemies of progress," he proclaimed in the published version of his diary. And: "Do you think that Christ would recognize himself today in His Church? It is in the name of Christ that we should oppose the clergy. It is not He who is hateful but the religious system built up after Him."

Severe words, these, and not easy to take for a devout son of the Holy Church. Yet those present agreed unanimously (including even Gide's most intransigent antagonist, Henri Massis) that the author of *Les Faux-Monnayeurs* commanded the greatest intellectual and artistic authority of all modern French writers—together with Paul Claudel, whose work had been discussed at the preceding conference of the Union. Nobody demurred when Ramon Fernandez suggested, in his penetrating introductory speech, that André Gide represented to French youth and to the international intelligentsia, much more than a literary style —namely, a style of life, a fashion of behavior, a complex and vital philosophy. Renan and Barrès were the two last ones, according to Fernandez, who had exercised a similar influence on the spiritual élite of the nation. Not even Massis contradicted. The speakers began to dissent from each other when it came to appraising the moral validity of this undeniable influence.

Massis, whose rôle was naturally that of an accuser, compared Gide's moral, or immoral, attitude with Barrès', and pointed out why he preferred the latter. Barrès, he held, was striving for self-perfection; Gide, for self-justification. "What really matters, however, is not that we justify ourselves but that we try to perfect ourselves. According to Gide's advice, we ought to accept our characters the way they happen to be; it is through this message that Gide, the artist, could become a 'reformer.' His reform rests entirely on his individual ethics. But after having accomplished everything attainable in this line; after having formulated a philosophy of man which may have had a liberating effect in certain cases but a literally mortal one in others; after having gone as far as possible in the direction of liberty, Gide felt compelled to fix on a cause transcending his own ego. He needed a new *raison d'être* to continue life. That is why he submitted himself to the communist orthodoxy."

This is the leitmotiv throughout the whole discussion: Gide's sensational "act of faith," its psychological reasons and moral implications. If the exposé made by Henri Massis is the most acute and most mordant contribution to this colorful symposium, it is Ramon Fernandez who finds the most sympathetic phrases to explain Gide's development. "The acceptance of a discipline coming after liberation is by no means a paradox," Fernandez points out. "Gide could accept a sound and practicable order after having struggled so long to get rid of a morality he deems sterile and obsolete."

He refers in this context also to an essential quality of Gide's artistic style—its tendency toward the dialectic reconciliation of seemingly incompatible contrasts. *Le Retour de l'enfant prodigue*, says Fernandez, is a typical example of this musical method of interweaving contradictory themes—in this case, the Christian element and its pagan counterpart. He might have mentioned also *Les Nouvelles Nourritures*, which seems to me the mature pendant to the *Prodigal Son*, equaling that early masterpiece in the purity of its texture and in the entrancing complexity of its ideological and emotional intimations.

The work of art is a magic mirror: it can solve problems, simply by reflecting them. In creations such as *Le Retour de l'enfant prodigue* and *Les Nouvelles Nourritures* the confusions and contradictions of the human drama in general, and of André Gide's drama in particular, are disentangled, purified, transfigured, by the heavenly touch of art. This artistic solution, however, is relevant only to the artistic sphere. Its validity becomes dubious when tested in the cold light of sober discussion. The same problems which, transformed into images, had ceased to be perturbing, become heavy and painful again. The artistic or artificial harmony fades away; we are confronted once more with actual confusions, palpable contradictions.

The chairman of the *Union pour la Vérité* conference asked Gide whether he thought his concept of "communist individualism" a logical and feasible program. "It seems," said the chairman, a certain M. G. Guy-Grand, "that your personal liberty is what you cherish more than anything . . ."

"I beg your pardon," Gide interrupted him. "The value I cherish more than anything is my art."

A few minutes later he confessed that he felt paralyzed as an artist since he had become a Communist. Asked by François Mauriac what prevented him from producing art, he answered: "What prevents me from writing is my fear of the index. Don't misunderstand me! I don't mean the exterior index. What disturbs me is my own anxiety to keep in line. The fear of transgressing the norm can become quite upsetting, once you have recognized that the norm is good. I have always been strictly opposed to all kinds of orthodoxy. Even now the Marxian orthodoxy seems as dangerous to me as any other; dangerous for the work of art at least. But as I am convinced that the Marxist orthodoxy is useful or even indispensable to guarantee the establishment of a new social order, I think it worth-while to sacrifice art, for the time being at least. The Party Line is necessary, perhaps. But, of course, an artist cannot work according to any line."

The devout Catholics present should have sympathized with his scruples and apprehensions. Gide's "fear of the index" must have sounded alarmingly familiar to many of them. And, in fact, they proved not without understanding for the intricacies of the Gidean conflict. The young revolutionary, Claude Naville, is right when he says in his pamphlet on *André Gide and Communism*, "François Mauriac, Henri Massis, Jacques Maritain, and other Catholic writers, at least tried very earnestly to understand Gide's conversion, although they could not approve of it. As for Louis Aragon, Vaillant-Couturier, and their comrades, they certainly approved of Gide's attitude but they did not even try to understand it. They just received the convert with open arms, with yells of admiration and fatuous flatteries. But this whole uproar was staged only for political reasons. The comrades utterly failed to appreciate the gravity of Gide's gesture, the meaning and the limitations of which they still completely ignore."

This was written about one year before Gide went to Moscow, following an invitation of the Soviet authorities.

The party accompanying Gide to the Soviet Union, in June, 1936, consisted mostly of intimate friends—Pierre Herbart (a young writer close to Gide for a number of years); Jacques Schiffrin (publisher, editor, man of letters, member of the inner circle of the *Nouvelle Revue Française*, director of the fine *Bibliothèque de la Pleiade*); Eugène Dabit (a young novelist of the popular-naturalistic school; literary protégé of Gide; author of some remarkable books—*L'Hôtel du Nord*, *Villa Oasis*, etc.); Louis Guilloux (as a novelist even more widely recognized than Dabit, but on less cordial terms with Gide); and, finally, as the one non-French member of the group, the young Dutchman, Jef Last, a proletarian writer of nervous talent, whose novel, *Zuiderzee*, had been much discussed, even outside the Netherlands.

Jef Last, in contrast to Gide's other companions, was not a political amateur but a sturdy professional. A member of the Communist Party, he had been in Russia before (his trip with Gide was his fourth one) and was in a position to converse with the natives without the assistance of an interpreter. He had been a sailor, and a soldier of the Spanish Republic, and a nuisance to the Dutch Government. His friendship with Gide began about one year before the Russian journey. Gide, at the peak of his Red enthusiasm, was particularly sensible to the popular wit, and to the almost savage vitality, of the husky rebel from Amsterdam. The contact with Jef Last was not without influence on the development of Gide's political adventure. The Dutch revolutionary was among those who initiated and prepared the Soviet tour. But, while he still stuck in general to the Party Line, he had already begun to dissent from certain trends and tactics of the Stalin Administration. If Last was at first instrumental in encouraging and intensifying Gide's pro-Communist inclination, he subsequently shared and fostered Gide's disappointment about what he saw in the Soviet Union.

This disappointment was inevitable, perhaps, considering the immoderate expectations Gide harbored when going to Russia. He was seeking the Utopian land, and what he found was just reality; as corrupt, bloody, woeful, and problematic as reality is always and everywhere. "What a distance between imagination and fact!" Lafcadio exclaims, in *Les Caves du Vatican*. And it is not only a distance that lies between imagination and reality, it is also a shadow.

Between the idea
And the reality
Between the motion
And the act
Falls the Shadow.

The shadow invoked in T. S. Eliot's poetic lament seems to darken Gide's Russian journey from its beginning to its end. It can manifest itself in many different forms, this murky companion, the shadow of disillusion. At times it appears in the prosaic disguise of boredom and irritation, in other moments it may assume the bleak grandeur of death.

The first speech Gide delivered in Moscow was a funeral oration. The State burial of Maxim Gorki, on June 20, 1936, was a grand, official affair, with a great deal of well-staged pomp and the usual mourning rhetoric. Gide joined the impressive array of speakers gathered at the Red Square. His speech is rather on the dreary side, conventional and grandiose, full of ornate clichés. He had no business to speak in Gorki's honor, anyhow. Why should the author of *Les Nourritures terrestres* pay homage to a Marxist fanatic and intransigent Puritan who defamed Nietzsche as a "morbid parasite"? What Gorki had to say about Dostoevski sounds hardly more polite or more intelligent. The author of *La Porte étroite* has almost nothing in common with an obtuse materialist who proclaimed that "in the Soviet Union the antagonism between faith and knowledge has long ceased to exist. Faith results from the consciousness man has of his own intellectual forces, and this faith, which creates heroes, will never create gods."

In no other period of his life, and in no country except the Soviet Union, would Gide have agreed to celebrate a writer, whether dead or alive, whose work and character are so strange or almost hostile to him. But in Moscow he was all compliance and courtesy. He who had always loathed and avoided big dinners, official inspections, gala performances at the opera, and the like, now allowed his guides to drag him from one sumptuous and tiresome occasion to another. A female functionary named Bola was in charge of André Gide and his party. I happen to know her: she couldn't be more jolly and enterprising. An excellent girl, at once dynamic and motherly, she shadowed and chaperoned the French visitors wherever they happened to go, and they did go places.

Gide inspected collective farms and sanatoriums, public libraries and the new Moscow subway, literary clubs and factories, picture galleries, battleships, and the famous recreation centers called "Parks of Culture." He inspected everything, unflaggingly, enthusiastically. He addressed organized novelists, organized students, and organized workingmen. The speech he had prepared for the writers in Leningrad turned out to be unduly bold, not to say heretic. He was naïve enough to believe that he would be welcome to discuss the issue of literature and opposition; or rather, the question he meant to tackle is whether literature can flourish when it is compelled to accept or even to glorify the official order.

Gide was advised, as tactfully and politely as possible, that this wouldn't be quite the right kind of thing to say, under the circumstances. Obediently, he composed another speech, much less interesting than the first one.

Michael Koltzov—at the time a kind of unofficial Minister of Propaganda in the Soviet Union—put a special Pullman car at the disposal of the Parisian guests. Each of the six gentlemen occupied his own little sleeping compartment. The meals were served in a spacious drawing-room. The food was delicious, the whole arrangement as comfortable as could be. The only pity was that the travelers had no opportunity to meet the less privileged passengers in the neighboring cars.

Gide thought Moscow an unusually ugly city. What he liked in Leningrad were, according to his own report, the souvenirs of St. Petersburg. They toured the country, visited the Caucasus, the cities of Tiflis and Batum, and the little town named Gori where Joseph Stalin was born. In Sebastopol, Eugène Dabit contracted scarlet fever and died there, on August 21, 1936. It was a saddening loss to Gide. He had been fond of this modest and serious companion.

The Shadow . . . The shadow over all earthly things; the shadow over Gide's journey.

Yet those who watched and guided him during the expedition were under the impression that he enjoyed himself. He seemed interested in everything, always alert and observant, quivering with curiosity. He studied rare plants in the forests of the Caucasus and the living conditions of the *Besprizornis*, the homeless children who had been one of the most alarming problems of the young Soviet Republic and still remained a perturbing feature of Russian life. He took notes about the anti-religious movement, the literary tastes of Russian workers, and the principles of recent Soviet legislation. He smiled graciously when people told him they had read one of his books in Russian translation. No doubt, he was having the time of his life.

All friends and propagandists of the Soviet Union were looking forward to the publication of Gide's travel account. But when *Retour de l'U. R. S. S.* came out, late in the fall of 1936, the same people wished that they had never heard the name of André Gide and that André Gide had never heard the word "Communism." The slim pamphlet, launched by the publisher Gallimard in a vast, inexpensive edition, turned out to be an unexpected blow to the cause of the Soviet Union.

Did Gide write his booklet *against* Communist Russia?

An active Party member and mediocre writer, André Wurmser, answered this question, rather wittily, in his extensive essay *L'U. R. S. S. jugée par André Gide* (published in *Commune*, January, 1937).

"Everybody remembers," he writes, "the laconic reply of the child who came home from Church and was asked what the pastor had been talking about.

" 'About sin,' said the child.

" 'And what did he say about sin?'

" 'He's against it.'

"It would certainly be unfair to judge Gide's book in the same laconic fashion. ('What does Gide talk about?' 'About the Soviet Union.' 'What does he say about the Soviet Union?' 'He's against it.') But this unfair simplification, if it is made, is not without sound foundation."

True, Gide uses the past tense, in the Preface to his pamphlet, when speaking of his devotion to the Fatherland of All Proletarians: "In our hearts and in our thoughts we confounded, resolutely, the glorious effort of the Soviet Union and the very future of culture. We repeated these things, over and over again. We wished that we could still believe in them." But the following pages, the opening chapter of the book itself, seem to indicate that the author has not yet lost faith in the Russian experiment. Right in the beginning Gide dwells on the "profound joy" he experienced when watching the serene and self-assured crowds in Moscow's "Parks of Culture." He appears equally delighted by other institutions, especially by the children's camps he visited, which he found full of healthy and handsome youngsters.

Gide's *Back from the Soviet Union* reads at first like a hearty panegyric. We are told that the people over there look beamingly happy; that they are hospitable and intelligent, eager to improve, joyful and polite. After this cordial introduction the scathing criticism of the subsequent parts sounds all the more perplexing. This disapprobation, first mildly and carefully phrased, becomes increasingly violent, in a furious crescendo. What commences on page 30 as a gentle reservation, has on page 60 the wrathful tone of an outright indictment. Towards the end of his essay Gide speaks of a "petty-bourgeois spirit" which, allegedly, prevails in Soviet Russia, and which, in Gide's opinion, is "profoundly and completely counter-revolutionary." And he continues: "But what they call 'counter-revolutionary' in the S. U. today is something entirely different. In fact, it is about the contrary. The spirit now considered 'counter-revolutionary' is the very spirit of revolution—the ferment which once made explode the decaying system of Czarism."

What grieved and irritated Gide most during his stay in Russia were two features of Soviet life, both particularly strange and repugnant to him, conformism and complacency. All Soviet citizens the French visitor came in touch with had the same ready-made, standardized, impersonal thoughts, and all of them thought themselves and their régime too fine and efficient for words. Gide was shocked and bewildered by the general ignorance in respect to conditions abroad. He met people who believed in all earnestness that Moscow was the only city on earth that possessed a subway. When the traveler dared refer to the good old Paris *Métro*, his Russian friends shrugged their shoulders and exchanged ironic glances: "Those foreigners! Always full of hot air . . ."

There were other things he disliked: the rampant cult of Stalin's personality; the glaring inequality of income and living conditions in the various groups of the population; the constant encroachments of the State bureaucracy on the rights of the citizen. No doubt, he was annoyed by the inordinate blare with which his visit was exploited for the purposes of governmental publicity. The suave journalist, Michael Koltzov, who represented to Gide Soviet officialdom, was hardly the type of man he may have hoped to find in power in the Fatherland of All Proletarians.

And yet Gide did not intend to write a diatribe. *Retour de l'U. R. S. S.* was conceived and composed as a piece of severe but friendly criticism. Gide is as sincere as always when he tells us, in the Preface, that it is an innate proclivity of his mind to be most exacting towards those to whom he feels the closest.

According to the same introductory paper, he was aware of the danger inherent in his attacks on the Soviet Union: that is to say, he realized that the enemy—namely, Fascism —might profit by his exposé. "And that would have prevented me from publishing my book," he adds candidly again, "if it were not for my unabated conviction that the Soviet Union will triumph in the end over the grave errors I indicate. Besides—and this point is even more essential!—the errors of one particular country cannot suffice to discredit an international, universal cause. The lie, and if only the lie of silence, may appear opportune under circumstances. In reality, however, to lie means always to play the enemy's game, whereas the truth, however painful, cannot hurt but wholesomely."

True enough; but the truth—particularly the truth about so vital and so delicate an issue—must be felt and formulated with striking clarity—precise, constructive, irrefutable; or else it will harm the cause it is supposed to promote.

The bad thing about Gide's report on Soviet Russia is that it is not quite good enough. Did I say before that I would choose *Corydon*, if I had to sacrifice one of his writings? Well, I have changed my mind. It's *Retour de l'U. R. S. S.* I would pick. If in *Corydon* the antithetic element is lacking, it is disturbingly obvious and unsolved in the Soviet pamphlet. The chiding reprimands of the second half contradict too grossly the eulogies of the beginning. If the Russian people are indeed as radiantly happy and healthy as asserted at first, all subsequent denouncements lose somehow their relevance and weight. Why should the citizens of the Soviet Republics not be self-satisfied, since their way of life satisfies them so completely? Why blame them for worshipping their leader and ignoring the outside world? If Gide's report is correct, they have no reason to distrust their Government or to envy the other nations.

It is a pity that Gide did not present his Russian notes the way they were probably couched originally—as fragments of his *Journal*. If he had stuck to this informal, typically Gidean pattern, the incongruities and superficialities occurring in his text might have lost their offensive character. Even in his judgments about the French administration in the Congo, Gide was more cautious and realistic than he appears in certain simplifying verdicts concerning the Soviet State. In *Voyage au Congo*, he contented himself with describing the individual cases of misery and injustice he happened to have watched. In *Retour de l'U. R. S. S.*, on the contrary, he seems inclined to jump to conclusions. "There are too many poor people in Soviet Russia." Too many? From what point of view? Might there be less? Under what circumstances? "Too many poor people" does not make much sense, as even one poverty-stricken person means a blot on Utopia.

And yet there can be no doubt that Gide's account deserves to be taken seriously and to be discussed with respect—first of all because of the greatness and integrity of its author, and also as a candid and instructive document containing a good many penetrating remarks and truthful observations. Even if the booklet were flimsier and more provocative than it is, however, the Communist reaction to it would be an embarrassing scandal. The same Marxist scribblers who had fawned upon Gide only yesterday, now slandered and smeared him. A furious outcry—"Traitor! Fascist agent! Double-crosser!"—rose from Party headquarters and reverberated throughout the Red press in several continents. There was only one voice among those loyal to the Kremlin: Gide is an impostor, a treacherous hypocrite, an insidious degenerate, and altogether a rat. Ilya

Ehrenburg called Gide a "wicked old man." It struck me
as slightly surprising as I had just published, in a magazine
I was then editing in Amsterdam, Ehrenburg's enthusiastic
essay about "*ce vieillard infâme.*"

Gide opened his pamphlet *Retouches,* a sequel to *Retour
de l'U. R. S. S.,* with this melancholy statement: "The publication of my book *Back from the USSR* brought me a
great many insults. Romain Rolland's gave me pain. I never
cared much for his writings, but at any rate I held his moral
character in high esteem. . . . This eagle has made his nest;
he takes his rest in it."

As for Gide, he had forfeited his nest, once again, if he
had ever had one. The sensational and transient interlude
of his partisanship was over. His first and only attempt to
join the ranks of a great, organized movement had failed
dramatically. He was alone, once more. The blatant chorus
of the disappointed comrades made him realize how isolated he was. Even more disconcerting, however, than the
invectives from the left camp were the unsavory flatteries
bestowed on him by the reactionary press. To be insulted
by *L'Humanité* was unpleasant but endurable; to be praised
and quoted by *Gringoire*—the scurviest Fascist sheet in
Paris—was more of an affront than any decent person could
stand. Even Hitler's *Völkischer Beobachter* considered
Gide an ally against "the Bolshevist danger." Never before
had his name been so frequently and respectfully mentioned in the big, popular newspapers, from the august
Temps down to the vulgar *Matin. Back from the USSR*
was a striking hit, from a commercial point of view: the
first best-seller Gide had ever produced. The succeeding
pamphlet, *Afterthoughts*—even more aggressive than the

first one—was also cordially received by all Red-baiters. Gide had the chance, or rather, he was in danger, of becoming the favorite of the most obscurantist and jingoist coteries.

But at this point he proved again his probity and his pride. Far from capitalizing his obstreperous glory, he discouraged his new admirers, whether reactionary or Trotskyite. He remained faithful to himself and to his unchanged, unchangeable ideals. Others may turn against a cause when they are disappointed with its representatives; not Gide. His love for liberty and progress is deep-rooted and authentic; his aversion to Fascism, implacable and instinctive. If he had been rash and immoderate in both his praises and condemnations of the Soviet experiment, he was firm and consistent in his hatred of brutal retrogression and in his striving for a sound and realistic formula reconciling freedom and discipline. The *Afterthoughts*, provoked by the venomous attacks from the Left, were his last statement exploitable by the powers of evil. Henceforth he was again a reliable, if lonely, fighter on the side of the angels.

I remember a luncheon with Gide in Paris, a few months after "the affair" had calmed down. Jef Last was with us; he, too, had severed his connections with the Communist Party.

It had been some time since I had last seen Gide. I was living in Amsterdam, at the time (where I made friends with Jef Last), while Gide sojourned mostly in Cuverville with his wife, who was in a poor state of health.

We discussed *Retour de l'U. R. S. S.*, the history, and the consequences of the little book and the complex drama it involved. I told Gide that I was not particularly fond of this work of his. He shrugged his shoulders and grinned his flitting, enigmatic, impish grin.

"*Que voulez-vous . . . ?*" he said, curiously amused. "One must be allowed to descend a little bit below one's own level, at times."

He reminded me of Goethe, who was told by friends that one of his plays, *Clavigo*, fell somewhat short of other things he had done, and who replied succinctly, "*Es kann nicht immer alles über alle Begriffe sein.*" Which means: "Why should everything I do be always excellent beyond words? I cannot be constantly at my best."

I quoted this modest and haughty word to Gide. He laughed.

Then he remembered that I had published somewhere an extensive article about his pamphlet, defending it against the rabid attacks of Romain Rolland, Lion Feuchtwanger, Ilya Ehrenburg, and others. He had already thanked me for this gesture, although there was nothing to it, I thought, worth mentioning. Of course, I had to come out for the man to whom I owe more, intellectually, than to anybody else, when he was abused by a lot of arrogant fanatics or cynical busybodies.

Now Gide remarked, with a transient frown, "You shouldn't have said that you do like my book since you don't like it really."

"What I tried to say isn't really that I liked this book of yours. I said that I like your books, and that I like you."

Then we discussed other things—the situation in Spain, for instance, from where Jef Last came and where I was about to go. And we talked about Hitler, and about the danger of war, and about Léon Blum's policy, and about what would happen to people we knew and to ourselves, in case war came after all.

Gide was in excellent shape, younger than ever, I thought; resilient and keen, of a certain grim, determined gaiety. It was good to watch him as he talked and smiled, his head bent somewhat sideways, his eyes narrowed to two glimmering slits, the cigarette dangling from his lips. While looking at him aside, I wondered what his face might have been like twenty years ago, or thirty or fifty years, long before I knew him, years before I was born. He was almost seventy now.

Probably he seemed older when he was twenty-five or fifty. Maybe he appeared sickly and blasé at that time. Now he was brisk and lively. The tanned skin was tight, if wrinkled, over the delicate curves of his lean, forceful face.

I remembered a word of Dostoevski quoted by André Gide: "I have lived; I have also suffered, but above all I have lived."

The epileptic genius said those words coming from Siberian exile. "Indestructible old warriors they are!" I felt, thinking of Dostoevski's tribulations and ecstasies, and also of Gide's adventures, his mistakes and his fights, his unending endeavor, the ultimate triumph of his incorruptible genius.

IX. THE DEBACLE

O Star of France!
Star crucified! by traitors sold!
Star panting o'er a land of death—heroic land!
Strange, passionate, mocking, frivolous land ..
WALT WHITMAN

I went to the Louvre—deserted. The end of a civilization?
ANDRÉ GIDE, IN 1914

"T H E truth is that I cannot dissociate myself from *Em.*; nor can I separate my brain from my heart," Gide wrote in 1933, after a visit to his wife in Cuverville. "That is the secret behind all my indecisions. There is nothing to be done about it. *You cannot serve two masters.* . . . Each time I see her again I realize anew that she is the only being I have ever really loved; in fact, it seems to me that I love her now more passionately and deeply than I ever did before. That is why every step forward causes me so much pain: it widens the gap between us. I cannot think without being cruel to her."

Five years later, in 1938, Emmanuèle died. His conscience and guardian angel abandoned him; his life, deprived of its balm and burden, seemed alarmingly empty. The long, seraphic romance, the secret drama of his biography had come to an end. He was quite alone, more isolated than ever and more unbound than he ever wished to be. "*Me voici libre, comme je ne l'ai jamais été,*" he exclaims at the end of his diary, the chronicle and confession of five eventful decades—"*libre effroyablement . . .*"

Absolute freedom and absolute solitude are not easy to bear. For the first time in his life the wanderer seems fatigued and depleted. "No, no!" he complains, "it was with *her* that I embarked on this venture. I feel derelict since she left me alone. I lose interest in the great comedy of life and wish to withdraw too."

Never before had he invoked the somber comfort of death; on the contrary, he used to be afraid of its gradual, unescapable approach. His attitude towards death was not romantic but philosophical; that is to say, he tried to overcome, through will-power and contemplation, the natural dismay which the thought of death always caused in him. In this sense he agreed with Montaigne that "to Philosophize is to learn how to Die." But his metaphysical concepts are curiously unrelated to the reality of physical decease. The delights and dilemmas of this worldly life bespeak God, or rather, they are our form of communication with Him, according to Gide's philosophy. The end of our biological drama may initiate a new stage of our eternal quest; but first of all, and directly, our organic decomposition removes us from God rather than brings us closer to Him.

All romanticists are in love with death. Gide is not a romanticist. Since the saturnine days of André Walter—his Werther period, so to speak—the specter of death had scarcely appeared in his work, except to dramatize the devastating energy of the demon. But, curiously, what Gide presents is always the agony of the victim, not the ordeal in store for the evil-doer. We witness the last convulsions of Marceline, in *L'Immoraliste*, but not Michel's inevitable atonement. We are admitted to the macabre and yet facetious scene of Fleurissoire's assassination, in *Les Caves du Vatican*, but the murderer, Lafcadio, apparently lives forever. In *La Symphonie pastorale*, Gertrude, the sightless angel, disappears in the floods like Ophelia, but the terrible Pastor remains alive to repent his sins and to renounce his pious trickeries. Young Boris, in *Les Faux-Monnayeurs*, perishes, another victim of the demoniac power, whereas Georges is spared, for other crimes or for his ultimate punishment.

Queen Jocasta commits suicide, but her son, lover, and murderer, Œdipus, continues his pilgrimage—"henceforth without home, without country," with nobody to prop and guide him, save Antigone, his saintly daughter.

Gide's eyesight was well intact when Emmanuèle left him; he did not, in contrast to Œdipus, depend on his daughter to find his way.

Did he still have a country?

This is the autumn of 1938, a dismal season pregnant with apocalyptic developments. Or is it a fall as other falls have been? Golden and serene, with its limpid skies and the melancholy splendor of its foliage?

Why can I not be happy? Gide muses. Why not enjoy these beautiful leaves and flowers, as long as I have time to enjoy them? What prevents me from relishing the wistful sweetness of this parting summer? Could I not forget, for a few moments, the bitterness of my loss, the massacres of Spain, the anxiety and tension with which the atmosphere is charged, all over Europe?

No, he cannot forget his anguish, nor can he ignore the ominous, dire signs. With disgust and apprehension Gide

listens, like everybody, to the rampant lies and affronts
Hitler broadcasts from Nuremberg throughout a paralyzed,
deluded, treacherous, trembling world. Even more frightening than the Führer's blatant enormities are the gales of
applause with which the German masses receive them.
Their delirium confirms that the blackmailing boasts of the
mustached monster are backed by the potential energies,
the wealth and power of a strong and dynamic people.

What is wrong with the Germans? André Gide wondered and mused, along with the rest of all thinking people. Did he not have the reputation of being a dogged
Germanophile? How often had he been abused by French
nationalists because of his penchant for the arch-enemy on
the other side of the Rhine! And, in fact, his mind and
vision had been molded in part by German poets and
thinkers. When he left France, in January, 1939, for his
last trip abroad before the outbreak of the war, his little
travel library consisted of only five books, three of which
were German: Nietzsche's *Birth of Tragedy*, *Joseph in
Egypt* by Thomas Mann, and Goethe's *Dichtung und
Wahrheit*.

But, on the other hand, it was Gide who had called
Goethe "the most un-German one of all Germans." Goethe
and Nietzsche, he said, are the two great German hostages
seized forever by French genius. One does not pay homage
to the Teutonic spirit by praising these two illustrious heralds of European culture in Germany. Why should France
disparage those who belong to her, her voluntary captives
and her natural allies?

Gide is familiar with the shortcomings and dislocations

of the German genius, partly thanks to certain penetrating exposés formulated by Goethe and Nietzsche. As far back as 1910, he speaks most aptly and most mercilessly of the German inability to design clearly and precisely the contours and the limits of a character, either in life or in literature. "And that is why their culture ultimately fails," Gide continues. "For the great instrument of culture is design, not music." Music, he tells us, is the principle of fusion and intoxication. Floating and irresponsible, it blurs the distinctions, merges the forms, it bewitches and dazes the listener. The design, on the contrary, stresses and clarifies the particular; it is the triumph of lucidity and criticism. "Criticism is the basis of art," Gide concludes, evidently in one of his most anti-romantic moods.

When speaking of music as if it were a narcotic and a public nuisance, Gide thinks of Richard Wagner—primarily of Wagner. It is certainly not Johann Sebastian Bach he refers to, nor is it to Chopin or Mozart. As for Beethoven, Gide's attitude is comparatively cool, considering the almost divine prestige of that master among French artists, from Victor Hugo and Hector Berlioz to Romain Rolland and André Suarès. Not that Gide was not sensible to Beethoven's vast persuasion; but his occasional praise of that great composer is hardly intense enough to counterbalance his statement to the effect that he prefers Bach and Mozart to "such musicians as Beethoven and Wagner." The association of the two names is scathing, in view of Gide's profound aversion to the Wagnerian style.

Whoever yields, without reservation, to the brutal hypnosis of Wagner's gestures and rhythms, has thus yielded to German imperialism. The genius of Lohengrin and Walkyrie is the genius of aggressiveness, reckless and gripping, ingeniously clever, for all its emotional exuberance. Nietzsche's fight against Wagner anticipates and symbolizes the inexorable hate with which he would have persecuted Nazism.

Gide, too, sensed the coming challenge in the redundant grandeur of Wagner's musical drama. To him, the rank splendor of this orchestration was both frightful and nauseous, not only in Wagner's operas proper but also, or even more so, in the voluptuous devices of his imitators.

"Last night, Salomé of Strauss," Gide noted, in 1907. "Ghéon repeats to us this mot of Madame Strauss, who felt that the Paris audiences were lacking in adequate enthusiasm for her husband's works: 'Evidently, it is high time to come back here with bayonets . . .'

"Hideous romanticism of this music. The turgid pomp of this orchestration could make you love Bellini. . . . Indiscretion of the artistic devices; monotony of the effects; bombastic repetitions, the most flagrant insincerity; incessant mobilization of all resources available. In this Victor Hugo and Wagner are the same; neither will choose among the many possible metaphors at their disposal to express a certain idea; they will spare us none. Barbarism of such a technique. Systematic amplification, etc. . . . It is not even interesting to analyze these deficiencies. I would much rather condemn such works en bloc, and await the bayonets. For this sort of art is really the enemy."

Do I need emphasize that Gide was not always so illtempered in his reactions to German art? Indeed, at other moments he was haunted by the idea that Germany might surpass France in vitality and creative force. It was on June 1, 1918, that he made this disquieting entry in his diary: "I think at times, with horror, that a French victory, for which all of us wish wholeheartedly, might turn out to be a triumph of the past over the future."

But when victory was attained—the victory of a fallible but well-intentioned civilization over a formidable military machinery—Gide was among those who understood and preached that the only feasible way to guarantee the maintenance of peace would be to bring about a general European alliance, a sort of continental Federation. As for Germany, she should be allowed, or even requested, to join this commonwealth and contribute her share to the enormous effort of reconstruction. "The European concert will always be fragmentary without Germany," Gide declared, in 1919. "*The important thing is to prevent her from dominating it.*"

Four years afterwards, he formulated, in the *Revue de Genève*, his European credo. *L'Avenir de l'Europe* (1923) is an eloquent and candid message of good-will and of considerable insight, claiming and elucidating the principle and program of international solidarity.

"No European country will be able henceforth to prosper and develop while abiding by an obsolete and sterile isolationism. Europe will be doomed, politically and economically, if the European countries continue to pursue their individual, selfish interests, regardless of the general well-being."

Gide finds his ethical leitmotiv relevant and applicable to this political context. He admonishes the nations as he used to admonish individuals: By overcoming your egotism

you will increase your own strength and happiness. By renouncing your arrogant individualism you will gain your
authentic individuality. To become European, indeed, to
become a citizen of the world, does not imply giving up
one's own national character. You may remain a good
Frenchman, a good German, Russian, or Italian, while becoming a good European. *It is in being the most particular
that we contribute most to the general cause.*

Gide did whatever he could to promote and deepen the
European consciousness of a common heritage and a common future. Thanks to his writings, the French intelligentsia became aware of certain aspects of the European
genius hitherto ignored or underrated in that country. It
was Gide, more than anyone else, who clarified the French
view of Nietzsche and Dostoevski; who reaffirmed and revived Goethe's cosmic grandeur, introduced Blake and
Kierkegaard, rediscovered Pushkin and the great English
novelists, publicized Joseph Conrad and Rabindranath
Tagore, hailed and elucidated the greatness of Walt Whitman.

But his efforts were not confined to the strictly literary
sphere. He proved and activated his good-will not only
through the medium of the printed word but also person-
ally, through the multitude of his international contacts
and through his participation in cosmopolitan conferences
and symposiums. One of the conventicles he patronized
was the annual meeting of writers and philosophers in Pontigny, a picturesque village in Burgundy. It was in a fine
old monastery that Professor Desjardins, Dean of the *Ecole
Normale Supérieure* and founder of the *Union pour la*

Vérité, presided each summer over a colorful and yet congenial group of men of letters. In an atmosphere of serene detachment, controversial and vital topics could be discussed, calmly and constructively, by an assembly composed of Frenchmen and foreigners, intellectuals from London and Rome, Amsterdam, Prague, and Geneva. Gide attended these summer meetings, together with many of his friends—Jacques Rivière, Roger Martin du Gard, Jean Schlumberger, Charles du Bos, and others. And it was there, in this oasis of tolerance, that German scholars and poets had the opportunity to rejoin a cosmopolitan circle, soon after the First World War. Men like Ernst Robert Curtius and Heinrich Mann were welcome in Pontigny, as far back as 1922, when the sound of a German accent still aroused public indignation on the Paris boulevards.

Happy, faraway days!—days full of hope and fervor. I like to visualize those urbane gentlemen walking about in the monastery garden or sitting together in the ancient hall —absorbed in cordial conversations and stimulating debates. After dinner they met in the drawing room to amuse themselves with what André Maurois calls in his memoirs "subtle and learned games." "One day," he remembers, "the keyword was: Mephistopheles. 'Is he one of your friends?' Gide, who was being cross-examined, was asked. 'So I flatter myself!' Gide affirmed between clenched teeth in his most metallically infernal voice."

If their games had usually a somewhat scholarly flavor, their disputes were not without a slightly playful touch. One day the discussion turned on the question of who were the three writers most instrumental in shaping the consciousness of modern man? The French participants agreed on Whitman, Nietzsche, and Dostoevski—a selection presently endorsed by the Germans. The Italian representative, Signor Prezzolini, demurred; he wanted Carducci and Croce. The English suggested Browning and Meredith. Finally Gide observed, "*J'ai besoin dans tout cela de Goethe.*"

When the distinguished party dissolved, some days afterwards, one of the British visitors said to the French host, "*C'était charmant, cher ami.*"

And the French professor responded, "My dear friend, it was *flawless.*"

When Dr. Paul Joseph Göbbels came to power in Germany, along with his talented crony, A. Hitler, he turned out to be particularly good at exploiting such lofty principles as European Solidarity, Pacifism, and the like. Many an upright Frenchman was fooled by the fiendish publicity manager of the Third Reich. Jules Romains, for instance, was naïve enough to mistake the Beasts of Berlin for the Men of Good Will he was writing a novel about. He believed in all earnest that he promoted the cause of European peace when he went to the German capital to lecture there under the auspices of Baldur von Schirach, supreme leader of the Hitler Youth.

It was quite an occasion when the illustrious guest from Paris delivered his speech on "Latinity and Germanism" in the big auditorium of the Berlin University. The brilliant crowd included Herr von Schirach, M. François-Poncet, Ambassador of the French Republic to the court of Hitler, and a certain Dr. Professor Fischer, Dean of the University. The audience as well as the press was smitten with the sparkling and tactful manner in which M. Romains defined his attitude towards the New German Order. Said the author of *Verdun* and of many other novels, "The new German 'Racism' revives and reaffirms an ancient drama, the longing of European man to overcome his present state of distraction and to regain his true, imperishable identity."

The platform from which M. Romains spoke was decorated with huge Swastika banners.

No doubt, André Gide could have had an equally good time in Berlin if he had cared to go there. There were plenty of invitations. His fame in Germany surpassed even that of M. Jules Romains. Not only Messrs. Schirach, Fischer, and François-Poncet, but even Dr. Göbbels, if not the Führer himself, might have attended his show. But he spurned the most flattering offers. Instead of wooing Nazi Germany, he challenged and angered her leaders.

Gide, pro-German with reasonable reservations, was anti-Nazi without reservations, openly and sternly. The masters of Berlin were finally compelled to acknowledge his intransigent attitude. They stopped sending him invitations. Gide's works got their honorable, well-deserved place on the blacklist of Dr. Göbbels.

Was Gide still a pacifist, at this point? Of course, he was. Every decent, civilized person loathes war and never ceases to do so. But the new situation created a new dilemma.

In August, 1933, the World Congress of Unconditional Pacifists and Conscientious Objectors urged him to send a message subscribing to their program. Gide's first reaction was all in favor of those peace-loving intellectuals who condemned war and vowed never to take up arms again, under any circumstances. He was on the point of endorsing their manifesto, when suddenly qualms and scruples began to perturb his mind.

It was a declaration from Einstein, among other symptoms, which impressed on Gide the utmost gravity of the situation. The eminent scholar, who had previously announced his passionate disapproval of war as a method of solving international problems, now modified his view. If and when, he said, it comes to war against Hitlerism, as it undoubtedly will unless Hitler falls, pacifism would be treason to the cause of progress and culture. In other words, even the horrors of war are not too high a price to get rid of the obnoxious plague which is Nazism.

"The case of Einstein is indeed extraordinary," Gide remarks in his journal. "As a German, he refused to take up arms. If he consents now to fight, he does so in his capacity as a refugee and in order to fight his own country, the menace of which he should be able to gauge. We ought to listen to him . . ."

And still it remains bitter for any civilized man to advocate the necessity of mass slaughter, Hitlerism or not. Was Gide in favor of war, in those crucial days of September, 1938? He wavered and wondered, torn by contradictory fears and wishes. What was he hoping for? Not for the sinister farce of Munich, to be sure. He realized that the treacherous bargain between Hitler and the democracies meant disgrace and disaster. But it meant also peace, for the time being at least. Gide could not help feeling relieved, for all his bitter misgivings. "Who knows," he kept asking, "if the Germans would have shrunk back from the extreme risk? And if Hitler had accepted the challenge and had declared war, who is in a position to predict the outcome? What if brutal force had triumphed over the righteous cause? Or if the righteous cause, in the course of its desperate struggle against brutal force, had betrayed its righteousness?"

He himself felt the futility of such questions. "What is the use of my repeating what everybody thinks and what all newspapers talk about? My feeble voice is drowned in the uproarious concert. Since I am unable to speak of anything except these disconcerting events, I may as well keep quiet."

Some years before, shortly after his return from Soviet Russia, Gide had said to Julian Green, "You are unpolitical. Remain so!" Now, in the dismal winter of 1938, he complains about the lack of consistency and honesty he finds in French foreign policy, "and, for that matter, in politics altogether."

How many debacles and disappointments during the last decade! The fiasco of the League of Nations, of the Kremlin, of the Holy See . . . Yes, the Catholic Church, too, wanted to appease the arrant enemy of Christian civilization. Catholicism had a unique, irretrievable chance, and missed it. The Papacy might have established itself as the spiritual leader of mankind, by proclaiming and organizing the Crusade against the Fascist anti-Christ. "The moral failure of Communism," Gide wrote, in 1939, "reaffirms the revolutionary mission of Christianity. Catholicism betrays itself by becoming conservative. What do they wish to conserve? Titles, fortunes, privileges . . . But it is only the Spirit that matters, not the formulas and rituals. I have never doubted that some Catholics are aware of these things. Could it be that now even the Church begins to understand?"

Another illusion? No, another hope, not without sound foundation, considering the courageous spirit prevailing in a group of faithful and firm French Catholic intellectuals. Gide certainly did not refer to Pétain and his dreary ilk when speaking of a potential renaissance of liberal Catholicism; nor did he mean Henri Massis or his old friend Claudel, both partisans of General Franco and altogether of definitely pro-Fascist tendencies. Among those he thought of are the late Charles Péguy, Jacques Maritain, François Mauriac, and a few others, including Georges Bernanos, the polemic genius of his generation. It was Bernanos who found the most poignant, most merciless formulations to cry out his grief and wrath, first about the Fascist-Catholic conspiracy in Spain, then about the craven and shortsighted deal of Munich. Like Gide, Bernanos reacts most violently against the stupidities and horrors of those he once deemed his allies—in his case, the extreme political right, from Georges Clemenceau to Charles Maurras of the *Action Française;* from the high clergy down to such abject "realists" as MM. Laval, Tardieu, Bonnet, and the like. It is against this array of decorated crooks and traitors that Bernanos darted the indictments of his two terrific diatribes: *Les Grands Cimetières sous la lune,* arraigning the outrages of the Spanish tragedy, and *Scandale de la vérité,* unmasking the intrigue of Munich.

"*J'ai honte,*" groans the offended, tormented Christian. "*J'ai honte de moi, j'ai honte de notre impuissance, de la honteuse impuissance des chrétiens devant le péril qui menace le monde.*"

He left France and escaped to Brazil—a gesture of protest, of shame, and of distress . . .

André Gide, many years older and many degrees less flamboyant than Bernanos, stayed in France; or rather, he returned to his country after a lonely journey which he undertook during the first few months of 1939. The day of his departure he noted, in Marseille under the date of January 26, 1939: "Obsessed with the idea of the atrocious agony of the Spanish people."

It was not long until even more gruesome visions were to beset and to afflict his mind.

Gide was in Paris when the Daladier Cabinet, after a breathtaking moment of hesitation, followed the example of the Chamberlain Cabinet and declared war on Nazi Germany.

He had kept silent from 1914 to 1918. He was not talkative in 1939 and 1940. Should he have joined the Office of Propaganda and Information headed by Jean Giraudoux? He would have been sadly out of place, between Jules Romains, former champion of Franco-Nazi *rapprochement*, and André Maurois, future apologist for Marshal Pétain in the United States.

It was hardly his line to compose patriotic manifestoes under the auspices of the Daladier-Bonnet Administration. Should he congratulate his Government on waging war against the "interior enemy"?—restive newspaper editors, stubborn liberals, parlor-pinks, veritable Reds, and the like —while the Nazi soldiers had the time of their lives exchanging dirty puns and pictures with the crew of the Maginot Line. And what could he say about his former friends, the Communists, who abruptly dropped the People's Front policy, when the signatures were not yet dry on the Hitler-Stalin Pact, and presently discovered "revolutionary potentialities" in Nazism? It would have been easy but somewhat cheap to denounce their scandalous conduct, nor was it possible to excuse them for their cynicism. Besides, Gide was just seventy years old when the war began. He withdrew to the South of France.

During the last war he had devoted most of his time and working capacity to the charitable organization of the *Foyer Franco-Belge*. This time, too, he took care of fugitives, if only in an informal and improvised fashion. His particular protégés were the anti-Hitler refugees from Germany, Austria, Czechoslovakia, and other countries. Tens of thousands of them had found a shelter in France; thousands lived on the *Côte d'Azur,* in the picturesque and inexpensive little towns or villages, somewhere between Menton and Marseille. There were many artists and intellectuals among these Riviera refugees. Some of them were old friends and admirers of André Gide. But not only his personal acquaintances besought his help and advice; strangers too approached him with their worries. He listened to their gloomy and monotonous confessions. He was patient and generous. The comfort he gave did not consist exclusively, or not even primarily, of money, letters of introduction, and other essentials of this palpable kind. Even more helpful than these material contributions was the example of his unshaken kindness and greatness.

They had great need of encouragement of this sort, the anti-Fascist exiles in the France of 1939 and 1940. True, some of them may have been traitors; others, weary and arrogant. But most of the refugees were sincerely and heartily loyal to the Allied cause. In their capacity as anti-Hitler fighters, they had claimed, and had been granted, the hospitality of the French Republic. Why should they be regarded as "enemy aliens," now, with the French nation engaged in an anti-Hitler war? Why should they idle and suffer in concentration camps, while the real Nazi agents, German, French, or "neutral," kept weaving their sordid plots, in Paris, Strasbourg, and elsewhere?

Or was this not a war against Hitlerism? Was it no war at all? Was it a "phony" war, as the Americans said? Premier Reynaud denied it. "I have tried to find out what that means—*phony*," Daladier's successor broadcast over the Atlantic. "It seems to indicate that this war is something made-up, something we do only feignedly—a counterfeit war. But, believe me, ladies and gentlemen, there is nothing 'phony' or counterfeit about our war effort . . ."

What, then, did cause this uncanny paralysis of a glorious people? What was the drama behind this pathetic collapse?

Gide, in the seclusion of his bachelor flat in Nice, spent his time delving into this weird, unfathomable problem. What has happened to France? Is she too civilized to resist? Or just too corrupt and weary? Is the French genius worn-out? Is our mission fulfilled? Has God lost interest in our endeavor? Does He no longer love our country? And if so, how can we continue to love it? Or has our beloved France already ceased to love her worried sons? Is she still faithful to us?

Only these questions matter, not the extraneous conditions responsible for the debacle in 1940. They scarcely counted, those minor and major blunders and treacheries, compared with this one cardinal issue: Is France still alive? Is her disgrace a lurid interlude and a gruesome lesson? Or does it imply and reveal the national disintegration?

Gide, the undaunted herald of sincerity and self-examination, faced the situation squarely, without delusion and without defeatism. He did not deny or mitigate the depth of his anxiety. He wrote: "Do not dodge, cravenly, your distress! Traverse it! Beyond, you may find the gleam of new hope. Go straight ahead! On the other side of the tunnel you will see light again."

It is dark, down there in the tunnel, bleak and black and stifling.

The Golgotha path of the French nation leads through the nether world of a fashionable if somewhat dusty watering place named Vichy. It was there that Gide happened to sojourn during the critical weeks of May and June, 1940. While Paris surrendered—her monuments spared: her honor sacrificed—the great old Parisian sauntered along the well-kept promenade of the quaint, elegant spa. Usually he carried two or three thick volumes under his arm. What did he read while the French Government, exiled in Bordeaux, wavered between the alternatives of a desperate last-minute stand and unconditional capitulation? Gide read Goethe.

He had promised Schiffrin, of the *Bibliothèque de la Pléiade*, a preface to his new edition of Goethe's dramatic work. An exciting, absorbing job! If only the provincial bookshops were a little better! "To do this work really well I need books which I can find only in Paris," Gide complained to his companion, walking through the park in front of the Vichy casino. "For lack of written information, I shall have to stick to generalities and to recollections of things I have read. After all, perhaps it is as well; in the same way, the novelist should not work directly from facts. The memory clarifies them, only retaining the essentials . . ."

The lady at his side—a lean, ageless figure, racy and aristocratic—was Annette Kolb, a gifted writer of half-French, half-German descent. Educated in Munich, she does most of her writing in German, but had become a French citizen again since Germany degraded herself to the Nazi mire. Annette is an old friend of Gide's.

"It happened that I left Paris at the end of May, 1940, meaning to return in a fortnight," Miss Kolb reported later, in an account called *Debacle*. "For we knew nothing. We were anxious, of course, and apprehensive, being aware of the uncanny sabotage committed from right and left. The war was unpopular with the people. 'It is not in Germany that there should be a revolution, but in France,' was a common saying. We suspected poisonous influences; we did what we could to counterbalance them without realizing to the full what formidable attempts were at work to undermine public opinion. Yes, we were anxious, but much less so since Weygand was commanding the army. And so I went to Vichy with two suitcases before an historic Vichy existed. There the news became darker every day. . . .

"André Gide was in Vichy, and we were seen sitting

together in the park, whereupon one of the pro-Nazi newspapers denounced us. '*Qui se ressemble, s'assemble,*' it sneered.

"But this was merely jocose compared with the following statement: 'And what about those foreigners who have lived in opposition to their governments, taking advantage all the while of our hospitality?' Thereby denouncing us for *not* being Nazis. '*A bàs les Juifs!*' was written with white chalk on many a tree. . . ."

What a curious picture!—this forlorn couple of aristocratic exiles, two Europeans of the good old stamp, sitting together in the shadow of a stately tree the bark of which is disfigured by the idiotically diabolic words, *A bàs les Juifs!* Annette shakes her head, distrait and sorrowful, unable to understand, speechless in front of such vandalism. As for Gide, he snuffs nervously and then shrugs his shoulders, his face slightly distorted in a transient grimace —disgusted, contemptuous, and a little bit amused, in a queer, bitter fashion. Then he opens his book and reads Goethe.

Does he remember what he said in Pontigny, years ago? "In this whole setup I miss Goethe's presence and authority . . ."

He might have thought of this statement if he had had to witness the triumphant entrance of the German troops, a few days after his hearty and gloomy rendezvous with Miss Kolb.

She was still in Vichy when the victors invaded the drowsy place. It was quite a shock, but Annette could bear it. She is a brave, resilient woman; besides, she had no choice. "Unless you fled in time into a café, you had to watch the terrific display of power and discipline," she reports. "Tanks as high as churches—and how else would Nazi churches look!—and other tanks, dangerously low, shaped like cannons and dashing along with indescribable impudence, swathed entirely in gigantic red flags marked with the swastika in flaming black. And the marching robots—inhuman tools of destruction."

No wonder she longed for a human face. "I looked for Gide. Friends had come to fetch him. He was gone."

He has always been in the habit of disappearing through trap doors, as it were. France was convulsed with new, refined, and cruel forms of agony and humiliation; Gide kept in hiding somewhere in the Midi, near Nice, in the house of friends—intent on Goethe and Montesquieu, trying to forget Herr Abetz in Paris and Marshal Pétain in Vichy.

Did he try to forget? If so, why did he not leave France as did many of his friends? Antoine de Saint-Exupéry escaped to the United States; so did Julian Green—American by nationality—and the political essayist Robert de Saint-Jean, both on cordial terms with Gide for years. Igor Stravinsky, who in 1934 composed the score for Gide's "melodrama," *Perséphone*, settled in California. Jacques Maritain, Gide's friendly antagonist in many a heated debate, too made his home in free America. Jules Romains refuted his own political theories and proved the noble substance of his character by abandoning the country now ruled by his former hosts, the Nazis. And some of Gide's old enemies went, along with his old friends—André Breton, for instance, the publicity manager of the Surrealist circus. How long ago was it that the business-conscious visionary had insulted Gide in an imaginary interview, just after having praised *Les Caves du Vatican* as a work of Surrealist inspiration? All these quarrels and intrigues seemed remote and meaningless now.

The world that had been Gide's cracked and crumbled. What, then, did hold him on a Côte d'Azur which turned bleak and lusterless, as if withered by a mortal blight? He intended to send his daughter across the Atlantic—a plan that was to be baffled by technical circumstances. As for himself, however, he preferred to stay where he was. Maybe he considered himself too old for transplantation. Or he disliked the idea of emigration, perhaps, out of pride and defiance: it would have offended his self-respect to give way to the inflated conquerors and their paltry stooges. Curiosity too may have retained him; the spectacle now unfolding surpassed the most hazardous fantasies in its outrageous sordidness.

But more compelling than all this was, perhaps, a simple and stringent emotion, new to him and almost surprising, in view of his nomadic past and his cosmopolitan credo. The old wanderer, who had never settled down, realized now that he could not live without France; that he needed and loved his country.

"How strange!" he mused, in his Mediterranean solitude. "How very curious!—the self-evident validity, the dynamic impact of those big, nebulous words: Heart, God, Country . . . We know very well what we mean by them, even if it is not easy to define their meaning. Certain emotions encroach on the spiritual and certain ideas are affected. It is possible that in the brain we have no emotions at all and that from it depend our feelings and our passions. But all the same this flood of blood to the brain comes from the heart, and we make no mistake about certain appeals from the brain which make our heart beat much faster. Heroism, sacrifice, fatherland: it is true that all these terms of heavy tonnage lend themselves easily to confusion. But it is for this very reason that they are useful. Certainly the word *country*, for example, does not include the same landscapes for the peasant from the North of France as for the peasant from the South; it is not understood in the same way by the agriculturist as by the intellectual; by the poor man as by the shareholder. But it is a rallying-cry. And when we hear that 'the country is in danger,' the important thing is for us to get up and unite to defend it; and what does it matter if what we are defending should be for the peasant, the farms; for the intellectual, culture; for the industrialist, industry; and even for the shareholder, his shares? The word *country* comprises all that; it is understood at the same time by the mind and by the heart."

"*Mon pays* . . ." He had avoided this irresistible formula when the whole nation shouted and blared it from 1914 to 1919. Now it had become dangerous to cry out one's devotion to the *Grande Nation*, with the Gestapo listening and the Nazi concentration camp around the corner. Gide, always fond of risks, admitted and stressed, at this point, his glowing patriotism, which he had concealed when it would have been convenient and profitable to proclaim it. The same Gide who had been defamed on account of his "uprootedness," now proved, manly and unafraid, his loyalty to the French cause, which still is the cause of *Liberté, Fraternité, Egalité*.

But what happened to those spirited jingoists who had reveled so long in flamboyant clichés? What a pitiful squirming and squealing among those who used to be so bold and eloquent, in the good old days! The great heralds of the Latin Tradition, the preachers of heroism, the rabid Germanophobes—now they quailed before the triumphant barbarians, licked the enemy's boots, fawned upon the invaders.

Look at those who smeared and slandered Gide as an agent of Pan-Germanism! Over night they have established themselves as the most vociferous and most ardent promoters of Franco-Nazi collaboration. Was it not a gentleman named Henri Béraud who once launched a venomous campaign against Gide and the other "long-faced Huguenots" of the *Nouvelle Revue Française*? The dashing humorist, author of the prize-winning novel *The Sorrows of a Fat Man*, blamed Gide, Proust, Valéry, Giraudoux, among others, for their lack of Gallic esprit and for their pro-German leanings. Now the fat man had sorrows of a different kind. He expressed them in the Fascist weekly, *Gringoire*, which featured his new declaration of faith under the sensational headline: "Great Britain must be reduced to a state of slavery!" A humorist, M. Henri Béraud . . .

Quite a Catholic, M. Henri Massis! Too subtle and too cunning to participate in the obstreperous treacheries of the literary jackals in Paris, he hides behind Pétain's back. His acute eulogies of the Axis are published in the august old *Revue des Deux Mondes*, semi-official organ of the Vichy-minded. There the neo-Thomist advocates, glibly and shamelessly, the alliance with neo-paganism. How many

years ago is it that, for M. Massis, Asia began right beyond
the Rhine?—and "Asia" means, in his terminology, the
abyss, the end, the inferno. To him, Luther is a Hun,
Goethe a half-wit, Bismarck a criminal. But Dr. Abetz is
great: the *Revue des Deux Mondes* is all in favor of him.
The aged dignitaries and bearded Academicians, the decorated bores and pompous mummies—all vie with each other
in paying flowery homage to the Führer, and to the Führer's representatives, and to the mistresses of the secretaries
of the Führer's agents.

They lie, they swindle, they deny and distort the truth,
they wallow in corruption, they humiliate themselves,
blinded by fear, ambition, stupidity, and juicy Nazi bribes.
MM. Fabre-Luce, Benoist-Méchin, Chardonne, and Chateaubriand are civilized and sophisticated liars; they repeat
the Nazi fabrications in a subtle and elegant fashion. Others,
like Fernand de Brion and Luchaire, Jr., are unabashed.
Göbbels pays them for translating his enormities into the
idiom of Montaigne and Molière. Charles Maurras seems to
forget his loyalty to the House of Bourbon, dazzled and
scared by the German saber. As for the great Claudel, he
is torn between his furious hatred of the German people
and their penchant for their authoritarian régime.

Is Gide disappointed in his illustrious friend? Maybe he is;
the relation between the two has recently become cooler.
However, Claudel is not an outright "collaborationist";
but a playwright who wants to see his drama on the stage,
and an adherent to law and order who prefers authority,
even with a Germanic accent, to liberalism in every form.
The eminent Catholic poet, however, is the only one
among Gide's personal friends who is plainly pro-Vichy

and even maintains contacts with the Abetz camarilla.

Louis Ferdinand Céline has certainly nothing in common with André Gide—not even the language. His rampant gibberish is not likely to appeal to an admirer of Racine and Pascal. The racial fantasies of Céline's book, *Bagatelles pour un massacre*, are indeed so glaringly absurd that an English author, Montgomery Belgion, could suggest in all earnestness that M. Céline intended to refute and ridicule anti-Semitism by exaggerating its ideas to the point of obvious fatuity. But the Nazis, used to the vilest and rankest humbug, take Céline seriously. Incredible as it may sound, this embodiment of "cultural Bolshevism" is a literary favorite in the Occupied Zone.

The abject behavior of Paul Morand does not come as a surprise, neither to Gide, nor to anyone familiar with the dreary career of that once sparkling jester. One might as well get excited about the political obscenities of the comedians Guitry and Raimu or of young Mademoiselle Darrieux and old Mademoiselle Mistinguette. Let Yvonne Printemps compete with Maurice Chevalier in wooing and pleasing the new bosses! Gide would be hardly concerned about those treacherous primadonnas (whether male or female), if it were not for a certain young man hitherto close to him. A successful movie director named Marc Allegret has joined the collaborationist camp. Marc, the companion of the African journey and of many other voyages and adventures; Marc, who was almost like a son, and more than a son, to Gide; Marc, a traitor, an opportunist. . . .

This loss and this disappointment are more painful indeed than the fact that a versatile climber, Drieu la

Rochelle, has taken over the *Nouvelle Revue Française* and turned the once illustrious magazine into a lukewarm and slimy organ of sophisticated skepticism and camouflaged Nazi propaganda. Gide's brain-child, the focus of his intellectual circle, the trustee of his lifework, the liberal and cosmopolitan *Nouvelle Revue Française* now carries stories like that of Georges Auric, who concludes his survey of the winter 1941–42 with a cheerful statement to the effect that "the season is excellent."

The season is excellent, says the talented composer, undisturbed by such trifles as the slavery of a few million Frenchmen in German camps; the starvation of French women and children; the martyrdom of innocent hostages. The season is excellent at the Opéra: Mademoiselle Germaine Lubin, the Wagnerian star and favorite of the Nazi chieftains, can afford several dazzling new Mercedes cars; Serge Lifar has a brilliant come-back—not quite so young and nimble, it is true, as he used to be when the late Diaghilev discovered his talent, a little swollen and hysterical, but still racy and rakish enough. The Marquise de Polignac and the Comtesse de Noailles have reopened their salons, elegant meeting-points of the collaborationist élite. What a season! It couldn't be more brilliant and colorful. So utterly gay and prosperous is Paris life under the Nazi yoke that even an exemplary Parisian like Jean Cocteau cannot resist the temptation. The most ingenious and most volatile performer in modern literature executes his last staggering somersault and makes friends with the illiterate murderers from Berlin and Berchtesgaden.

It amuses and somehow comforts me to imagine the diabolic fashion in which Gide may have grinned and

smirked when he heard of Jean's desperate cynicism. "*Ah!
Celui-là! Quel blagueur! Enfin, passons.*"

Their friendship has always been somewhat one-sided;
that is to say, Cocteau never ceased to woo Gide, assidu-
ously and naïvely, whereas Gide remained chilly, inaccessible. "My first contact was Gide," says Cocteau in the
preface to *Le Rappel à l'ordre* (which is dedicated to
Georges Auric, incidentally). "Our friendship encouraged
me."

Grateful by nature, he paid homage to his master whom
he would like to call his friend. It was Gide, allegedly, who
stimulated Cocteau to write his memoirs: "*C'est à Gide
que je dois ces Portraits-Souvenir . . .*" And, one year later,
in 1936, he reaffirmed his indebtedness in the dedication
of *Mon Premier Voyage,* the book edition of his travel
articles for the *Paris Soir*: "To André Gide, who taught
us how to travel."

As for Gide, he proved cruelly impervious to so much
good will and humble admiration. "Cocteau?" he once said.
"Who is he? A flatulence in the bowels of the rich . . ." A
terrible word, malicious to the point of unfairness. It
sounds as if Gide were without receptivity to Cocteau's
intense, if irresponsible, inspiration. The uncanny bril-
liancy of such masterpieces as *Les Enfants terribles* and
La Machine infernale not only fails to captivate Gide but
rather seems to irritate and annoy him.

No doubt, there is a moral element, a touch of Puritanism, in Gide's disapproval of Cocteau's desultory feats.
To Gide, creative writing is primarily an ethical exercise;
to Cocteau, a sport, a narcotic, an aimless thrill. Gide's contempt of Cocteau is organic and inevitable, as is Edouard's

contempt of Robert de Passavant, in *Les Faux-Monnayeurs*.
There is a definite resemblance between Edouard's attitude towards Passavant and Gide's towards Cocteau. The
aversion, in both cases, is not quite free of jealousy.
Edouard-Gide not only scorns the elegant frivolity of
Passavant-Cocteau but also envies secretly his sprightliness
and immorality. Edouard and Passavant are rivals, not only
because both happen to be interested in Olivier, but also in
a more complex and more general fashion. Of course,
Edouard is infinitely superior to Passavant as far as character and talent are concerned. But Passavant commands a
flippant wit and a dashing agility with which Edouard
cannot compete. Edouard might say in reference to Passavant what Gide said about Cocteau: "He has that enviable
carelessness of the playboy. And when I am with him I
always feel particularly clumsy, heavy, downhearted."

This revealing statement occurs in a diary entry dated
August 20, 1914, and the beginning of which reads as
follows: "Jean Cocteau and I got together at an 'English
tea.' . . . I did not look forward to seeing him again, despite
his exceedingly friendly nature. For he is incapable of
being serious, and all his thoughts, his puns, his feelings,
this extraordinary flavor of his chatty talk, was a shock to
me like some luxury object on display at times of starvation and mourning. He is dressed almost like a soldier, and
under the lash of the day-to-day developments he looks
much better. Otherwise he has not changed, and just
ignores the martial atmosphere around him."

There they are again, the times of starvation and mourning, and in the twenty-five years which have passed since
the last tribulation Cocteau has become even more chatty

and cynical, while Gide has increased in gravity and courage. Cocteau enjoys the "excellent season"; Gide joins the
"interior emigration" scattered throughout a torn, smolder-
ing France.

For General de Gaulle and his soldiers are by no means
the only guarantors of French honor and of French resistance. Within the humiliated, tormented country itself,
the spirit of patriotism and democracy could never be
broken or bought altogether: it survived in heroic individuals, in underground organizations, in the thoughts and
actions of undaunted, incorruptible men and women. It
may be that the attitude of the average Frenchman toward
his nation and toward the outside world had become somewhat sluggish and skeptical. The French, being the most
civilized nation on earth, were the first to overcome the
devastating stupidity which is Nationalism. A Frenchman
could write, in 1938, "Let us not deceive ourselves! France
is not big enough for the notion we want held of France.
Her glorious doggedness from 1914 to 1918 has deceived
both the world and us Frenchmen." And, "But there must
be a choice. We must decide whether we want to be
mighty or happy."

The majority of the French people did not intend to
sacrifice honor by choosing happiness. They wanted to
cultivate their garden, unaware of the sinister forces under-
mining its ground, from without and within. The shock
of the debacle awakened the gardeners.

True, the French Communists sabotaged the war effort,
together with the generals and the industrialists. But while
the Fascist coteries are guilty of deliberate high treason, the

misguided Jacobins were just muddled and ignorant. Many of them are expiating in 1942 their sins of 1939: the same saboteurs who once harassed the decaying Third Republic do the same thing now to their real enemy, the Third Reich.

If such men as Giraud and De Gaulle reaffirm the military honor of France, Edouard Herriot embodies and dramatizes the pride and common sense of the liberal bourgeoisie. His resignation from the Legion of Honor, of which he held the great Chevalier's Cross, is a gesture in the grand French style, an eloquent and impressive answer to the men of Vichy who granted the national decoration to a Frenchman in Nazi service.

Vichy may be on the most cordial terms with the Vatican; but the truly Christian spirit is not with the clerical collaborationists. This spirit may be found in the ranks of the Catholic Action—an organization to which flock, at this point, many young, unyielding Frenchmen, who act and feel according to these words of the Archbishop of Toulouse, Monseigneur Saliège: "It is the future of Christianity which is at stake in the present struggle, the outcome of which may decide the shape and spirit of centuries to come. Many priests, many Catholics fail to see this. That is why I admonish them officially to beware of notorious errors and of words the meaning of which remains vague and ambiguous. It is our mission to save and to promote the true Christian spirit—not a clericalism of which the Church disapproves and which we sternly reject; but the salvation of the world under the auspices of the Christian Cross, manifestation and symbol of divine, infinite Love."

This is not the language of compromise and caution. The Archbishop could speak out, protected by his ecclesiastic authority, what many another upright citizen—Catholic or not—feels with equal fervency but is forced to conceal. While an incessant, sickening concert of lies blares from Paris and Vichy, the truly distinguished Frenchmen (except, of course, those in exile) have to keep quiet or to whisper. One hears little from Mauriac, Malraux, and Giraudoux, from Valéry, Duhamel, and Martin du Gard. They all live somewhere in the unoccupied zone, hoping and waiting in silence. "Patience is a great and rare virtue," according to André Gide.

Gide, patient and unafraid, just shrugs his shoulders when the jackals bark against him in the Paris press. One by the name of Maurice Martin du Gard (not to be confounded with Gide's friend, Roger Martin du Gard!) referred to him as "old Narcissus who leans over the eddies of expectation and lies in wait for the drunken whispers of the defenders of the gold-standard."

"Isn't it curious?" says Gide. "This need to search for vile reasons for other people's opinions . . ."

At times they grow bolder and more unpleasant; they become snappish and dangerous. A semi-Fascist organization, the French *Anciens Combattants*, launched a furious protest when Gide's name appeared on the speakers' list of a literary group in Nice. The announced subject of his address was completely unpolitical. Yet the irritable legionnaires considered the whole affair an unbearable provocation. Gide was bombarded with anonymous letters and dire phone calls to the effect that he would be beaten to death if he dared to attend the meeting.

He went there all the same—to the surprise and fury of the martial jackasses. They had threatened to kill him, and still he had the nerve to show up! What a stunning old fellow! He seemed calm and serene as he mounted the platform and produced a letter. All sovereign dignity, he read the blackmailing epistle to his flabbergasted audience. After having concluded this extraordinary recital, he said, smilingly: "So I am here to beg your pardon, ladies and gentlemen. For I am afraid the remarkable document you have just heard will be my only contribution to this literary program. Not that I mind a good fight, quite the contrary. But, alas, I am not so young as I used to be. Besides, I am here by myself, whereas our valiant legionnaires, as you know, make it their policy to appear in masses."

He made an elegant bow and withdrew, leaving the ruffians aghast and the audience in raptures. "It was a tremendous success," said a friend who witnessed the incident, "a real triumph for Gide. If my information is right, those louts haven't bothered him since."

But Gide had to be careful. When he was urged to contribute to an American magazine I was editing at the time, he answered, somewhat apologetically: "I shall try my best to write something for your new review, as soon as possible. But I am not in a position to make a definite promise. Four days out of five I feel terribly remote from my work. Besides there are so many 'considerations' that slow down my writing . . ."

The quotation marks around the word "considerations" seem to suggest a gloomy and dangerous story which the letter conceals.

No "considerations," however, could prevent Gide from conducting what an American observer recently called "a subtle rear-guard action against Paris." This definition is indeed subtler than the action it is supposed to describe. In fact, I know of no other prominent man of letters in a Fascist country who has been as courageous, not to say foolhardy, as is this admirable old man, André Gide of France.

The English review of literature and art, *Horizon*, meritorious in many respects, had the privilege of presenting the English version of Gide's literary "rear-guard" campaign, which at times looks ominously like a frontal offensive.

"When *Horizon* was founded," the editors tell us, in the "Comment" to their issue of June, 1942, "a letter was written to Gide asking him to contribute, to which he replied that he was under a vow of silence not to write anything till the war was over. This vow he has now broken, and this month we conclude the series of *Imaginary Interviews* which appeared at the beginning of this year on the literary page of *Figaro*, a Vichy paper which has been once or twice suspended for its views, and which clearly preserves the nearest possible likeness to a pre-war French newspaper. Apart from the interest attaching to anything written by Gide, who is the greatest living writer in Europe, and who writes most consciously for the future, the articles reveal how much can still be said in unoccupied France, and what lengthy grammatical involutions are necessary to say it."

It is indeed quite a lot that can still be said by a writer who commands the indispensable amount of tact and of prestige. Of course, Gide has to be diplomatic; for his imaginary interlocutor is a plain, vulgar Fascist. Gide, absent-minded and not very time-conscious—as old people are apt to be—mistakes his visitor at first for the interviewer he used to receive in the old days of *L'Immoraliste* and *Les Nourritures terrestres*. But the contemporary journalist, type 1942, is much more alert and perky, a dynamic representative of the New-Order species. At times Gide seems nonplussed in front of the smart young man. "Long live our National Revolution!" exclaims the dashing son of a defeated nation. What can an old man reply to such a puerile euphemism? "There was a silence for a minute. . . ." A terribly eloquent silence it must have been.

"Do not insist!" Gide begs of the interviewer, who keeps plying him with questions about current, which means, therefore, untimely, events. "There is a quantity of subjects it is better not to talk about today. I have made up my mind to it: literary affairs will be my only concern with you."

But the demarcation between literature and politics has become somewhat indistinct, nowadays. Does the recent book of Jacques Chardonne, *Voir la figure*, belong to the literary category? The interviewer suggests that the book is full of topical interest. "Yes," says Gide, "but he blows with the wind." In other words, Chardonne is a collaborationist. Gide dismisses him with a few scathing phrases. "Let us take leave of Chardonne, I beg of you, and go back to literature."

The interviewer dwells on the current French penchant for poetry. "Collections of poems are appearing everywhere, and never has the public shown itself so eager or greedy for poetry."

Whereupon Gide observes, "It would seem as if the public were taking refuge in it."

They discuss several recent lyric anthologies, and Gide discloses his plan to edit such a collection himself. It will be stimulating, not only to correct the limitations and prejudices of other editors, but also to modify one's own premature judgments. Take Victor Hugo, for instance! Gide has done his bit to deflate this bombastic genius. How long ago is it that he gave his oft-quoted reply, "Victor Hugo, alas!" when asked who was the greatest French poet? At this point, however, he deems it pertinent to reaffirm the glory of the great lyricist, "the greatest in our Pantheon." "Let us add," Gide says, a bit abruptly, "that he excels in abuse." Does he feel like repeating the spirited invectives Hugo coined against "*Napoléon le Petit*"? And if so, against whom would he like to use them?

Far from indulging in coarse talk, however, they continue their chat about poetry. Gide perceives and hails a renaissance of light and popular verse. Does the interviewer know by any chance, that stunning young woman, Lil Boel, who is now reciting her ballads in a small music hall near the Place d'Italie, in Nice? The interviewer has read the introductory poem from her repertory, recently featured in *Figaro*. He does not like Lil Boel, for one reason or another. As for Gide, he thinks her excellent.

They talk also about novels. Gide, after having admired various English and American masterpieces, admits that there is a new rise noticeable in the French novel as well. "Jean-Paul Sartre, today, gives us, with exceptional skill, a picture of the despicable; he is never flabby." (Nor is he a collaborationist . . .) "The works of Giono, Malraux, Saint-Exupéry, Montherlant, their aims and their value give me great hope of getting out of the often muddy rut in which our literature was stuck. Dignity, nobility of heart, heroism, find an echo, I believe, among the young people of today."

Gide adds some illuminating remarks as to the connection between the novel and individualism. "The great producers of the novel are those peoples among whom the individual is most distinct from the mass. On the other hand, the type of literature most specifically German is the lyric drama, a synthetic type in which Germany excels and triumphs, in which music and poetry join in such a total effect as flowers in Wagner's tetralogy; in this, it seems to me, where a whole people gathered together listens religiously and where a true social fusion is attained, it achieves its most perfect expression."

A dubious homage to the Teutonic genius, considering Gide's opinion about Richard Wagner and his musical theater. In this context even the expression "total effect" seems maliciously chosen. It somehow connotes the ominous term "totalitarian" . . .

There he is, the grand old man of French letters, in his modest Riviera retreat; heckled by a callow stranger who is neither the Nathanaël of *Les Nourritures terrestres* nor the Comrade of *Les Nouvelles Nourritures*. He is just a pretentious young careerist, and the ideas he expresses seem to Gide "more confused than new."

Yet the patient old man remains good-tempered. "I had

not the heart," he tells us, "to get angry with such a worthy chap." Besides, they are in the same boat, the placid eremite and his unstable visitor. Both are subjected to the same privations. The grand old man says, "It is true I am wearing old clothes as I am unable, as you are, to get any new ones for myself. Those you see on my back have been relined three times; I have had the elbows patched. For food, there are certainly very few meals on top of which I would not willingly accept a beefsteak with fried potatoes; but I am glad to hear that the other districts are better provisioned than ours. I also know that some have much less, and that even in the most favored, a number of people are shorter than I am. As a matter of fact, I am very glad not to eat too much meat and have never felt in better health. I do not miss coffee as I had not been in the habit of drinking it. The shortage from which I suffer the most is, I admit, that of tobacco, having formed the cowardly habit of smoking while at work. At the beginning, I thought, what a good chance to break this habit. . . . This was without reckoning on the solicitude of several friends who, by not smoking themselves, kindly facilitate my vice when it is a question of action. I am stubborn and preserving but prone to temptations."

What a familiar tune! The cigarette leitmotiv. . . . Our first luncheon, near the Luxembourg Garden; Pastor Vedel's obsession . . . Stubborn and preserving as he is, Gide sticks to his traditional vagaries—apocalypse or not. He, for one, remains faithful to himself.

He remains keen and receptive. Even the national tribulation might seem exciting to him, if it were not so cruel. "But so much novelty intimidates us. The mind and

specially the heart have great difficulty in adapting themselves."

He remains confident. He quotes Montesquieu: "One of
the things most noticeable in France is the extreme facility
with which she has always recovered from her losses, her
illness, her decrease of population; and the resources with
which she has always endured and even overcome the
internal vices of her various governments."

He remains realistic. When the interviewer suggests that
a new kind of national unity might result from the stirring
experience of the national calamity, Gide replies, rather
dryly: "Well, if I may speak frankly, I believe that this
kind of unification of minds, which you admire, is far more
apparent than real and far more desired than existing. The
French, although afflicted by a common misfortune, remain as divided as they ever were."

"If this is true," says the interviewer, "do you not find
it distressing?"

"No. We have often been told that the variety of France
constitutes her value."

He begins the new year, the year of 1942, in a faithful
and sober spirit. "Let us hope," he says gravely, "it will be
less dark than these two wretched years of disgrace."

And the interviewer, in his callow, optimistic fashion
says, "Fortunately, some reassuring gleams are beginning
to appear."

Bitterness and faith, stoicism and the unyielding will to
resist, are curiously fused in André Gide's simple answer.
"In a tunnel, artificial lighting does its best. Before seeing
the real light, I am afraid that we shall have to sink much
deeper into darkness. Meanwhile let us not lose hope."

EPILOGUE

What a piece of work is man! how noble in reason! how infinite in faculty! in form and moving how express and admirable! in action how like an angel! in apprehension how like a god! the beauty of the world! the paragon of animals!

SHAKESPEARE

Mais cette certitude: que l'homme n'as pas toujours été ce qu'il est, permet aussitôt cet espoir: il ne le sera pas toujours.

ANDRÉ GIDE

A N D R É G I D E'S interviewer seems ready to withdraw at last. "Heil Pétain!" he crows cheerfully. "Long live the National Revolution!" The old gentleman, looking very distinguished in his shabby, discolored clothes, makes a wry grimace as if tasting something foul or bitter. Then he sighs and smiles. "Au revoir, young man. Look after yourself! And be good, if you can . . ."

There is a stillness. The Interviewer has gone. The old man sits alone, dreaming in a quaint, plush-covered armchair, on the terrace of a modest Provençal villa.

There are a few other houses one can see from the terrace, five or six white, cubic buildings half-hidden by the foliage of the olive groves. That is all Cabris-sur-Grasse has to offer—an unassuming village somewhere in the hinterland of the *Côte d'Azur*.

The evening sky is cloudless and transparent over the Mediterranean landscape, with mellow, floating tints where the sun went down. How strangely transfigured appear

the familiar things in this pallid twilight! The black sil-
houettes of the cypresses against a limpid horizon; the
silvery hue of the olive trees; the aimless flights of the birds;
the flowers, the house, the path—how curious, all this! how
real!

A peasant woman comes from the vineyard, striding
slowly and solemnly, carrying a weighty basket on her
proud, white-haired head. The motionless old man on the
terrace watches her, a living part of the landscape, all in
keeping with the rhythm and color of this Latin land.

"*Bon soir, Madame*," says the old man from the terrace,
smiling at her, but still motionless.

"*Bon soir, Monsieur*."

It sounds grave and yet hearty, the salute of an upright
person who knows her rights and her merits and respects
those of others.

"She wouldn't say, *Heil Pétain*," thinks the old man as
she passes by. "Not she. She is French enough—and proudly,
consciously so—without invoking that old bore of a Marshal. But those callow young men with their dashing manners always have recourse to some bearded authority. What
a dreary lot! At once rude and servile . . .

"That clever busybody of an Interviewer got on my
nerves with his rudeness and with his servility. When I
spoke about Goethe and his 'serviceable individualism,' he
had the impudence to interrupt me, rather snappishly,
'Have you not said all this already?' What an affront!—
all the more annoying as he is not quite wrong . . . What
could I do? I hurriedly invented a friend of mine, also
seventy years of age, and who was being accused of repeti-
tion. Said my fabulous friend, 'At my age we must agree

to repeat ourselves, if we do not wish to say stupid things.'

"But it didn't work. The irritating young chap had the nerve to ask me, insidiously, 'Is not your friend a relative of those imaginary characters that Sainte-Beuve pretends to quote when he wants to show himself in a good light?' I tried to make my voice as glacial as possible when I observed, all disdain, 'You are very subtle.'

"Not that I would mind his being a little fresh, if only he were more courageous and more attractive. Here, in Cabris-sur-Grasse, such a little nobody can be flippant and captious. In Vichy or in Paris he swallows everything. He blames me for repeating some things I may have said before, in a different context. But he repeats the tritest cliché when it comes from an authoritative side. What blatant nonsense he said about those French poets and novelists in disgrace with the new masters. I could have slapped his face when he spoke of 'certain pre-war writers,' —and amongst them the best—'who were lacking in civic virtues.' Why did I allow him to accuse men like Proust and Valéry, yes, and like myself, of having 'discouraged and devitalized the French nation'? Not our corrupt politicians and inefficient generals are responsible for the fiasco, but we, the prophets and victims of the debacle, are being denounced as the culprits!

"It is always the same trick—the writers and intellectuals as scapegoats. Even the dead are smeared. We often hear a whole epoch or a century covered with shame. Sometimes from Léon Daudet it is 'the stupid nineteenth century'; sometimes a critic makes a victim of the eighteenth century. The Catholics reproach Diderot, Renan, even Montaigne; and the freethinkers, Bossuet. The old chorus is taken up again. '*C'est le faute à Voltaire* . . . *c'est la faute à Rousseau* . . .' Michelet and Hugo are spat at by Claudel. A recent anthology of French poems only praises our sixteenth century at the expense of the sublime flights of our Romantics, and only includes a few isolated verses of theirs. This is ludicrous; and it would be just something to laugh at if the books concerned were not in process of being effectively banned from the bookshops. What sad and sickening mischief! The nation of Stendhal and of La Rochefoucauld, famed for its psychological perspicacity, is now forced to accept such clumsy and deceitful slogans as 'corrosive literature,' 'uprooted intellectualism,' 'cultural Bolshevism,' and the like.

"There may be mistakes and sins to hold against us writers, the generation under Nietzsche's spell. Not quite the kind of errors, though, the Fascists blame us for. To reproach us with having 'discouraged and devitalized' French youth is indeed nonsensical. Our fallacy is rather of the opposite kind. Haven't we overrated and unduly glorified the value and grandeur of vitality and dynamics? —of vitality as such, no matter what its purpose and its direction? Haven't we encouraged the anti-intellectual and anti-humanitarian vogue? Haven't we been prone, at times, to the diabolic bacillus of madness and barbarism?

"Yes, Zarathustra bewitched too many of us with his dangerous catchwords. Let us be hard! Let us defy the code of Christian ethics! Revaluate all values! . . . How thrillingly adventurous life seemed, up there, in glacial height, immeasurably beyond good and evil. How enthralling it was, to disregard all conventions, to transgress all taboos. The cult of instinct and intuition; the worship of energy; the panegyrics of the *élan vital*—it was ever so stirring and intoxicating. But from Nietzsche's Power philosophy it is only one step to Sorel's Defense of Violence and to Spengler's Decline of the Western World.

"The decline of the Western world . . . *C'est la faute à Nietzsche* . . . *c'est la faute à Bergson* . . . *c'est la faute à Gide* . . .

"Why not admit it? I too have sinned and have contributed my bit to the general disarray. Now I recognize the germ of anarchy in the exuberance of my *Nourritures*, in my individual ethics, and in my concept of the gratuitous action. Is not Lafcadio's capricious crime an offense against the very principles on which our society rests? Did I not urge Nathanaël to burn books?—an ominous piece of advice, considering certain recent developments . . . The demon of *Les Faux-Monnayeurs* is double-faced, a disquieting fruit of the marriage of heaven and hell. Did I not realize what I risked as I kept experimenting with high-explosive energies?

"But would it have been better to conceal our insights into man's contradictory and demoniac nature? Should we delude ourselves and our followers into shallow and fallacious optimism? We know better. The nineteenth century refuted, once and for all, the generous illusions of the eighteenth. How is it possible to ignore the sinister qualities of modern man, after the bold and tragic revelations of Rimbaud and Dostoevski, Stendhal and Nietzsche, Flaubert and Baudelaire, Tolstoi and Kierkegaard? How could we indulge in euphemisms about man's intrinsic goodness and simplicity, in view of their cruel and admirable truthfulness? 'The masks,' Montaigne says, 'must as well be taken from things as from men.' And, too, La Rochefoucauld: 'Weaklings cannot be sincere.' Do we want to be weaklings?

"But I would much rather be an optimistic weakling than one of those gruesome charlatans who think themselves profound when they are pompous and nebulous; realistic, when they are greedy and cynical; superhuman, when they are inhuman. They despise man because they take it for granted that all of us are as despicable as they are. But man is not despicable. He is lovable and disquieting—God's striving, problem child.

"Of course, man is neither good nor evil but a mixture of both. To all those who simplify and thus distort the human problem I would like to quote this extraordinary page from Montaigne's *Essays*:

" 'Our composition, both publike and private, is full of imperfection; yet is there nothing in nature unserviceable; nothing thereof hath beene insinuated in this huge universe but holdeth some fit place therein. Our essence is cymented with evil qualities; ambition, jealousie, envy, revenge, superstition, dispaire, lodge in us, with so natural a possession, as their image is also discerned in beasts: yea and cruelty, so unnatural a vice: for in the middest of compassion, we inwardly feele a kinde of bitter-sweet pricking of malicious delight to see others suffer; and children feele it also.

" 'The seed of which qualities, who should roote out of man, should ruine the fundamental conditions of our life: In matter of policy likewise some necessary functions are not only base, but faulty: vices find therein a seate and employ themselves in the stitching up of our frame; as

poysons in the preservations of our health. If they become
excusable because we have neede of them, let us resigne the
acting of this part to hardy Citizens, who sticke not to
sacrifice their honors and consciences, as those of old, their
lives, for their Countries availe and safety. We that are
more weake had best assume taskes of more ease and lesse
hazard. The Commonwealth requireth some to betray,
some to lie, and some to massaker: leave we that commis-
sion to people more obedient and more pliable.'

"Could it be that Providence, at this point of the human
adventure, employs certain hardy men as its unpleasant
tools to teach us a cruel lesson? Do the modern barbarians
fulfill their historical task, unwittingly and paradoxically,
by betraying, lying, and massacring? Did we need the
ghastly spectacle of disorder and tyranny to remember
the double fundament of our civilization, Freedom and
Discipline? Would man become too sluggish and self-
assured without occasional shock-cures like the one we are
now passing through? We took too much for granted—we
here, in France, and people everywhere. Our freedom and
our security, our conveniences and our luxuries—we believed naïvely that we were entitled to possess all this and
that we could never lose it. Did I not admonish Nathanaël
not to hang his heart on possessions and institutions? *For
whosoever shall save his life shall lose it; but whosoever
shall lose his life, the same shall find it* . . .

"Did the French people lose their spiritual life because
they clung to their material security?

"One has to take chances, must not shrink from hazardous games and risks. Not to stand still! To move! Too long
we have drowsed and dallied—leaving all initiative to the

enemy. The very concept of progress tarnished and stagnated. The bourgeois notion of democracy was lacking in
drama and color: that is why ignorant, impressionable
youth fell for the glaring and blaring stunts of reckless
demagogues. But the well-meaning gentlemen in our camp
continued their unctuous sermons. For every enigma and
paradox had its clear-cut, shallow solution.

"I remember how irritated I was when I read that
English book, *Our Present Philosophy of Life* (according
to Bernard Shaw, André Gide, Sigmund Freud, and Bertrand Russell). The chapter about me was fairly good on
the whole. But the following sentence disturbed me: 'Man
by nature is, Mr. Gide feels, good.' Is that so? Do I agree
with Rousseau that man in his natural state is without guile
and sin? Do I blame civilization and society for all our
shortcomings and vices?

"No, the faith in man's primeval perfection seems naïve
and romantic to me. I do not believe that man has ever
been perfect; but I do believe he may eventually become
better than he is now. He is capable of improvement. And
to improve does not mean, to overcome the 'evil' and to
develop the 'good'; it means, to integrate good and evil,
to render all energies—virtues and vices, love and hatred—
serviceable in the interest of progress.

"To harbor *both* tendencies; to reconcile the contrasts;
to accept and dominate the contradictions and complexi-
ties inherent in our nature—what do the fanatics and the
hypocrites know about that exciting feat? Montaigne knew
about it, and Goethe, and Nietzsche when he wrote: 'Man,
in contrast to the animals, has developed a profusion of
contradictory impulses and qualities. Thanks to this syn-

thesis within his character he could become the master of the world.'

"Man, the master; man, the hero; man, the promise of the superman—thanks to his ability to scrutinize his own problem, to transform his substance, to move, to change, and to suffer.

"Man, the master of his destiny, by virtue of his spirit. For man's spirit functions according to the rules of homeopathic medicine: at once poison and remedy, it cures the disease that it produced itself. Are the restlessness and the irreverence of our minds responsible for the present crisis? Well, then, the same forces will be instrumental in overcoming the emergency. The energy that proved bold and dynamic enough to upset an obsolete way of life, will never yield to the foul substitute now imposed on us as a new order.

"The new order is neither anarchy nor stagnation: it is movement, experiment, and constructive adventure. I, an old adventurer and experimenter, am avid for new discoveries and new risks. Do you realize, you smug and ruthless young men, how much anguish and bliss this implies?—still to long for things to come, after having witnessed the frustration of so many hopes, so much bafflement and betrayal. To remain faithful in spite of all disappointments—*malgré tout, trotz allem, after all!* To be in love with man, for all his meanness and stupidity: to be in love with his potential greatness, his future trials and triumphs, his yet secret glory . . . How I pity you, obtuse, selfish, unhappy conquerors, unable to grasp or to imagine the solemn sobriety of this faith: *the faith after the disillusion.*

"How can one despise or hate man for what he *is*, when he still is in the process of *becoming? L'homme devient*, and I, *toujours amoureux de ce qui pourrait être*, shall never cease to be fascinated by the spectacle of his growth.

"It may be a long, tedious growth, interrupted by painful relapses. Patience is a great and rare virtue, to know how to wait and to mature, to correct oneself, regain control and, as the apostle says, aspire to perfection. But the taste for perfection is going astray. It is a pity, as man's finest accomplishments are due to precisely that taste. But nothing that has already been imagined or achieved will be lost forever.

"Those who are obsessed with the most insatiable curiosity will give the world an example of patience and endurance—indispensable virtues for anyone really interested in the future.

"Those who understand and love the concept of the Infinite will reaffirm the value and necessity of voluntary limitation and discipline. This is Goethe's constant and secret drama, and not only Goethe's: the struggle against the Infinite in which he is involved by his too broad and too universal genius, whereas he feels and knows that the community in which he lives and the work of art he wants to create require limitation and concentration—neither of which is attained without sacrifices.

"Those who have been most deeply enthralled by the inconsistency, the perpetual flux and change of all things, will in the end conceive the opposite law in nature and human life, *continuity*. The logic and constancy of organic or historical developments may be more difficult to discern than the erratic leaps and vagaries. Yet no phenomenon is disconnected, and even the most desultory motion is not without aim and reason. There are transitions and transformations but there are no gaps.

"I often feel like urging the younger generation: Please stop believing in gaps! If you drift or slip, don't think that everything goes downhill from now on. Life travels upward in spirals. And if you go any further than we have been able to go, so much the better; but remember that it is all on the same road: whither my good wishes and my hopes will follow you, even if they have not preceded you."

It is dark and still. The cypresses and olive trees seem frozen in the hazy garden and up there, on the black, distant hills. How chilly the air is now! The old man on the terrace shivers. It is high time to go into the house, supper will be ready; friends expect him, he is not alone.

"You are not alone!" This whisper, familiar and yet strange, does not come from the lighted dining room but from the floating mist with which the garden is filled. What wondrous procession hovers between the cypresses! You are not alone, André Gide. From the hazy darkness emerge your heroes and saints, your jesters and criminals.

Young André Walter opens the curious parade. His gait is stooping and stumbling, but his sunken eyes radiate an unquenchable flame. Behind him, there are Hubert, the melancholy clown of *Paludes;* Urien, the eloquent traveler who never left his studio; Narcissus, disquieting and entrancing with the deadly smile of his introversive passion. Nathanaël and Ménalque, all in Bacchic raptures, brandish bunches of gaudy flowers and fruits. In contrast to these

Dionysiac vagabonds, the two haunted kings, Saul and Candaulus, seem all the more dismal and neurotic. Michel and Marceline—the Immoralist and his victim—stride in a pallid, phosphorescent aureole; but around Alissa the air is placid and pure, bathed in heavenly hues. Jerome, her lover, fades away at her side, sacrificed by his bride as an oblation to the deity, as Michel sacrificed Marceline to the Evil One.

They pass by, they glide through the fragrant night, an array of specters bearing the unmistakable features of that extraordinary old man smiling in reveries. There is Lafcadio, a jaunty and elegant spook, teasing the Calvinist minister, who tries to hide behind a screen of self-delusion and hypocrisy. "From now on I will live chastely," mumbles the clergyman. "No more cigarettes!" For the hero of *La Symphonie pastorale* has transformed himself into Pastor Vedel, the director of the boarding school where the boys amuse themselves with murder and forgeries. Look at old La Pérouse carrying his tragic head as if it were too heavy and woeful a burden. Look at Vincent, who thinks himself the Devil, intoxicated by Lady Griffith's kisses as by poisonous wine. His brother Olivier, at once airy and resilient, escapes from Passavant's velvety clasp, to be received by Edouard. Bernard needs no protection: alert and pugnacious he meets his demon alone and wrestles with him without anybody's assistance. But if he turned his head and glanced back, he would recognize the Prodigal Son, his saturnine double, oscillating between repentant and rebellious impulses, now the penitent kneeling before his father, now his older brother's restive antagonist, now again the simple son of a simple and anxious mother, and now—what has changed him?—the demoniac seducer who whispers glowing words to a keen, corruptible child.

The younger brother of the Prodigal Son—his name is perhaps Caloub?—will wander and go astray and seek God in debaucheries and in prayers. They all are compelled to wander, to continue their quest, always in search of their own intrinsic identity and of the Strait Gate that leadeth unto life: Alissa and Narcissus, André Walter and Nathanaël, the Immoralist and Lafcadio, Olivier and Edouard, Bernard, the Prodigal Son, and the three tragic kings—Saul, Candaulus, and Œdipus. The last has perhaps the best chance to find the narrow way; for he has renounced his crown and his eyesight for an inner light that will guide and protect him. They are unafraid, the illuminated blind man and his obedient child: they have each other and they have the world. Wherever their disquietude may lead them, they will find brothers and sisters with whom to share their sorrow and their joy.

King Œdipus, experienced in all kinds of errors and transgressions, delusions and blasphemies, finally arrives at certain simple and basic truths. Only he who has bitterly suffered from man has the right to repeat, with Œdipus and Gide, these words of Sophocles, "Many things are admirable; but nothing is more admirable than man."

He passed through the infernos of despair and skepticism, to conclude his lifework with this plain and heartening message: "Comrade! Do not accept life as a *fait accompli!* Never cease to believe that it could be richer and finer—your life, and the lives of your fellow-men. Take nothing for granted! Question everything! Insist on proofs for every theory! Help bring about amelioration for every evil! Some day you will understand that it is man—not God—whom we should blame for the disarray of our wordly affairs. From that day on you will no longer acquiesce in evil."

He who experienced every form of sorrow and sacrifice sums up his wisdom, succinctly and cordially: "Nature indicates beyond doubt that man is destined for happiness."

A spirited explorer of iridescent mysteries, he followed his demon on many a crooked and devious path. "Hell, like paradise, is within ourselves," says Gide, and cries out, with the Miltonic Satan: "Which way I fly is Hell; myself am Hell."

There was always a fiery token luring and guiding him. The relentless flame parched his skin and wounded his sensitive heart; it often led him astray and at times almost destroyed him. But he is proud and tenacious: he survived. And as he continues to live and to struggle, the diabolic spark reveals its divine origin: behold, it triumphs and shines; it is spirit and love, life and light.

The old wanderer, overwhelmed by his vision, covers his aching eyes with his hands. He weeps. He jubilates. And he prays:

O trop claire lumière
Transperce mes paupières!
Ta vérité, Seigneur,
M'a blessé jusqu'au coeur.

BIBLIOGRAPHY

THE WORKS OF ANDRÉ GIDE

Les Cahiers d'André Walter (Libr. de l'Art Indépendant, 1891)
Les Poésies d'André Walter (Libr. de l'Art Indépendant, 1892)
Le Traité du Narcisse (Libr. de l'Art Indépendant, 1892)
La Tentative amoureuse (Libr. de l'Art Indépendant, 1893)
Le Voyage d'Urien (Libr. de l'Art Indépendant, 1893)
Paludes (Libr. de l'Art Indépendant, 1895)
Les Nourritures terrestres (Mercure de France, 1897)
Philoctète (Mercure de France, 1899)
Feuilles de route (Mercure de France, 1899)
Le Promethée mal enchaîné (Mercure de France, 1899)
Le Roi Candaule (Libr. de la Revue Blanche, 1901)
L'Immoraliste (Mercure de France, 1902)
Saül (Mercure de France, 1902)
Prétextes (Mercure de France, 1903)
Amyntas (Mercure de France, 1906)
Le Retour de l'enfant prodigue (first in *Vers et prose*, March
    1907)
Bethsabé (L'Ermitage, 1903; *Vers et prose*, 1908–1909)
La Porte étroite (Mercure de France, 1909)
Oscar Wilde (Mercure de France, 1910)
Nouveaux Prétextes (Mercure de France, 1911)
Charles-Louis Philippe (Figuière, 1911)
Dostoiewsky, d'après sa correspondance (Figuière, 1911)
Les Caves du Vatican (Nouvelle Revue Française, 1914)
Souvenirs de la Cour d'Assises (N.R.F., 1914)
La Symphonie pastorale (N.R.F., 1920)

Morceaux choisis (N.R.F., 1921)

In Memoriam Oscar Wilde (Mercure de France, 1921)

Incidences (N.R.F., 1924)

Corydon (N.R.F., 1924)

Les Faux-Monnayeurs (N.R.F., 1925)

Journal des faux-monnayeurs (N.R.F., 1925)

Si le grain ne meurt (N.R.F., 1926)

Numquid et Tu . . . ? (Schiffrin, 1926)

Voyage au Congo (N.R.F., 1927)

Le Retour du Tchad (N.R.F., 1929)

Essai sur Montaigne (Schiffrin, 1929)

Un Esprit non prévenu (Kra, 1929)

L'Ecole des femmes, suivie de Robert (N.R.F., 1930)

La Sequestrée de Poitiers (in the "Ne Jugez pas!" collection, N.R.F., 1930)

L'Affaire Redureau (in the "Ne Jugez pas!" collection, N.R.F., 1930)

Œdipe (N.R.F., 1931)

Divers (N.R.F., 1931)

Pages de journal, 1929–1932 (N.R.F., 1934)

Perséphone (Music by Strawinski) (N.R.F., 1934)

Les Nouvelles Nourritures (N.R.F., 1935)

Nouvelles Pages de journal, 1932–1935 (N.R.F., 1936)

Geneviève (N.R.F., 1936)

Retour de l'U.R.S.S. (N.R.F., 1936)

Retouches à mon Retour de l'U.R.S.S. (N.R.F., 1937)

Journal, 1889–1939 (Bibliothèque de la Pléiade, 1939)

Œuvres complètes (N.R.F.; started in 1932; 15 volumes; to be continued)

* * *

Miscellanies (not included in the Collected Works)

Preface to *Vol de nuit* by Saint-Exupéry (1931)

"Traversée" (Poem) (*Die Sammlung*, Amsterdam, 1933)

"Le Treizième Arbre" (Farce) (Simultaneously in *Mesures*, Paris, and *Die Sammlung*, Amsterdam; 1935)

Preface to *Avertissement à l'Europe* by Thomas Mann (1937)

Preface to Shakespeare's *Collected Works in French* (1938)

Preface to *Dangerous Acquaintances* by De Laclos (London, 1940)

Preface to Goethe's *Work for the Theater* (Bibliothèque de la Pléiade, 1942)

"Imaginary Interviews" (three instalments, *Horizon*; London, 1942; reprinted from *Figaro*)

TRANSLATED BY ANDRÉ GIDE:

Joseph Conrad, *Typhoon*

Shakespeare, *Antony and Cleopatra; Hamlet,* Act One

Rabindranath Tagore, *Poems* ("*L'Offrande lyrique*")

Walt Whitman, *Poems* ("Morceaux choisis")

William Blake, "The Marriage of Heaven and Hell"

Alexander Pushkin, *Tales*

Gottfried Keller, Fragment of *Der Grüne Heinrich*

* * *

AMERICAN EDITIONS OF WORKS BY ANDRÉ GIDE:

(*All published by Alfred A. Knopf, New York: except the two last items*)

Strait is the Gate (*La Porte étroite*) (1924)

The Vatican Swindle, later called *Lafcadio's Adventures* (*Les Caves du Vatican*) (1925)

Dostoievsky, with an Introduction by Arnold Bennett (1926)

The Counterfeiters (*Les Faux-Monnayeurs*) (1927; taken over by the Modern Library in 1931)

The School of Wives ("*L'Ecole des femmes*") (1929)

Travels in the Congo (*Voyage au Congo* and *Le Retour du Tchad*) (1929)

The Immoralist (*L'Immoraliste*) (1930)

Two Symphonies (*Isabelle* and *La Symphonie pastorale*) (1931)

Return from the U.S.S.R. (1937)

If It Die (Si le Grain ne meurt) (Random House, New York, 1935; limited edition)

The Living Thoughts of Montaigne: Presented by André Gide (Longmans, Green & Co., New York, 1939)

DOCUMENTATION

(*Confined to Writings by Contemporary Authors*)

Montgomery Belgion, *Our Present Philosophy of Life: According to Bernard Shaw, André Gide, Sigmund Freud and Bertrand Russell* (London, 1929)

——, *News of the French* (London, 1938)

Georges Bernanos, *Scandale de la vérité* (Paris, 1939)

Charles Du Bos, *Le Dialogue avec Gide* (Paris, 1929)

Ernest Boyd, *Studies from Ten Literatures* (New York, 1925)

Paul Claudel, *Ma Conversion* (Paris, 1913)

Jean Cocteau, *Le Rappel à l'ordre* (Paris, 1926)

——, *Portraits souvenir* (Paris, 1935)

——, *Mon Premier voyage* (Paris, 1936)

Ernst Robert Curtius, *Die Literarischen Wegbereiter des Neuen Frankreich* (Potsdam, 1923)

——, *Französischer Geist im Neuen Europa* (Berlin, 1925)

Henri Drain, *Nietzsche et Gide* (Paris, 1932)

Ilya Ehrenburg, "Der Weg André Gide's" (Article: *Die Sammlung*, Amsterdam, 1934)

Bernard Fay, *Panorama de la littérature contemporaine* (Paris, 1925)

Ramon Fernandez, *André Gide* (Paris, 1931)

E. M. Forster, *Aspects of the Novel* (London, 1927)

Wallace Fowlie, *La Pureté dans l'art* (Montreal, 1941)

André Maurois, *I Remember, I Remember* (New York, 1942)

Julian Green, *Journal: 1928–1934* (Paris, 1938)

——, *Journal: 1935–1939* (Paris, 1939)

Albert Guérard, *Preface to World Literature* (New York, 1941)

"André Gide et Notre Temps" (Protocol of the *Union pour la Vérité*) (Paris, 1935)

Annette Kolb, "The Debacle" (Article: *Decision*, New York, 1941)

Minna Lederman, "France's Turncoat Artists" (Article: *The Nation*, New York, 1942)

Jacques Maritain, Preface to *Témoignage sur la situation actuelle in France: Par un dirigent français d'Action Catholique*" (Montreal, 1941)

Claude Naville, *André Gide et le communism* (Paris, 1935)

Léon Pierre-Quint, *André Gide: sa vie, son œuvre* (Paris, 1933)

Henri Peyre, *Le Classicisme français* (New York, 1942)

Peter Quennell, "André Gide" (Article: *Horizon*, London, 1942)

Jules Romains, "Deutschtum und Latinität" (Lecture: reviewed and quoted in the *Berliner Tageblatt*, 1934)

Maurice Sachs, *André Gide* (Paris, 1936)

André Wurmser, "L'U.R.S.S. jugée par André Gide" (Article: *Commune*, Paris, 1937)